The Crisis of RELiGiON

Second Revised Edition

ADEBOWALE OJOWURO

VERITY PUBLISHERS
Pretoria

THE CRISIS OF RELIGION
Second Revised Edition

Copyright © 2019, 2012, 2010 by Adebowale Ojowuro

First Published as Verity Paperback 2010

Reissued in 2012

This edition is published in paperback and digital in 2019

© 2019 Verity Publishers

Pretoria 0001

www.veritypublishers.co.za

ISBN 978-1-928348-82-5

Cover Design by Aletia Lensink

*****

"It is a blessed thing that
in every age someone has had individuality
enough and courage enough to stand by his
own convictions, -- someone who had the
grandeur to say his say. I believe it was
Magellan who said, 'The church says the earth
is flat; but I have seen its shadow on the moon,
and I have more confidence even in a shadow
than in the church.'
On the prow of his ship were disobedience,
defiance, scorn, and success."

– Robert G. Ingersoll

*****

Acclaim for
The Crisis of Religion

"This book is a masterpiece, a passionate and intellectual skewering of religion that gives a fresh perspective from a new author. I couldn't put it down! I found this author's command of the English language rather like that of great authors of the past, able to describe difficult concepts eloquently, clearly, and passionately keeping the reader glued to the conversation, wanting more..."
— **Stephanie D. Norris Anthropologist / Archaeologist, in a review that earns** The Crisis of Religion **a 5 Star rating on Amazon.ca (Canada)**

"I read the manuscript of The Crisis of Religion *with great interest and concentration. I agree with most of your charges regarding the gullibility of the majority of religion believers... In short, your entire presentation is a bitter but perhaps necessary pill to swallow."*
— **Mokgethi Motlhabi, Professor of Systematic Theology and Theological Ethics, University of South Africa**

"Thank you! You have captured my sentiments exactly... You have touched on a subject that most people fear to even contemplate. I hope your book will create a space for mind-blowing debate. I felt society needs this."
— **Ms. Choene Nkoana, Pretoria, South Africa**

"This book is a mirror image to the religious fallacy in the Philippines... eloquently written by Adebowale... I do not have enough words to describe the elegance of this book. "
— **Marissa Langseth, Founder, Humanist Alliance Philippine, International**

"I have just finished Adebowale Ojowuro's amazing book, "The Crisis of Religion." And, I salute him for the great work he has produced. He has examined the Jewish/Christian Bible in more depth than I've ever seen before...Very fresh. Very startling. Very growth promoting."
— **Arthur Jackson (San Jose, California)**
Author of How to Live the Good Life: A User's Guide for Modern Humans

Contents

Preface

"All great truths began as blasphemies"

– George Bernard Shaw

*E*xactly three weeks to the official launch of the first edition of this book—*The Crisis of Religion*—one of my childhood friends visited my residence in Pretoria to recount how his mind came directly to me during the course of his pastor's sermon in the church, earlier in the day. According to the details of his account, his passion strongly signified the certainty that the Holy Spirit must have in particular inspired his church pastor to deliver this picky sermon as forewarning to those of us who hold the conviction that there is no God.

He recounted the theme of the sermon was drawn from the first verse of the fourteenth chapter of Psalms; the King James Version of the Holy Bible reads: *"The fool hath said in his heart, "There is no God."* The translation of this same verse in my mother tongue —Yoruba — rendered the word *'fool'* as *'mad.'* Therefore, my concerned friend reproached me to repent from my 'insane' contention that, *"There is no God,"* so I could be saved from eternal condemnation into hellfire.

I thereafter inquired from him if he has a copy of the first edition of *The Crisis of Religion*. He admitted having one, but hasn't had the time to read through. I, at once, advised him to read some of the very elucidating topics the book has intrepidly uncovered, before he could come to any conclusion of who between the two of us is actually afflicted with madness, and needed deliverance from the bondage of pernicious ignorance.

Let me emphasize it once again that I am not a credulous sceptic of religion. I became an unbeliever after I've carefully read the 'Holy

Scriptures' and found its numerous claims to divine inspiration and command to be very much ridiculous for the belief of any rational mind. In the immortal words of Sir Richard Francis Burton, *"The more I study religions the more I am convinced that man never worshipped anything but himself."*

Without a doubt, the scriptural God is a divinity of human invention whose character is terribly fashioned by primitive men after their very own evil and despicable mode of life. The God of organized religion is a typical fiction not different from the Zeus and Thor, Orunmila, Chiuta, and Ngai of ancient mythologies. Therefore, the prose and poetic fancies of mankind are what the architects of religion have cunningly glued together and shoved down the throats of credulous believers as the *"word of God in print."*

The tragedy of this case is that our generation has lost the battle of saving the lives of the next generation of our offspring from being indoctrinated into institutionalized misfortunes of theocratic lies. However, the hope remains that, if the world harkened the voice of reason and judicious observations of Scientists and the Secular Communities, we might replace every error of theological gibberish with uncontaminated truth of our natural world, to save the lives of unborn generation from the calamities of dogmatic beliefs that, through the handiwork of incredible priest-crafty, ruined the lives of their feuding ancestors.

It is undeniable, therefore, that professing dogmatic faith in popular superstitions and ancient myths handed down by our primal ancestors are shared errors that have incredibly retarded Africans from keeping a steady pace with global scientific, social, economic, and technological progress at a time when a swift focus in these areas of development is exceedingly crucial for the survival of African civilization.

When God does not make sense in our world anymore, we should be courageous enough to cast him/her/it off our shoulders, and let the superstitious God of savages rest in peace. It should be morally prohibitive to teach illusions to our children in this modern age. We ought to do our utmost best to give our children up-to-date knowledge that's profoundly proportionate with intellectual faculty of modernity. Children should be taught the science of going to space and not the fantasy of going to imaginary heaven that does not exist anywhere in the cosmic space.

I also wish to mention that my foremost aim for publishing this work is to re-echo my dissenting opinions to the entire world concerning the ills and tribulations of religion, especially the way religion is being delivered to the general populace of Africans. My intention for doing this is to discourage the baffling gullible nature of Africans and motivate extensive interests of my kinsmen in the values of secularism and common humanism. This is because the God of sectarian faith had awfully failed in a continent where the stronghold of organized religion has chronically bred very awkward delusions of terrible nature for the entire black race to be contented with not understanding the world they live in.

Before I bring this Preface to a close, I wish to recognize it in good faith that a number of difficulties have attended my life from all prospects since the release of the first edition of *The Crisis of Religion* into the book market, as numerous colleagues, associates, families, and friends could neither grasp nor welcome the purity of the motive that provoked me into writing against their religion. I, however, do not blame anyone of them for their alarming actions towards me, since I'm very much aware of the naked truth that the entireties of Africans have been strictly tutored under extreme tyranny of faith never at all to question or reason where religion is concerned. Thus, in all, extensive population of my compatriots totally lack whatsoever exposure to any other line of critical thinking, except the dogmatic belief system they have been programmed to accept hook, line, and sinker from childhood. And this, of course, has turned the bulk of my people into gullible belief engines that never at any point in their entire life have the incisive bravery to scrutinize the gross absurdities that impose the reign of stupidity upon their land in the name of *God*.

It's hard to imagine the level of extreme delusion that terribly engulfs such a nation of people where a 33-year-old graduate of Mechanical Engineering does not have the least idea that Jerusalem and Damascus are cities of this world, much less considering the precepts of the phantom of God he so fanatically embrace as incredible con job that originates out of downright fallacies of primitive men. It's not funny at all! Hence, I hold no feeling of resentment against anyone.

However, it is very important for my people to pay attention to this commonsensical advice from the brave author of *The Satanic Verses*, Salman Rushdie: *"Freedom of expression ceases to exist without freedom to offend."* For that reason, I do not think that moral justice allows for any group of people to suffer unfair discrimination in the society, because they have chosen to correct the errors and ills of religion through the astute path of telling the people the cutting truth they do not want to hear.

Amazingly, in the midst of all the odds, I have had the resolute individuality and tolerant optimism to stand by my convictions. Through thick and thin hath the power of rationality capably shepherd me, and well preserve the blotting of my inner conscience from the drench of naive self-deceit; and this has ably empowered me to prevail over brutal repressions petrifying from the den of the faith merchants.

Because I truly know that my total disbelief in contradictory theologies of fictionalized gods does not in any way constitute a crime against humanity and the law of any land, I shall dutifully continue to echo my dissenting opinion against the despotism of faith in our modern society. So long as I still hold the liberty of speech as my civil right, I shall, with all sincerity of purpose, carry on stimulating Africans to the apparent exigency of our modern civilization, which of course is the crucial need to relegate religion to the back seat where it actually belongs.

It is a fine thing in the right direction that we allow for science and secularism to lead the way in our modern age. Africans can no longer afford the dangling of its future hope upon vain belief systems that unreasonably abhor the use of critical thinking. As the German Poet and Freethinker, Heinrich Heine, has aptly observed, *"In dark ages people are best guided by religion, as in a pitch-black night a blind man is the best guide... When daylight comes, however, it is foolish to use blind, old men as guides."*

Organised religion is an apparatus of mental slavery. It is controlling, dividing, extorting and by all appearances hostile to human liberty and suppressive of honest inquiries. It is incumbent upon us all to curtail this adversary of mental freedom in whole nine yards, to attain upright liberation from the shackles of dogmatic creeds that burden the reign of stupidity on the minds of gullible Africans in the name of God. There is no time better than now to open closed minds, so the world can break free from mythical dogmas that seek to compel obedience of organized superstitions upon modern men.

Attentive readers of this book would evidently discern how staggering and incredibly infinite the human stupidity truly is where it concerns religion. For, I methodically beamed extensive spotlight on the extreme folly to which the credulity of man could go at the silly influence of dogmatic faith. It is mindboggling how the untamed excesses of the gullibility of man still awfully obey spurious commands of fictionalized gods, even when these false commands dubiously encourage and promote the most detestable of human stupidity.

I wish to bring this preface to a close in the immortal words of Mohandas Ghandi, *"Truth alone will endure, all the rest will be swept away before the tide of time. I must continue to bear testimony to truth even if I am forsaken by all. Mine may today be a voice in the wilderness, but it will be heard when all the voices are silenced, if it is the voice of truth."*

Reading Notes

I have consistently used the male pronouns 'man', 'he', 'his', and 'him' throughout this book in the place where I intended the generalization of the entire humankind. I have purely adopted this writing style on the ground of perspicuity, orderliness of self-expression, and reading clarity, to avoid the common confusion of word usage. Therefore, my consistent references to 'man' does not in any sense imply gender inequality. Sincere apologies to our mothers, wives, sisters, and daughters.

I have indicated in bracket, all Biblical quotations from the New International Version as (NIV). All Biblical quotations from the King James Version are also in bracket as (KJV).

Where quotations indicate dots, thus ... this signifies the deliberate omission of some sections of the passage for being direct to the point.

Your friend in reason
Adebowale Ojowuro

Chapter

1

The Prelude

"Thinkers aspired to know, or dared to doubt, where bigots had been content to wonder and to believe."

– Lord Thomas B. Macaulay

My agitation to investigate Bible truth and the certainty of religious doctrines and dogmas, as offered under the auspices of the church, started a long time ago. I am not particularly sure of my school grade at that time, whether primary two or three. Routinely, in those days, it was mandatory for the pupils of Saint Paul's Anglican Primary School, then the only primary school in my village, to attend Sunday school classes where village children studied the word of God from the Bible.

I could distinctly remember that, on this particular Sunday, I was ill with malaria fever, but managed to attend church. The theme of our Sunday school sermon came from the fourteenth verse of the nineteenth chapter of the book of Matthew. The King James Version reads, *"Suffer little children and forbid them not to come unto me for of such is the kingdom of heaven."* After the classes that Sunday, I excitedly returned home with the picture of our heavenly residence, sometimes in the near future, not far from that of Uncle Jesus' in the heavenly paradise.

Previously in our Sunday school, the children had gained knowledge of the unique love that Jesus Christ allegedly had for little children. We had also learnt of how Jesus had received special spiritual promotion from his heavenly Father — the Almighty God — on his arrival to the heavenly kingdom in 33CE. With our beloved friend, Jesus Christ, now standing at the right hand side of God as second in command, *"with all rule and authority, power and dominion, and every title that can be given,"* placed under his feet (Ephesians 1:20-23 NIV). I eagerly envisioned, should I happen to die in my sickness, how I would frequently visit our benevolent Deputy God's palatial home in the heavenly kingdom. If possible, sit on his lap, while listening to those interesting stories, parables, and illustrations he normally told on Mount Olives and all other mountainous sites in ancient Israel during his earthly ministry. For some days, after I had listened to the sermon of Matthew 19:14, my heart regularly tickled with excitement that the little ones would also inherit the kingdom of God.

After that, came the death of an old woman in my village. During her funeral service, I sceptically noticed, with curiosity, some contradictory declarations in the Reverend's sermon. These were his indictment of Satan as the cause of all human deaths, alongside his conflicting affirmation that, *"God giveth and God taketh."* My other specific notes included the Reverend's affirmed certainty that the holy angels had gracefully carried the old woman, whose corpse laid inside a coffin in front of the church congregation, to the bosom of the Lord in heavenly paradise. Of particular interest to me as a child was the premise of the Reverend's prayers, which entreated everyone to grow old like the deceased woman before dying and departing to heaven. I cautiously discerned the prayers as being at odd with our previous Bible lessons regarding children and the kingdom of heaven.

When I arrived home, I immediately questioned my grandparents whom I had followed to the funeral service to explain the contradictions of how Satan could possibly be the cause of human deaths, if actually, *God giveth and God taketh,* as the Reverend had earlier sermonized. I also inquired from my grannies concerning the possibility of little children becoming a part of God's heavenly kingdom, as the Reverend's prayers were fervidly against the death of little ones, much less their going to heaven. *"Wouldn't the kingdom of heaven be over-crowded with too many old people?"* I childishly questioned my grannies.

In their replies, my grannies had both supported the Reverend's point of view, but equally added (as I now think) the pagan belief they held before their change of faith into Christianity. They narrated that when a child's lifetime is cut short by sudden death, his spirit or soul does not go directly to heaven; instead, it hovers somewhere around the middle of heaven and earth until a rebirth into life again to complete the number of years that God had appointed the person here on earth. In addition, they affirmed that, it is only upon the completion of God's appointed number of days on earth that such a person might eventually die; thereafter, his spirit or soul would finally gain entrance into eternal kingdom of heaven or hell, depending on the person's life deeds while on earth. Honestly, my grannies' explanation illustrated further mysteries to my keen mind, as it totally ruled out the prospect of children being partakers in the heavenly kingdom of God.

The following Sunday, I hastened up to church to raise these same questions with my Sunday school teacher. All the same, he rendered some clarifications that I was the one who got the wrong end of the stick to his teachings regarding children and heavenly kingdom. He then explained, *"For the kingdom of heaven belongs to those who have such guiltless and sinless heart as that of children."*

Furthermore, I instigated a probe into what becomes of the destiny and fate of the dead little ones. At the same time, I engaged him in questions like how Satan could possibly be held liable for all human deaths, when the Bible plainly affirmed the notion of *"God giveth and God taketh"* in the books of Job and 1Samuel 2:6 (NIV), *"The LORD brings death and makes alive."*

In addition to that, I drew his attention to the conflicting references to Jesus as the son of God, and at the same, God himself; which hoisted the confusion in my head as to how 'God the Father' could possibly downgrade himself to 'God the Son' on earth, and subsequently again get promoted to hold new office as 'Deputy God' in heaven?

Instead of my Sunday school teacher answering my questions and addressing my deep concerns, he conversely scolded me, hauling my rational queries over the coal. He then admonished me to desist from asking such probing questions anymore, but to just believe and accept whatever the church told me.

From that moment onwards, I began to suspect certain fundamental teachings, dogmas, and creeds that severely encumbered ethical and natural truth inside the religion into which my parents had initiated me. However nauseating the code of these religious creeds manifest its absurd trumperies, the Holy Scriptures and its advocates are never wrong; thus, the supremacy of their deceptive teachings absolutely placed above the questioning of any sceptical devotees, even when they appeared nothing more than blatant lies. Accordingly therefore, the cartloads of irrational doctrines are made fittingly relevant amid the torrents of convoluted misconceptions; while the gimmick of godly command subtly provides the spiritual influence by which gullible devotees are led into the path of unreason idiocy.

As a child, I tamely agreed and questioned no more whatsoever my church told me. But, as I progressed in age, I all over again became doubtful like Thomas. I needed solid evidence to prove the God of my inherited faith truly existed in the skies. I actually wanted to be blessed by knowing, and not by hearing and sheer belief. This persistent agitation duly prompted the process of my fervent search for God, which therefore resulted in my crisscrossing the different denomination of churches and other mystical institutions available in my homeland, seeking God and the truthfulness of the apostolic testimonies surrounding Bible miracles.

Regrettably, throughout my fervent search for God, establishing the natural truth of Him in all the several denomination of churches and sanctuaries I have so far attended becomes exceedingly intractable. Unto this day, what I empirically discovered is man's inordinate search for security and not a fragment of his search for gospel truth and faithful worship. Furthermore, my findings evidently revealed the deceptive imposition of man's word upon great multitudes of gullible devotees as the word of God, which has grossly malformed into booming organized trade for extortion, mind control, and authoritarian influence of those who pretend to be oracles of God on earth. All of these findings have clearly confirmed the strong suspicion and doubt I have held from childhood against the Bible being the true word of the creator of the universe, if there exists any.

In writing this book, I took into solemn cognizance, the bare fact that our ancestors in Africa could never have resisted the cartloads of strange religious falsehoods that were forcibly imposed upon their life, because they did not have the basic education to detect them as utter fallacies. However, the case should cease being the same with modern Africans; for it is a debasing sin at this modern age to blindly persist in following the religions imposed upon our ancestors when they were slaves.

It is therefore wise for Africans to pay considerate attention to this sensible advice of Samuel Butler, instead of allowing false religions to mislead them perpetually into the path of stupidity: *"If God wants us to do a thing, he should make his wishes sufficiently clear. Sensible people will wait till he has done this before paying much attention to him."*

It is my hope that this book would offer those who stagger under the confusion of what to believe or disbelieve, the rightful precept to make informed choice and not gullibly accept every strange system of belief in an exceedingly baffling manner.

I find it exceptionally vital at this modern age to sensitize the entire human race to the resolute exigency to wipe out, in totality, all manners of religious conflicts and hates; and entirely expunge every act of religious terror and violence that dogmatic extremism largely engenders all over the world in the name of God. The age has now come for the entire human conscience to eradicate all facets of religious bigotry and fanaticism out of our modern democratic society. The bane of religious dogmas has eaten too deeply into our world, turning countless number of people into dangerous character of extremists who live under bizarre delusion of abiding by the word of God. The act of killing in the name of God must be routed out of our modern way of life. The fraternity of humanity-to-humanity should not engender any act of pious brutality, bitterness and violent conflict amongst humankind, for they are simply not worth the while.

In the beginning was the word, and the word was 'GOD' — the supreme fraud of all times. In the hope of helping our modern society eradicate the nuisance of religious extremism, which sprang out of accepting reprehensible fallacies of savages and ancient con artists as testaments and decrees of the creator of the universe, I here expose the clouds of religious deception to the entire world.

Chapter

2

Our Ignorance is God

*"Faith is the determination to remain ignorant in the face of
all evidence that you are ignorant."*

— Shaun Mason

Throughout the history of humankind, from civilization through civilization, the proclivity of every human culture has profoundly searched through many spiritual pathways for their creator, and the invisible provider of the vast depository of wealth and marvels that thrive in the world they live in. The passionate quest for God has throughout recorded and unrecorded history spread at an explosive rate; resulting in uncountable numbers of religious faiths all over the world.

Patently from the ancient world down to our modern civilization, humankind's intense exploration for God has fanatically passed through the course of several trails and directions. All races of humankind have applied different names and titles to describe the Supreme Being they conceive as the creator and ruler of the universe, the same way they have devotedly invented divergent creeds, dogmas, and religious rituals in the worship of Him.

Like the bountifulness of the colourful rainbow, the fantasies of human intellect and mental prowess have through various appearances contrived series of hypothetical postulations, speculative abstractions, as well as imaginary revelations in all manners of sacred books to depict the image of the supreme spirit they figured out as their Almighty Creator. Various human thoughts have employed countless tales to portray imaginary characters of the creator of the universe, his celestial abode, powers and wishes, as well as his mightiness, alongside that of his invented foe and adversary — Satan — the devil.

All known races, tribes, and societies that spread out across the globe have constantly engaged themselves through one way or another in attentive reverence to some forms of worship, adulation, or religious ritual. Through all ages, it is evident that all species of humankind are deeply conscious and mindful of the existence of some mystical forces they conceived as greater than mortal powers. As a result, the human race has constantly venerated these supernatural forces for appeasement and security, to find imaginary favour and divine support in the life here, and the life they fancied to live hereafter. Thus, unto this day, religion has devotedly attached the conscience of humankind to the worship of the gods.

Many people of diverse background have endlessly told tons of stories about the origin of religion. Multitudes of theologians, mythologists, superstition organizers, historians and anthropologists, including evolutionary biologists and scientists, and many other experts have propounded theories and opinions to describe how the first religion actually evolved on planet earth.

A number of hypothetical indications affirmed the first religion originated with God revealing himself to man. Many theories are prevalent with the speculations that religion actually evolved with man. While several others specified that humankind evidently evolved to become *"belief engines;"* and that the invention of religion is simply an expression of the innate gullibility in the human systems.

The seasoned Professor of Anthropology (Pascal Boyer, 2001), in his book (Religion Explained: The Human Instincts that Fashion Gods, Spirits and Ancestors) theorized that, *"Religion is the result of the psychological mechanisms shared by all normal human minds."* The Roman poet, Titus Lucretius Carus, in his day believed that, *"Fear was the first thing on earth to make gods."* The list of these theories and opinions are as numerous as the sands of the sea.

For several years of my life as a dogmatist, I have time after time devoted attentive thoughts to regular religious sermons, doctrines, and commentaries that habitually proclaim the universe and all of nature's wonders as intelligent designs under the direct creation of an Almighty Maker, commonly known as "God." My keen intellect has for so many years approved the vast magnificence that are of the sun and moon, rivers and oceans, air, fire, rain, thunder and lightning to the clever design of an omniscient creator. In this manner too has the intuition of my inner-self endorsed the splendour of the starry heavens, the complimentary beauty of the rainbow, the picturesque vistas of mountains and valleys, lakes and waterfalls, including the minute details in atoms and molecules, marine creatures, insects and winged birds; together with the spectacles of our abilities to live intelligent life, *etc.,* exclusively to the clever design of an all-wise creator. How better could I have comprehended the entire marvels I often behold in the structure of the universe, if not to attribute the incomprehensible whole to the glory of an intelligent designer?

What else could account for the orderly plan with which the vast machinery of the universe precisely operates? What, as well, could account for the microscopic details of how our cells correctly replicate, in addition to how our DNA transmits the gene of the parent to the progeny in specific details? To what credit could I have endorsed the distinct gender of all animals, if not to attribute it to scriptural doctrines of *"male and female created He them"* Genesis 1:27 (KJV). What, as well, could account for the power of our reproductive abilities, not just to procreate, but also enjoy sexual intercourse with opposite sex? How do we account for the complex design of the eye to capture the sight of distant objects in distinct colours; and with all the different parts of our body components performing various exclusive functions to exacting details?

The entireties of these amazing marvels surrounding us, with utmost good grace, apparently point to the handiwork of a grand designer — *God the Perfect Creator* — rather than some random chances. This true to life insight has been what I constantly perceived in the sermons of *Natural Theology* — the testimonies of what I behold in nature that openly appeal to my sense of reasoning, as well as the sympathy of my experience and ignorance. This factor has been the most convincing basis for which the sincerity of my intuition keenly approves of the reality of the *designer-God* hypothesis for considerable number of years as a theist. For, I had credulously accepted my theistic beliefs conclusively within the confines of my religious viewpoint and bias. As it was then my habitual stock in trade to search for scriptural answers to confirm what I already believed from childhood to be 'true,' rather than apply the rational basis of my common sense to search for what actually is truthful in this whole business of religion. Interestingly too, this same viewpoint remains the most compelling factor that has persistently glued the adherence of extensive number of people of faith to the worship of *Vishnu, Olodumare, Yahweh, Allah, Orisa-Gbodo,* and other countless gods of earthling religions, too numerous to itemize in this book.

Let it be known to the reader that the exact origin of the theological *Argument from Design,* which Theists have hijacked in all times to support the *creator-God* hypothesis, is primarily derived from the evidence of what *Natural Theology* holds forth in the structure of the universe. The proposition of the *Designer Argument* entails that nothing as complex as the universe could ever exist by random chance, unless it be by the skilful design of some sort of intelligent forces, attributable to an '*Almighty God.'*

In all honesty, my Scepticism has no disagreement with the phantom of *God* as a substitute for the ignorance of humankind, especially in the actual face of the unknown. In point of fact, explaining the unknown with the custom of popular superstition should somewhat be explicable and acceptable during the gloomy eras of the human evolution. Therefore, my bone of contention intrinsically lies not with the illusory gods that primitive ignorance of ancient cultures have fashioned, primarily in the absence of logical certainty, to explicate the mystery of the unknown.

When, from the mind of a naturalist, I reflect on the immensity of the marvellous things I often behold in the structure of the awesome universe, my intuition regularly approves of the hands of intelligent creator(s) in the perfect finesse of the natural world; signalling the possibility that these objects and creatures have not merely evolved haphazardly at random. The Magnetic Field of the Earth that protects our planet's atmosphere from space radiation tells me so. Thus sayeth too, the definite laws that power the engine room of the vast mechanisms of the universe. So sayeth the amazing designs I constantly observe in my physical form as a human being — my wonderful set of teeth structured in sparkling enamelware, my eyes and eyelids, the hormonal properties that effect physiological activities in my body, as well as the glands that synthesize substances needed by my body to function ably and eliminates the non-required. In similar manner sayeth the remarkable beauties that I constantly observe in various species of insect, animal, marine creatures, and vegetation life. For these reasons, I have always referred to the supreme creator(s) that I envision as the designer of these marvels as *'Mother Nature.'*

It is, therefore, imperative for the reader to note that my doubt about the truth of religion is not due to the absence of good grounds to believe that the universe and all its infinite products might possibly be the handiwork of intelligent designer(s). Neither is my reason for rejecting the gods of religion due to lack of good grounds to accept the *Argument from Design* as logical enough for my belief in an intelligent creator or multitude of marvellous creators. The very fact that life exists on earth could simply stand as enough evidence for me to think along the line of entertaining the idea that intelligent creator(s) might probably be behind amazing creations of the wonderful world. Moreso, observable evidence of amazing things in nature, in addition to the several complex processes under which various components of the cosmos perform their unique functions to every demanding detail, could also stand as enough evidence for me to accept the existence of a grand designer or numerous excellent designers; especially in the absence of any acceptable scientific data that clearly explicate the origin of the universe and how life's early chemistry begat biology.

Although, vast number of scientists and other truth seekers are still furthering their explorations into the origin of the universe and its intricate mechanisms; it is excellent that they are making appreciable progress in their various areas of endeavour. However, the progress made thus far is certainly not enough to cut the hands of intelligent creator(s) off the origin of the universe and entire matter and creatures therein. This is for the simple reason that we have through the aid of modern scientific observations conducted detailed studies of the universe; and we have thoroughly examined our planet from all possible angles. Through the means of science, we have discovered the vast depository of natural wealth with which the earth is richly furnished for varieties of life to flourish in every bit of material comfort. New breakthroughs in technology have enabled us to exploit the earth's colossal fortunes to our utmost benefits. The course of modern enlightenments has facilitated the discovery of the invisible magnetic field — the protective guard — that shields the earth from space radiations. We have systematically carried out intimate studies of the entire components of our planet's protector — The Earth's Magnetic Field. Even so, the fact of how it has formed, and how it has effectively protected our earthly home from getting irradiated from lethal toxins emitting from outer space has been totally elusive to us.

Of course, we know the sun and all other stars are giant flaming orbs of gas floating in a vacuum, but have wondered as to why these trillions of gigantic orbs of blazing gases have not razed beyond the specific boundaries they have naturally flared for billions of year, as to blot the marvellous symbol of radiant beauties the sun and all the stars display to us in the skies.

The anthropic principle denotes that the physical laws that govern our universe are precisely those that allow for complex life to develop as we know it on earth today. The remarkable balance of these laws — how amazing the universe appears so finely tuned for life — continually poses incredible wonder to several scientists who have devoted ample time into studying mechanisms behind the efficient organization of these laws; as any little change or defect would so drastically alter the universe ecosphere to the extent that life would totally become impossible to exist anywhere in it. But these physical laws have for billions of years performed their different functions to perfect details with no significant disorder. Which brings into rational enquiry as to whether the hands of extra-terrestrial controllers do not actually exist behind the process of these physical laws that govern the amazing universe?

It is undoubtedly true that the evidence of how the universe came into existence and the exact proof of the origin of life on earth still very much remain obscure to researchers unto this day. Although, several theories in *ABIOGENESIS* — the scientific principles that describe the origin of life — endeavour to shed some detailed insights into the origin of life and evolution of species through the process of natural selection, but the substantiations they present have only explicated how life evolved once it got started in the terrestrial world.

In addition, proof of fossil record presents a reasonable case for evolution; however, some critical questions still remain unanswered, as many of the underlying principles of evolutionary strings just do not read well to the discernment of those who would like to identify some obvious examples of the theory of evolution in practical reality. This is especially when they cannot, in most cases, relate any of the evolutionary transition to any clear disclosure that is analogous to natural life as we examine it on daily basis in our world.

Most scholars agree that evolutionary theory runs contrary to quite a lot of evidential facts we behold in nature, in the same vein as the theory of creationism. A good example of this is how the theory of evolution cannot account for why the lower species of apes still thrive in the world according to their kinds, when all the supposed *"ape-men"* that evolved into humans have all gone into outright extinction. According to the theory of evolution, *'ape-man'* is the most superior species of apes, which then makes its kind the most capable of survival than the lower species. The question that here arises is why had the superior species of *'ape-man'* gone into total extinction without affording humanity the prospect of knowing their so-called evolutionary ancestors; when, in fact, the lower species have had continued existence unto this day?

The fossil record also gives no tangible clue that any basic type of animal has ever changed into another basic type. Moreover, no in-between forms have ever been discovered unto this day. Also, evolutionary theory could not explicitly assign ancestors to numerous species of multi-celled life available on earth today. In addition, the theory of evolution still cannot present any evidence to show that humans, animals, or any vegetation life will most likely change into other basic type in the near or distant future. In short, several other unresolved questions have simply tagged the precept of evolution as both theory and uncertain fact. Meanwhile, the growing approval of evolutionary theory in the secular community has in effect provoked intense conflicts between believers and sceptics of the long-established teachings of creationism.

Is a Supernatural Being Truly Up There?

Howbeit, is a 'God' truly up there in the image of man who has caused the universe and all its infinite wonders into being? Well, at this stage, it becomes very vital for us to undertake a systematic enquiry into the information supplied in several of the religious books that informed humans of the existence of a *creator-God* or multitude of creator-deities, to enable us verify whether we can give any credible recognition to the information they narrate to us as containing any reliable matter-of-fact.

According to Ruth Hurmence Green, "*There was a time when religion rules the world. It is known as the dark ages.*" It is evident that the origin of several of the mythical books that are today called the 'word of God in print' by theologians and those with pious reputations dates back to the age when religion rules the world — the Dark Age — the era of vast ignorance in human history.

Great evidence abound within the internal contents of these 'sacred books' that all of its ancient authors were primitive men who modelled their dealings and relations entirely towards the essence of superstitions — unfounded beliefs that an object, action, or circumstance not logically related to a course of event allegedly influences its outcome. These beliefs are usually devoid of experimental reasoning concerning matters-of-fact, as they merely attempted to explain the course of events they did not understand with primitive cosmological myths by attributing their existence to the gods.

Biblical Creation Myth

A good example of how bible writers merely described the course of events they did not understand with primitive cosmological myths is how the author of the Bible book of Genesis has laughably described the clouds of the sky — a visible mass of water vapour or frozen ice-crystals suspended in the atmosphere above the earth — as 'firmament' that God created on the second day and called, "heaven" (Genesis 1:6-8 KJV). The book of Genesis asserts that God created the firmament as a vault of solid structure to separate the oceans from the waters above. However, evidence from ancient Jewish culture reveals that several of these biblical creation stories are, in fact, directly derived from oral traditions of primitive Jews, rather than supernatural revelation from the divine. The Jewish Encyclopaedia describes the belief held by ancient Jews regarding the idea of the sky as follows:

> *The Hebrews regarded the earth as a plain or a hill figured like a hemisphere, swimming on water. Over this is arched the solid vault of heaven. To this vault are fastened the lights, the stars. So slight is this elevation that birds may rise to it and fly along its expanse.*

It is here easy to detect that traditional beliefs prevalent in ancient Jewish culture actually suggested the narration of the firmament story in Genesis account of creation. Although, the idea of a rock-solid sky has been widespread from first to last of all ancient cultures. However, in sharp contrast to the accounts given by the author of Genesis, our modern knowledge of cosmology has plainly revealed the irreconcilable opposite to us in the structure of the universe that there are no **firmaments** above the earth; thereby exposing the emptiness of the work which the Bible alleged God to have performed on **Day Two** of the Genesis creation story as blatant fiction. Indeed, God did not perform any work on **Day Two** as the Jewish Bible has falsely narrated the story in the book of Genesis.

Previously, on the first day, the Genesis God also did not perform any work, as our in-depth knowledge of cosmology has again revealed the irrefutable fact to us that **light** cannot exist in the universe without the sun and the stars — the great luminaries that were allegedly created in biblical accounts of creation on the fourth day. The fundamental issue arising from this case is that, if God did not perform any work on **Day One** and **Day Two** of creation, or rather had performed imaginary creations as nature's evidence has revealed the actual facts to us, how then can we trust the 'creation' God had purportedly performed from **'Day Three'** through **'Day Six'** as inscribed by the author of Genesis?

Several facts available to the knowledge of astronomers and observational cosmologists whose enormous explorations, vis-à-vis the study of the universe, far transcend the boundaries of our Milky Way Galaxy, evidently validate the reality that the sky is plainly an atmospheric expanse; rather than an arched firmament made of solid crystalline material. No astronomer since the day of the martyred Giordano Bruno, through the day of Galileo Galilei, onto our present day, has spotted anything close to the trace of firmament which God called 'heaven' in the eighth verse of the first chapter of Genesis. Astronomers have launched their spacecraft, probes, and telescopes far and wide into the gigantic cosmic space, but nothing like this biblical firmament has been spotted anywhere in the universe; neither did we hear of reports from these highly educated people that the firmament has once obstructed their spacecraft and probes from flying freely across the length and breadth of the cosmic space.

Right from the dawn of recorded time, extensive enquiry had been expended to verify the nature of the biblical firmament; and all verifications positively reveal the proof that *'firmament'* as described in the book of Genesis is downright misconception that represents nothing but blatant betrayal of the ignorance of primitive men who perceived the clouds as a solid ceiling-like dome arched over the earth; and to this ceiling-like vault were fastened great multitude of stars, the sun and moon.

After far-reaching study of the mysteries surrounding the falsehood of the biblical firmament had been exhausted from the late Middle Age through Early Modern Age, John Calvin, renowned Protestant theologian of the Calvinism fame, proposed to the church in 1554 that the biblical firmament be correctly interpreted as clouds. He wrote: *"...Genesis had to conform to popular prejudice regarding cosmology... Moses had to respect us rather than the stars."*

It is to be noted that a similar creation myth denoting the sky as a solid dome arched over the earth was first recorded in Sumerian mythology. The Sumerian sky-god, *Anu* (the god of heavens, king of gods) ruled these firmament-like "heavens," which the wind-god had separated from the flat disc of the earth below, and there were primordial seas above the firmament (Encyclopaedia Britannica). This prehistoric fable is exactly what the book of Genesis has again updated and listed in its mythical story as second creation of Jewish/Christian God.

How, for example, can modern biologists believe the invalid report of Genesis that vested the naming of all species of animal upon Adam, when they truly know the definite fact that new species of organisms are continually been discovered, identified and aptly named by various divisions of biological taxonomies — the branch of biology that deals with the science of classifying and naming living organisms?

We can also find another example of the absurdities of ancient scriptures in the ninth chapter of the book of Genesis; therein, the author oddly attributed the prismatic effects of raindrops that materialize in the sky as rainbow to be the *covenant sign* between the Jewish God and the nation of Israel, as well as the entire living creatures and the earth:

> *And God said, 'This is the token of the covenant which I make between me and you and every living creature that is with you, for perpetual generations: I do set my bow in the cloud, and it shall be for a token of a covenant between me and the earth.'* Genesis 9:12-13 (KJV).

It is to be noted that:

- The primitive author of the Norse mythology had described the rainbow as the **'road'** between the worlds of the gods and man.

- In related odd manner too had the primordial Irish believed that a **'pot of gold'** lies at the end of a rainbow.

- The ancient Greeks also believed that the rainbow was the sign from the gods to foretell **'war and heavy rain.'**

- While primitive Indians believed that rainbow was the sign between the living and the dead.

It is today clear to all modern men through our knowledge in science that the rainbow does not signify any bogus covenant sign between the Jehovah of the Jews and humankind. We today know that the Norse mythology that represents the rainbow as the road between the gods and man is utter fallacy. We also can evidently observe the fact very well that the rainbow contains no pot of gold in either of its ends as the ancient Irish had then believed. It is also evident to modern men that primitive Indians were totally wrong in their belief that the rainbow was the sign between the living and the dead. The true picture of what rainbows really are is provably far from what the primitive author of Genesis has misled the world into believing it to be. It is, therefore, obvious to all that the biblical explanation for rainbow is perceptibly not different from any of the outdated ancient mythologies.

The rainbow is, in reality, a prismatic effect of raindrops — an arch of particular colours formed in the sky, in certain circumstances, caused by the refraction and dispersion of the sun's light by rain or other water droplets in the atmosphere. The rainbow therefore is not any false covenant sign between any imaginary God and any nation of people in the Middle East or the entire human race.

Yet again, in the same absurd manner, had the primitive author of the third chapter of Genesis preposterously attributed the painful parturiency of childbirth to represent divine curse from the Jewish God upon Eve — the first woman in the Bible and her offspring — because she ate the forbidden fruit in the Garden of Eden. It is also easy to detect that the circumstance of the pains that women experience during childbirth had merely suggested the idea of the fable in Genesis 3:16. (KJV) *"Unto the woman he said, I will greatly multiply thy sorrow and thy conception; in sorrow thou shalt bring forth children."* It is a fact on scientific records that human feminine folk is not the only creature that bears the monopoly of painful childbirth. In actual sense, most animals that fall into the category of mammals — the class of warm-blooded vertebrate animals whose females have secret milk glands to feed their babies — also suffer painful labour during childbirth. The giraffes, impala, horses, cattle, including apes, goats, zebra, sheep etc., are all examples of animals that suffer great agonies, as their tears, groaning noises, and gesticulations suggest severe pains like that of female humans during childbirth. However, the Bible did not tell us that any of these animals also ate of the forbidden fruit in the Garden of Eden which, in addition, consigned them under divine spell of painful labour during childbirth.

Any reasonable person can see how invalid and unreal the explanations of ancient mythologists concerning the clouds above the earth, the rainbow, and painful labour during childbirth really are. We all can see that the entire beliefs of the ancients are pretty much absurd. In addition, we can clearly see that the alleged *'word of God in prints'* are downright fallacies of primitive men, which they dishonestly ascribed to heavens and the gods. And that those who still believe in these absurd stories, despite the proof of our modern scientific observations to the contrary, are very much delusional and ignorant in exact manner similar to that of primitive people that lived in dark ages.

It is, thus, evident that the fairy-tales surrounding the sun god, moon god, rain god, sea god, Zeus, Ra, Thor, Isis, the gods of iron and thunder, and all the gods of antiquity that have withered and shrunken into the monotheistic *God* of organized religion, including their Satan, Messiah, angels, and self-styled prophets, are altogether fantasies of primitive men. They are nothing more than mere attempts of these primitive authors to explain things they do not clearly understand with false and fanciful stories, which credulous people in their day have subsequently come to believe and accept as both true and foundational identity of their particular tribe or race.

According to American Heritage dictionary of the English Language, "*Ignorance is wilful neglect or refusal to acquire knowledge which one may acquire and it is his duty to have.*" Therefore, our credulous belief in the totality of these absurd myths as the word of the creator of the universe (if there exists any) is primarily the depth of our wilful neglect or refusal to acquire proper and accurate knowledge in the areas where religion is concerned.

The fact is very clear to all rational people that all the gods that theists have described in their *'sacred books'* are far from being the creators of any component of the universe, because they are all imaginary gods. On the other hand, the fact is also very clear that no definite scientific data is currently available to the human race, as to how the universe and life truly began. Therefore, recognition of this fact should sensitize Sceptics and Freethinkers into reappraising the proposition of a designed universe by looking into other probable directions; because we cannot adamantly ignore the revelation of what our knowledge of cosmology has so far made known to us through several scientific observations. Hence, I still hold the conviction very close to my heart that it is imperative to allow for a game of permutation and combination of all possible positions that intelligent creator(s) might probably exist in the extra-terrestrial world.

Evolutionary theory categorically reveals some logical proofs that limitless mortal lives have consequently evolved in the terrestrial world owing to the very conducive ecospheres that prevail for life to flourish in its environment. And, out of these uncountable varieties of evolved life, also evolved **Man-the-Maker**, who happens to be in control of creative affairs on planet earth. Rational lead that therefore springs out of the validity of what evolution teaches us, most reasonably imply that varieties of wide-ranging life — immortal and the supernatural — could also have possibly evolved according to their kinds in any of the most conducive ecospheres in the extra-terrestrials. Conceivably too, out of this possible evolution of the supernatural, intelligent creator(s) could also have possibly evolved to take charge of cosmological creations in the universe. We simply do not know, therefore we cannot out of our deficiency in knowledge rule out such probability. This is the exact point where our ignorance still faces *'epistemological black hole,'* as we obviously do not have experimentally provable information that credibly detach the hands of intelligent creator(s) from the structure of the universe.

The point I am making here is that the partial confirmation that our progressive knowledge of cosmology has so far afforded us implies that the possibility of intelligent creator(s) of the universe is indeterminate and very much unclear. The firm certainty that is undeniably definite to the perception of every rational human being is that the stories surrounding supernatural revelations from the gods of religion are altogether fables. Therefore, if the universe is in point of fact the handiwork of intelligent designer, it does not in any way mean that the designer is correctly the *God* of religion who, by theists' accounts, inspired all the grossly unintelligent 'holy books' available on planet earth. In the meantime, the more our search for the truth progresses, the more the barrier multiplies against the claim of these supernatural creations from the *God* of religion.

Let me reiterate it clearly to the reader that the basis upon which I have rejected the countless gods of religion differs in a number of ways to that of several other nonbelievers. My scepticism concerning the gods of religion aligns most comparably with the firm declaration found in Charles Bradlaugh's essay of 1864, entitled, 'A Plea for Atheism:'

> *The Atheist does not say "There is no God," but he says, "I know not what you mean by God: I am without idea of God; the word 'God' is to me a sound conveying no clear or distinct affirmation. I do not deny God, because I cannot deny that of which I have no conception, and the conception of which by its affirmer is so (confused) that he is unable to define it to me."*

Errors of Teleological Argument

The teleological argument for God as the intelligent creator of the amazing world is, for the most part, erected upon the proposition that the universe is too complex for it **not to have been designed** by an intelligent creator. It is undoubtedly clear to every reasonable person that this is a proposition ably informed by every atom of common sense, and I sincerely have no problem with that.

However, my dispute with the basis of this argument is upon the fact that, if at the resolve of common sense, theologians conclude that the universe is too complex to have evolved at random chance, how then should the same common sense not equally appeal to the rule of their judgments that the creator-God must also be far too complex than all of its supposed creations for him/she/it to have evolved merely at the behest of random chance? This is taking into cognizance that there is no way an unintelligent idiot could have designed a complex universe. Therefore, the complexity and grandeur of this creator-God should by any standard surpass all of its supposed creations. Even if the creator-God is just as complex as the universe, it would also have been impossible that he/she/it could have just evolved abracadabra without a creator of greater relevance to his/her/its grandeur primacy. For that reason, the creator-God must equally require a designer as much as the universe to be able to derive his/her/its existence. Whence, then, cometh the God of religion?

As Philosopher, Douglas Adams, has appositely posed the pertinent question to theists:

> *If we imagine a designer, that implies a design and that therefore each thing he designs or causes to be designed is a level simpler than him or her, then you have to ask 'What is the level above the designer?'*

The deficiency in the designer argument greatly bothers on the fact that it simply does not reveal where factually the designer came from.

Argument from Ignorance

Despite the fact that several colours of conflicting arguments (for and against) the existence of God have been very much over-flogged in different dimensions by numerous sceptics and religious enthusiasts in recent past; kaleidoscope of postulated opinions in these arguments have not been of any convincing help to establish the true existence of any God.

As new concepts of hypothetical conjectures are on daily basis emerging to argue for the existence of God, thus too are significant objections arising from sceptics for its rebuttal. I, therefore, do not deem it necessary to start another dry-run all over again in an attempt to debunk confidence hypotheses of those who pretend to be oracles of God by reinventing endless arguments over baseless suppositions in history books that contain chronic lies from cover to cover. For, it is entirely redundant to continue preaching the same old sermon to the choir; especially when all the choristers in both camps know the facts too well that no amount of arguments for the existence of God, without cogent evidence, can ever make it plausible that the gods of religion truly exist. Therefore, the complete absence of evidence in these arguments, at best, characterized its basis as hypothetical rationalization based upon ignorance.

However, I shall endeavour to shed lights on a number of points I consider necessary to further enlighten innocent souls who stagger under the confusion of what to believe or disbelieve, the equitable precept to moderate their confused state of minds. And, in the same vein, stimulate rational believers into utilizing reason — the free gift of nature — to reflect more deeply on the absurdity of adverse delusion that hoodwink them into believing counterfeit word of God that looks suspiciously like the word of man.

From whichever point of view that one might choose to examine the collection of pious opinions put forward by theologians and countless advocates of religion in their efforts to transform the word of man into the word of the creator of the universe, if there exists any; all their arguments have proven to every single extent as unfounded conjectures of men who speak of things they obviously do not at all discern.

I have committed ample time into reading a couple of numerous hypotheses emanating from religion apologists in support of the arguments for the existence of their God. It is necessary to add that I could draw no other conclusion from the philosophy of these arguments than series of personal opinions formulated in calculated attempts to provide consoling answers in the face of utter ignorance. I, moreover, perceive the bulk of these hypotheses for God entirely as guarded notions limited by lack of objective authenticity, but wholly bent on strengthening the propagation of faith over and above the truth of validating the real existence of God. The eccentric fabrications contained in these pious arguments are comfortable opinions that typify fanatical commentaries of diehard bigots to fill unsolved gaps in knowledge with baseless propositions, out of extreme desperation to preserve the pious trade, regardless of what on earth the penalty of massive societal deceit might bring upon the progress of the human civilization. The totality of these arguments wholly represents express betrayals of the peculiarity of accustomed deceit that flows directly from the inner heart of the original theology that is widely called the 'word of God in print' by attorneys of organized superstitions.

Rabbi Moshe Averick, author of *Nonsense of the High Order: The Confused and Illusory World of the Atheist* — a literary work that aptly represents its illogical title — asserts the reality of God thus in his rejoinder to Atheists' Objections to the Design Argument:

> *At some point in the progression, we are faced with the inescapable conclusion that there must be a creator who is not physical matter at all; a creator who does not need to be created; a creator who is not subject to the limitations of cause and effect. There must be a creator who is the first, who is the beginning of it all. There must be a creator who is outside of the physical universe. A creator who is outside of the physical universe, not existing in time and space, and composed of neither matter nor energy, does not require a preceding creator. There is nothing that came before him. He created time, he does not exist in time; there is no "before."*

I would like to learn just one more thing from you, Rabbi! Did you receive this revelation through the spirit or by believing what your ancestors told you? Otherwise, are these your critical effort of thoughts? If so, are you now trying to attain your goal by human efforts, in express contradiction to Paul's advice to the Galatians? Galatians 3:1 (KJV). For

verily, verily I say unto you, Rabbi: Your affirmation, *"There must be --*
There must be," sounds very much like the chant phrase of ancient
conjurers who made gods by the dozens into the human world.

The truth is very obvious to every discerning mind that the precept of
several theological arguments for God, as presented under the umbrella
typology of organized religion, wholly falls within the category of
arguments that merely appeal to ignorance. They altogether signify
'informal logical fallacy,' established upon stated premise that entirely
disconnect from providing support for the proposed conclusion for which
the objects of the arguments have been invented. The foundation of such
arguments is wholly erected upon the odds that some false propositions
may never be disproved with absolute conviction, because they cannot be
empirically evaluated by the means of science. The proponents of these
arguments basically take advantage of the constrictions that scientists
cannot experiment some of the specifics of their claims, or test the
hypothesis that God exists. Therefore, several of the mythical points in the
arguments primarily rely on exploiting the loophole that there is not
enough knowledge at hand to detect or arrive at an explicit conclusion
regarding the conjecture of *God* as the creator of the universe.

Evolutionary biologist, Douglas J. Futuyma correctly asserts in his
book, 'Evolution': *"The fundamental claim of creationism that biological*
diversity is the result of supernatural powers is not testable. This is equally
true of 'intelligent design' theory; it cannot be evaluated by the methods
of science." As a result, such proposition cannot be considered a
downright lie simply because there is insufficient knowledge at hand to
expose its falsehood to the world.

The definition that various religions — Brahmins, Shintoists, Judeo-
Christian-Islamist, and all other religions known to humankind in this
world have offered to describe their respective God is that of eternal and
absolute existence, uncreated and self-existed supernatural being of
infinite power and wisdom. For millennia, most religions have at all times
described their God as unalterable divine entity who is present
everywhere and very much in control of all natural events and matters in

the entire universe. The concept of a monotheistic God to all people of faith is that of supreme reality in power and wisdom, holiness, and virtue, who is often conceived of as a personal being, the three Omnis' father-figure, who has human attributes and personal acquaintances with every aspect of earthling needs and practices — language, money, sex, love, jealousy, hate, marriage, suffering, slavery, theft, war, adultery, including the 10% rules, etc. The monotheistic God of religion is customarily regarded as the universal grand provider who enacted specific guidelines in various holy books, under which humankind is compelled to live their life and dutifully worship him as their Almighty creator.

Going by the concept of God that theists have described to the human race, the question of how the three Omnis father-figure have come into existence will certainly be by no other means but evolutionary course. Since he could not have created himself and no other higher God is here available in the picture that could have created him; for that reason, his mysterious existence could not have been otherwise explained except by evolutionary course. This is the only possible option we can conceive of the inexplicable existence of any uncreated God.

Therefore, if a complex, three-headed God or multiple of gods could so evolve at the behest of random chance, why then could the less complex, single-headed human, animal, and vegetation life not evolve at random chance? In other words, if theologians could agree to the proposition that their God had derived his existence through the process of evolution, why should they refuse to accept the proposition that the less complex mortal life had also derived their very existence through the process of evolution, without the need of a creator? Isn't it the height of downright confusion for theologians to grant the existence of their God to random chance evolution, but obstinately refuse to accept all the evidence that certify the existence of the less complex earthlings as products of evolution by the means of natural selection? This is where the **'fallaciously valid'** points that embellish the *Argument from Design* entirely disconnect from its stated foundation, as it basically aligns more with evolutionary theory than the creation myth for which it has been invented to safeguard from downright collapse.

Trace it back and front, the idea of an uncreated God could only be acceptable under evolutionary theory, as the supposed 'First Cause' could only have come into existence through evolutionary course (if this mystical father figure is uncreated). This is the only reasonable way we can conceive of any idea relating to the existence of an uncreated God anywhere in the terrestrial or extra-terrestrial world.

The entire argument for intelligent design is preposterously based on logical fallacy of false dichotomy. For, it deceptively imposes a fictitious God not logically related to the cause of creating the universe as its conjured maker. Another major flaw in the Designer Argument is that the details of creation process, allegedly made known to us by the supposed creator of the universe, are highly suspect materials. These fallible details, especially as inscribed on the pages of the professed guidebook that purportedly originated from the throne of the 'creator-God,' by the accounts of evangelical propagandists, are inversely proportional to all proofs that nature constantly display to the knowledge of humankind in the structure of the universe. The entire 'revelation' in the alleged 'Holy Scriptures' apparently **agrees not** with the reality of what the sermon of nature evangelizes to us in the structure of the universe. In other words, creationism as offered to us in the book of religion is gravely at discord with several valid observations we behold in the book nature. It is therefore evident from abundant discrepancies in these 'Holy Scriptures' that the imaginary 'God' which theists have contrived in their sacred books and their subsequent arguments for intelligent design is undoubtedly a fake creator. The God of religion is certainly not the creator of the universe we behold, if there exists any.

For any proposition to be considered valid, all of its components must be convincingly seen to a wide-ranging extent to be well-founded on categorical truth. The **evidence of clear-cut truth** is grossly deficient in every of the alleged guidebook that theologians have imposed upon humankind as the word of the creator of the universe. Credible authentication of anything called **'truth'** is, noticeably, not present at all in that which is called the 'word of God in print.'

According to Bertrand Russell, *"It is undesirable to believe a proposition when there is no ground whatsoever for supposing it is true."* When a proposition is offered to any reasonable person, a critical and unbiased assessment of the validity of the evidence adduced to the proposition is the only reasonable way under which to ascertain the truth of its claim.

Touching the Record of Constant Evidence

In 1903, innovatory automobile manufacturer, Henry Ford, proclaimed to the entire world, *"I will build a car for the great multitudes."* Five years later, he made good his words, and rolled out his first batch of Model T cars with instruction manual that carried the signature and official seal of the Ford Motor Company. The instruction manual itemized every component part in the new car according to their exacting positions. It was very obvious to the discernment of all users and mechanics that this, indeed, was an authentic guidebook duly issued and certified by the rightful manufacturer of the product; as every detail could so be fittingly confirmed to the clear observation of all, just exactly as the authentic designer of the product had documented it in the instruction booklet.

True to brand quality assurance certification, all users and mechanics were able to locate the propeller, radiator, head lamp, spark plugs, and all other component parts accurately at the precise spot the designer had clearly outlined they were to be found in his guidebook. Definitely, the record of *constant evidence* in Henry Ford's instruction manual required no defence of compulsory professional *'argumentators'* to safeguard his assertion as the legitimate designer of Model T series, because every confirmation that reality could afford us, especially from the merit of his bona-fide instruction manual, clearly approved of Mr Ford as the true designer of Model T cars. Therefore, not a single case of doubtful inkling could rear its ugly head anywhere next to the reputation and character of Henry Ford anytime the debate arose as to who the original maker of the Model T car truly was. However, basket cases of suspicion, inconsistent forgery, and mistrust would naturally mount against the claim of Mr Ford only when people detect his guidebook as nothing more than spurious and absurd contradictions, as well as patent forgery of flight-by-night impostor, which is no different to run-of-the-mill tales that normally do the rounds in fiction books. It is, obviously, in the light of such doubtful cases that the service of professional *'argumentators'* and skilful attorneys of superstition are most obligatory to fill the heads of gullible bigots with absurdities of validating corrupt and illegitimate manual through the fraud of inconsistent rationalization based on fallacy.

Beginning from when the first *'Sacred Scripture'* emerged on planet earth, mystery has ever since encircled its true origin. Different salvos of relentless arguments unleashed upon the general public by professional argumentators and people with pious status have not helped in any palpable way to clear the clouds surrounding the true origin of the their 'Holy Book.' I therefore consider it a fruitless exercise for theologians to divert our attention from the original root of these mysteries into another superfluous level of postulating different colours of arguments financed by religious groups to bolster up the existence of their gods in peoples' mind — when, in fact, the rickety and fallacious foundation upon which they have erected the basis of their arguments is extremely doubtful.

In our sincere efforts to disentangle the mystery that engulfs the truth of religion and set the record straight, I truly believe we have no duty to uphold these Arguments from Ignorance to sustain the existence of God in peoples' mind. Rather, it becomes very important that we start by tackling disturbing questions that shadow the true source of these holy books; in that our bias and preconceived notions may not inflict wrongful verdicts upon any judicious insight that may exists in whatever credible arguments thereafter proposed. And, that we may, in addition, determine with exactitude whether there is sufficient authority for believing any of the Holy Scriptures as the true word of the creator of the universe, or whether there is not. This is what sceptics and theologians must coherently do in successive measures, until we discard every vague matter that is **fallaciously invalid.**

As Charles Bradlaugh has critically observed, *"The best policy against all prejudice is to assert firmly the verity."* Even the Bible urges believers to examine every claim into exacting details in order to establish the reliability of that which is the truth. *"Prove all things; hold fast that which is good"* 1 Thessalonians 5:20 (KJV). This counsel is very obligatory upon us all; on the reward that, that which is doubtful and contrary to reason might, with no trouble, be denounced as fallaciously invalid.

The first step is to ascertain the fact very solidly on rational grounds, whether or not sufficient authority truthfully exists at hand for humanity to believe the suspicious tales in religious *sacred books* as the true inspiration of the creator of the universe, if there exists any. It is, therefore, rash and equal to downright use of *'fallacy of false choice'* for theologians and advocates of religion to resort to the means of speculative arguments to drive collective obedience of the masses to the belief of their professed gods. It is only when we have very accurately established the true origin of the Holy Scriptures as the product of divine inspiration and command, along with when we have accurately confirmed the true identity of their respective authors that we can then proceed to the second episode of determining whether any valid argument truly exists to believe the existence of the gods of religion. Until this is done, the dispute between sceptics and religionists will forever remain unresolved.

Is God an Unavoidable Redundancy in Human Life?

It is very obvious that the record of doubtful stories in sacred books has not truly convinced majority of the people that one god or the other has given any revelation from On High about him/herself/itself as the creator of the universe to whichever self-styled prophets, theologians, rabbi, imams, priests, clerics, and professional preachers. The truth of this case is that over two billion Christians all around the world are unreceptively suspicious of the reality of divine revelation that Moslems assert for the source of the Holy Quran; the same way as they vehemently disbelieve the validity of the Hindus' Bhagavad-Gita as divinely inspired word of the creator of the universe. In the same vein that over one and a half billion Moslems worldwide have critically expressed outright rejection of the biblical story of Jesus as the four gospel accounts have recorded it. While another set of one and a half billion Hindus and Buddhists jointly reject the tales of both the Bible and the Quran as utter fallacy. The indication is quite clear from all fronts that the God of religion is an unavoidable redundancy amongst the different races of the human species, as it is evident from the distrustful scepticism with which every sectarian faith has rejected the claim of one another to divine revelation. If the testaments and revelations of the creator of the universe truly exist in any printed book, it is certain that the whole world would believe it alike. In other words, if the valid creator of the universe has indeed spoken to humankind, the word of the creator-God should have credibly convinced the entire world, but the case isn't so.

Emerging proofs from several investigations of religious studies scholars, in addition to our modern enlightenments through science, have enabled us to discover without any atom of doubt that ancient narratives of revelations from On High and supernatural tales that purportedly emanate from the throne of the creator of the universe are utter fallacies and doubtful hearsays originating from nowhere, but confidence tricks of ancient theologians. Therefore, the bulk of these contemptible deceits to divine revelations from an imaginary God that does not exist, undeniably represent unsound and fallacious claims that further disprove the God hypothesis rather than ascertain its precise validity in definite clarity. It is upon this ground that I reasonably erect the basis of my disbelief of all scriptural gods and the entireties of the highly suspect materials that several religious people today refer to as the *'word of God in print.'*

As I have earlier stated, it is not my intention to start another rehearsal argument in this book, as is too often the inordinate longings of those with pious reputations to fabricate colours of baseless arguments and commentaries to protect their religious trades. I honestly do not intend doing this, because my previous investigations into these so-called *'Holy Scriptures'* in the first edition of this book, clearly exposed the alleged 'word of God in print' as ramblings of ancient liars. This same conclusion goes for all those apologetic arguments for the existence of scriptural God, as they typically constitute the ramblings of modern liars. So, no authority whatsoever exists for believing the tales of the alleged 'holy books' as the 'word' of the creator of the universe any more than we can believe the philosophy of these arguments. For, it is more than obvious that they lack any cogent evidence to prove to rational minds that the cartloads of contemptible fallacies in the supposed 'Holy Scriptures' that narrate the existence and testaments of God to humankind are truly divine products of the creator of the universe, if there exists any.

I did mention in the earlier part of this chapter that the sermon of *Natural Theology* — evidence of what we behold in nature — is noticeably what theists have hijacked to sustain the *Argument from Design* in support of their God as the *creator* of the universe. Unfortunately, every attentive enquiry into the validity of the 'Argument from Design' has, in fact, rendered the theological account of creation very much absurd; since the argument could not uphold the basic foundation of scriptural account of creation for which it has been invented.

A good example of this is how the *Designer Argument* could not give any credible support to biblical fallible account of creation that dates the earth's age and all organisms and physical elements in it to be a little over six thousand years old. Every scientific enquiry has evidently confirmed the realistic truth that organisms and physical elements in the universe have had sustained existence for several millions of years, in direct contradiction to the creation myth in the book of Genesis. It is to be noted that in year 2006, a scientific consensus validated the research result that dates the earth's age to about 4.5 billion years old as evidence-based fact. The fundamental issue arising from the verdict of this scientific consensus is that it, in effect, nullifies the Genesis account of revelation from God that relates the course of divine creation to humankind, together with all ensuing *Arguments from Design,* as baseless and downright fallacy.

In short, it is evident that no argument in whatever form has been able to give a clear-cut answer to the puzzling question of how God and the universe have truly come into existence; the same way as all the pages of the 'sacred books' that claim to contain the revelations of God in print could practically not offer any clue. From the *First Cause Argument* through *Ontological Argument* to the *Intelligent Design Argument,* including the *Moral Argument*...etc., all these artificial and incoherent opinions of pious men have merely succeeded in painting the existence of their fictionalized gods in total obscurity. The conclusion arising, thereof, denotes that our ignorance is God.

For the factor of causal deficiencies that largely constrain the knowledge of humankind, from the dawn of recorded time unto this day, in decoding accurate data of how the universe actually came into existence, along with how life's early chemistry begat biology; it thus becomes explicable as to why the phantom of God has preposterously reigned supreme over all human civilizations, all the way through the Dark Age into our modern era. It is absolutely clear from this plain reason that our ignorance is **God.**

Why My Apostasy

My fall out with religion lies not with whether a God or a host of gods truly created the universe or not. Neither is my trouble with religion in any conflict with who the supreme governor of the universe really is; nor who the deputy God might be; be it Prophets Moses, Jesus, Mohammed, Lord Ganesha or Buddha. Whether the celestial Congress Leader is angel Gabriel and the Chief Whip is Satan the devil, constitutes none of my business. For, I bother not myself with that which merely exists on the basis of supposition and fabrication that stem from humans' awkward delusion. Nonetheless, my dispute with religion lies with the massive deceit under which the cartel of organized religion had very craftily manipulated the control of the human minds in collective obedience to what is totally not true in this whole business of religion, for the purpose of extortion, mind control, and authoritarian influence of those who pretend to be oracles of God on earth.

The foremost of these problems is the network of outrageous lies and falsehood that organized religions have built across the length and breadth of the blue planet. My dispute with religion bothers greatly on the supreme chieftain that theologians and priests have hijacked in the society to take charge of how the mortals should be indebted to live their lives. It is baffling to imagine how self-styled prophets have continued to rule the entire world in deceit. How artificial 'holy men' have continued to control the lives of humans under the pretence of being custodians of sacred authority of an imaginary God that does not exist. How could a fiction character, who merely existed in the cock-and-bull story of human ignorance, truly have spoken to these pretended men of God; when all evidence, in fact, show the embroidered myths in the alleged holy books, featuring 'God' as a lead character, are far from being the products of divine wisdom? Rather, the doubtful tales that these so-called sacred books have fallaciously related to mankind are untrue stories, gross exaggerations, and deceits that originated from nowhere other than the mindset of ancient con artists. It is evident from all enquiries of religious studies' scholars that the big claims in all the holy books are nothing more than speculative theology of evangelical propagandists, as well as sheer impositions of charlatans to turn misguided judgments of humans into divine commands, primarily for the purpose of power and lucrative profits. It's a big failure of society to allow a group of people with bogus claim to usurp the control of how humans should live their lives, as is presently the case all over the continent of Africa. The time has now come for rational people to speak up against this illegitimate and morally obscene situation in our society, for it is totally an improper, abhorrent, and baffling imposition.

It is bare naked to all unprejudiced minds who desire the path of truth that the contents of these holy books that confer Divine Power of Attorney upon these artificial men of God are plainly human inventions that should never at all be trusted or taken seriously any more than we can rely on fiction books. Moreso, the validity of the true identity of the scribes who penned down the inspired word on behalf of the alleged heavenly author, together with their bogus claim to divine revelations, largely remain a mystery unto this day. Every evidence that nature and scientific observations constantly afford the earthlings has obviously rendered the holy books of organized religion as invalid forgery and downright falsehood in its entirety. It is clear from this reason that the proof of the official seal and signature of whosoever the divine creator of the universe might be, is conspicuously missing therein.

As the reader may be aware, I have in the past employed substantial time to examine these so-called 'word of God in print' in my first revolt against the supreme tyranny of theology in the first edition of this book— *The Crisis of Religion*. The outcome of my probe into the 'Holy Scriptures' clearly incriminates all of its stories as ramblings of ancient liars. It was, indeed, with devastating evidence that I probingly spotted doubtful, dubious, and questionable holes in the alleged holy inspiration of the creator of the universe. Of course, these invented Holy Scriptures, enormously bear internal holes within its pages that gravely expose the suspicious hands of inconsistent, fly-by-night liars. Very shocking and ineffable fallacies that undeniably confirm the alleged word of God in print as fantastic works of ancient con artists are widely patent for the verdict of all discerning minds; as not a single thing in that which is called the 'word of God,' at least, points to any particular evidence of divine revelation and wisdom. As Bernard J. Bamberger has resolutely asserted in 'The Story of Judaism:'

> *The Bible as we have it contains elements that are scientifically incorrect or even morally repugnant. No amount of 'explaining away' can convince us that such passages are the product of Divine wisdom.*

This same analysis holds true of Albert Einstein observation regarding the alleged word of God in print:

> *The word of God is for me nothing more that the expression and product of human weakness, the Bible a collection of honourable, but still purely primitive, legends which are nevertheless pretty childish. No interpretation no matter how subtle can (for me) change this... For me the Jewish religion like all other religions is an incarnation of the most childish superstition.*

Honestly, this book is all about what Jerry told Juliet, and what Columbus narrated to Sandra, including an 'upward of a thousand lies.' Hmm ... word of God indeed! Funny how humans are always doing the talking!

Any book that reinforces stupidity in the society cannot be a holy book in any logic and wisdom. No one will deny or dispute the fact that the highlight of the growing conflicts between believers and sceptics mainly stem from the highly suspect materials embedded in several of these alleged 'holy books.' All proofs that reality exhibit to the knowledge of humans entirely have rendered the so-called 'word of God in print' as cartloads of pious fraud, collated under the cover of artificial and faceless authors, with every identity of profane deception impressed beneath the motives of their inventions.

In fact, the root cause of my doubtful suspicion about the validity of the Holy Scriptures bothers greatly on the question of how divine inspiration and command could possibly have originated from an imaginary God. Investigations of several scholars into the true source of these so-called 'Holy Scriptures' empirically reveal there is no *Pot of Gold* at the end of the rainbow. It is curious to note that not a single line of the internal books of the Bible is penned down by the authors for whom they are named. But, in contrast, they are deceptive forgeries of mysterious writers whose real identity cannot be established or confirmed to this present day. I shall deal with this topic in greater details in a later chapter.

Whenever I listen to that which the Theists call the 'voice of God' in his divinely authorized guidebook, I continually hear the voice of man chatting audibly at full volume: *This is what sayeth Hieronymus to Amanda, and what Athanasius decreed his credulous disciples.* Ooh...word of God indeed! But funny how humans are always doing the talking?

*****

"Religion is comparable to a childhood neurosis. The whole thing is so patently infantile, so foreign to reality, that to anyone with a friendly attitude to humanity it is painful to think that the great majority of mortals will never be able to rise above this view of life."

— **Sigmund Freud.**

*****

Chapter

3

Man the Maker

"Men create God after their own image, not only with regards to their form but with regards to their mode of life."

– Aristotle

$\mathcal{D}$own the ages, in round about every society of the human race, the vast majority of the people passionately profess belief in invisible supernatural beings they usually refer to as "**gods.**" The three subsidiaries of Abrahamic religion, Judaism/Christianity/Islam, altogether affirm monotheism—the model of one God—whom they adore and worship as the supreme creator of the universe. However, these religions have varied conception of this monotheistic God, as well as the mode of worship they devote to his reverence.

Civilizations at large, undoubtedly, have assumed the idea of God and the quaint grotesque of religious practices from primitive cultures that far predated our modern age. But how did the idea of God originate into the human culture?

Who or what is 'God?' Is God an abstract word coined to designate the hidden forces of Nature, or rather a mathematical point having neither length and breadth, nor thickness? Is 'God' simply *"a prostration of the human intellects on the threshold of the unknown,"* as Charles Bradlaugh has described it in 1864? Moreso, is 'God' an unnecessary postulate or merely an unavoidable redundancy in human life? Alternatively, is 'God' truly the eternal existence who is conceived by Theists as the perfect, omnipotent, omniscient, and omnibenevolent creator and supreme governor of the universe?

The fact is very certain to all rational people that the idea of a creator-God actually evolved into human civilization through Natural Theology — the plain evidence of what 'Early Man' constantly beholds in the book of nature. These are indications of natural phenomena that openly appeal to his sense of logic and common sense, as well as the sympathy of his emotions and ignorance. Obviously, **Natural Theology** is the accurate source known to humankind as the exact origin of how the idea of 'God' has, down the line of history, developed into the human culture. Although, several scholars have also propounded numerous theories as to how the idea of God has evolved into human civilization, but none of these theories seem as valid as the clear evidence of what **Natural Theology** holds forth in the book of nature.

Philosopher, Douglas Adam, provides a very applicable and coherent insight into where the idea of God had possibly originated into the human world in this piece extracted from one of his essays titled, *'Is there an Artificial God?'*

> *Now imagine an early man surveying his surroundings at the end of a happy day's tool making. He looks around and he sees a world which pleases him mightily: behind him are mountains with caves...in front of him there's the forest—it's got nuts and berries and delicious food; there's a stream going by, which is full of water—water's delicious to drink...I mean this is a great world, it's fantastic. But our early man has a moment to reflect and he thinks to himself, 'well, this is an interesting world that I find myself in' and then he asks himself...'So who made this then?' Who made this?...Early man thinks, 'Well, because there's only one sort of being I know about who makes things, whoever made all this must therefore be a much bigger, much more powerful and necessarily invisible one of me, and because I tend to be the strong one who does all the stuff, he's probably male.' And so we have the idea of a god.*

As we clearly can discern from this remarkable presentation of Douglas Adams, it is evident that the necessity for the concept of God naturally stemmed from fantastic reflections of *"Early Man."* After Early Man had, thus, postulated the idea of God from the perspectives in which he sees the world around him, what then followed?

As much as necessary, evolutionary strings of religion began to develop into various aspects of the human culture, and our ancestors effectively commenced the worship of elements and the physical powers of nature. Thus, the ancient foundation of religious belief and practices began to dominate the life of humankind, and more and more imaginary gods started to take shape in the natural history and likeness of man.

As the ever-increasing offspring of Early Man progressively developed into literate beings, and bit by bit became conversant with the progress of the world around them, they subsequently compiled their divergent ideas of God into works of art, poetry, folklores, and fables. Majority of the descendants of Early Man, therefore, integrated and weaved the mythical tales surrounding these imaginary gods into tribal version of events prevalent in their oral traditions. They fittingly fashioned their fantasized gods in their own likeness—wearing their exact look and behaving in the same authoritarian and cruel manners as they did—love your own and unleash untold hatred upon others.

Even as early as the fifth century BCE, the detail is revealed to us in historical records of human civilization that ancient Greek philosopher, Xenophanes of Colophon (c.570 BCE – 475 BCE), penned down in one of his earliest works, unequivocally denouncing every particular portrayal of the gods of religion as manifestly man-made. He wrote:

> *Both Homer and Hesiod have attributed to the gods things that are shameful and a reproach among mankind: theft, adultery, and mutual deception. And this he held was due to the representation of the gods in human form. But mortals suppose that gods are born, wear their own clothes and have a voice and body. The Ethiopians say that their gods are flat-nosed and black, while the Thracians say that*

> *theirs have blue eyes and red hair. Yet if cattle or horses or*
> *lions had hands and could draw, and could sculpture like*
> *men, then the horses would draw their gods like horses,*
> *and cattle like cattle; and each they would shape bodies of*
> *gods in the likeness, each kind, of their own.*

Aristotle (c.384 BCE – 322 BCE) in similar manner, also observed very accurately the representation of God that looked suspiciously like human inventions in the internal pages of all religious books, and expressly concluded that the God of religion is manmade:

> *Men create God after their own image, not only with*
> *regards to their form but with regards to their mode of life.*

As belief is an obsession of the human mind, it therefore became compelling for succeeding offspring of **Early Man** to profess credulous belief in those imaginary gods, which their ancestors had primarily fashioned in their own likeness. It was then persuasive for them to find a supreme chieftain in the idea of imaginary gods their ancestors had postulated out of utter ignorance of nature's world. Consequently, successive offspring of **Early Man** were left with no choice, but to recognize and profess credulous beliefs in those mythical collections that their forebears had compiled into historical documents from oral traditions, as the 'word of God in print.' Mythology books such as the Bible, Bhagavad-Gita, Quran, Sanskrit, etc., are all examples of historical documents that later became 'revealed' word of God in print. These are primarily mythical books that organized religions have transformed, by deceit, into the status of Holy Scriptures, which they subsequently impose upon credulous worshippers as guidebooks from their invented gods.

Without a doubt, the idea of God actually instigated from the ignorance and deficiency in humans' perspectives of the natural world they found themselves. Majority of the human tribes and races have developed mythical stories, which later became written accounts, to describe how the earth was made and how life came into existence in it. Some of the narrations in these accounts also describe how humans have lived life and populated the earth since the beginning of their existence.

For example, the huge collections of ancient stories and traditions in the Jewish culture consist a set of superstitious rule and religious sacrifices they specified as desirable to their own God, as well as specific moral conducts by which their God expected their people to live a righteous pattern of life.

It reminds me of my childhood days, when I used to live with my grandparents in the village. Every evening, after the fatigue of farm work, and after we had all had supper of our regular dish of pounded yam with any variety of Yoruba traditional soup, my grannies and I would usually recline at night in the frontage of our little home. These were the times when I habitually found enjoyment in the narratives of various colours of tales from my grandparents, most particularly under the brilliance of the moonlight, as our village then had no electricity. Many were those times then when my grandparents would jointly contemplate and appreciate the glory of the supreme powers behind all the remarkable spectacles they observed in the structure of our awesome planet. Several times, they would loudly voice out their reverence and veneration for the enormity of the source of these predominantly wonderful powers that constantly aerate the cosmos without a break; illuminate the entire skies both day and night with sunshine and with moonlight without flaws, and so on ...

In gratitude to these omnipotent powers, which my grannies believed were the controlling forces behind the marvels they behold in nature's splendid scenery, they would naturally burst into offering mystical incantation and adulation that glorified these magnificent powers. In some occasions, they would offer sacrificial live fowls in appeasement of these mighty powers to guarantee the continued security of our life, and the prospering of our farming endeavours under the divine control of these great supernatural forces. In this same manner, the first religion might have as well initiated on earth by the first Adam and Eve.

Please note that the Adam and Eve I have referred to above are not the biblical Adam and Eve that the mythology of Genesis portrayed as typical robots who could not discern their left from their right, because they possessed no knowledge inside of them, until a serpent came to their rescue. The Adam and Eve in this context are the anthropological Adam and Eve; the authentic **'Early Man'** who truthfully first walked the surface of the earth from the time when the science of anthropology and other relevant branch of science revealed to us that man first started to inhabit our earthly home some hundreds of thousand years ago.

The basis of the hypothetical answers that the first human generation had then offered to several of their keen queries concerning the wonders of nature must have subsequently led them to the conclusion that some higher powers indeed existed behind the operations of virtually all that surrounded them in the universe. Of course, as a matter of common sense, the first human generation would have enclosed it in their minds that these powers are truthfully higher authorities with more superior powers than they possessed. As a result, they would have initiated the reverence and worship of these powers out of utmost respect, gratitude, fear, and adoration for the astounding beauties of the wonderful creations they conceived that these higher forces have perfected in their world. For this reason, the first humans on earth would have idolized the powers behind the sun, thus in all probability giving birth to the sun god. They would have also deified the powers behind moonlight and, in consequence, beginning the worship of the moon god. The different stars they could possibly count and name, they have on the whole idolized. As they fantasized a god for rainfall, so too they did for every river, sea, and ocean they could give a name. The gods of iron, trees, thunder, fire, the atmosphere, and all other forces of nature would have subsequently emerged out of their inventions and fancies. What's more, they would afterwards convert all the ethereal elementals of nature into deities, and religiously adore them as gods and goddesses. In short, all of their fictionalized gods and religious worships they had, of course, bequeathed to successive generations. Thus, unto this day, the conscience of humankind has faithfully remained connected to religious adorations.

From the lingering evidence of history that past generations have left behind for the grasp of our present civilization through the narrative process – the tradition of storytelling – my father and my mother told me so and so ... that our ancestors believed ... so and so ... in ancient times.

It is apparent that polytheism (a belief in many gods) was the first religion of the ancient world, which obviously transpired out of the connections of what the ancients could then comprehend from the marvellous forces of Nature.

For example, the ancient Yoruba (an ancient tribe in western Nigeria) professed a deep-rooted belief in one Supreme God to whom they referred as *Olodumare,* meaning the King of the people of many colours. In Yoruba ancient polytheism, Olodumare (the Supreme God) has numerous Orisa (gods or deities) that are subject to his authority. These deities also include Esu (God's Special Messenger). Before the advent of foreign religions into Yorubaland, the ancient Yorubas revered Esu as the special messenger of the Supreme God who takes man's supplications and sacrifices from these subordinate gods directly to Olodumare the supreme God. In primordial time, the Yoruba people had faithfully deified Esu as the spiritual custodian and administrator of God's judicial system. Even up to this day, remnant of the Yorubas who remained steadfast to their tradition would always deify Esu very close to all their gods and goddesses; and at all times, offer a portion of every sacrifice they provide to their various gods also for the appeasement of Esu, to earn his spiritual favours.

The ancient Yorubas believed that these gods and deities were the rulers or controllers of all natural events—storms, fire, rainfall, sunshine, fertility, rivers, oceans, and the atmosphere, etc. Therefore, whenever there were famines in their lands, the Yoruba people would appease Orisa-Oko (the earth fertility god) to promote the fertility of their land in order to enhance ample harvesting. During, or shortly after harvesting, they would also make elaborate sacrifices to Orisa-Oko in appreciation of their bountiful harvests. During the chaotic ire of the sea, or the chaotic crash of thunder and lightning, they would render sacrifices to Olokun (the sea god) and to Yemoja (the sea goddess) to calm the angry sea storm. Similarly, they would placate Sango (the god of thunder) to avoid the rage of thunder and lightning.

Even though, the different tribes in the ancient age had then lived thousands of miles apart from one another, with no access to mass communication devices as in our modern civilization, striking similarities then existed as regards their religious beliefs and practices. The religious practices of the ancient Yoruba had very close connections to that of the ancient Rome, Assyria, Babylonia, and Greece, including ancient Mali, Egypt, and many other nations of the world. This sensibly suggests the plain fact that the ancients had naturally invented their religions out of what they behold in nature.

In short, whatever natural forces the Orientals comprehend in Nature, so too do the Africans, the Europeans, and every other race and tribe comprehend alike. As the sun radiates it rays and energies to Adelaide in Australia, the same it does to Timbuktu in Mali. The compositions of oxygen that aerate the winds in Australasia are the same as those that blow across the entire globe.

At some point in the ages past, it is clearly definite that all the nations of the earth have naturally agreed on an identical face of religious worship and equality before Mother Nature—their only known creator. The aspirations of the primordial men to religious worship were then totally devoid of any contrivance of their spiritual priests claiming false superiority for one religion over the other, as well as the preferential treatment of the creator of the universe for one nation at the bloodshed of another. The several religious faiths in existence in the ancient world were not encumbered with brutal thorns of persecution amongst each other. Their primary religious convictions were devoid of bitter discriminations, intolerance, and extreme dislikes; save for being in overall likeness that upheld the most admirable cordiality of spiritual values, which were purely conformable to true worship and reverence of the amazing powers the ancients could wholly identify with in the natural world.

It is very obvious from the evidence of history that the pioneers of primordial faiths had then set up their religious convictions purely with intent to contemplate and revel in the munificence and magnificence of the powers they discerned in Mother Nature. And these were totally against the backdrop of artificial beliefs that arrogated unfounded falsehood of God's preferential treatment for one nation at the bloody expense of another, as it now prevails in the religious convictions of our modern world.

Even in the face of a wide range of religious diversities, devotees of the different sects often fraternized together in past ages to observe various religious rituals, sacrifices, and seasonal festivals with one another. Their unity in diversity had then provided for genuine spiritual influence that supported the growth of moral and cultural welfare within their various clans, contrary to what the case has now turned out to be in our modern civilization. The religion of the ancients were not the machinery of some organized trade that took pleasure in amassing wealth and authority, together with encouraging the reproach of other disciples of a different faith as infidel. The amiable practices between devotees of the ancient African religions had then encouraged deep trust, mutual respect, and religious tolerance amongst their people, as opposed to the cruel acts of distrust, bigotry, and conflicts that organized religions of our modern world now engender in our various societies.

Extinction of the Gods of Antiquity

Extensive races of humankind have invented uncountable number of religions, through the ages, to sustain the belief of successive generations in the worship of their gods. They have devotedly erected assortments of Synagogues, Temples, and Pyramids, including Shrines, Oracles, and Monuments to provide shelter for their gods, as well as to signify their extreme devotion to the worship of these deities.

For instance, the ancient Egyptians had dutifully held the reality of their gods very close to their heart, to such extent that they erected colossal structures like the Great Pyramid to the reverence of these gods. Despite the vast scale of labour-intensive enterprise the ancient Egyptians had then committed into constructing the Great Pyramid, the entireties of modern day Egyptians have today turned their back on all the gods of their ancestors. At present, modern Egyptians no longer believe the heaps of mythical stories concerning the existence of these ancient gods. They now know better than their primitive ancestors that God Osiris and

Goddess Isis, Horus and Ra, and the totalities of Egyptian ancient gods were created out of the imagination and ignorance of 'Early Man.'

For the reason that modern Egyptians are now fully aware of the fantastic stories behind the fabrication of these gods, they no longer bother themselves with redundant rituals of venerating imaginary gods whose existence are pretty much unreal. Therefore, the Egyptian Great Pyramid, one of the original '*Seven Wonders of the World*', now serves as tourist attraction in today's Egypt.

A comparable situation, similar to that of ancient Egypt, also existed in ancient Greece and Rome, where primordial Greeks and Romans likewise erected magnificent Temples made of marble for their gods. The ruins of these bravura Temples, which the ancient Greeks and Romans had then devoted rigorous times to build in honour and worship of Zeus, Jupiter, Apollo, Juno, etc., nowadays serve as tourist attraction in their respective cities. It is remarkable to note that the Statue of Zeus at Olympia also ranks amongst the **'Seven Wonders of the Ancient World.'** However, modern Greeks and Romans have totally deserted the worship of these ancient gods, because they longer believe their existence to be real.

Amplified knowledge of humans that resulted in the death of ancient Egyptian, Roman, and Greek gods also, by the same token, resulted in the demise of several ancient Sumerian, Persian, and countless of African and Oriental gods.

Ascendancy of the Modern God of Monotheism

Noticeably, all ancient gods without exception have gone into total extinction to give pre-eminence to a monotheistic God describe by theists as a father-figure who has human attributes and personal acquaintances with every aspect of earthling needs and practices. Today's Egypt consists predominantly of Muslims, while modern Romans and Greeks are mainly Christians, with their religious beliefs strongly rooted in monotheism — the model of one God.

Abrahamic religions (Judaism, Christianity and Islam), the three major monotheistic religions, altogether originated in what is today known as the Arab World; and belief in the doctrines and teachings of these religions is widespread across our modern world.

All the same, is a supernatural being truly up there in the image of man whose existence is infinitely beyond the vastness of the cosmic space, and with divine capability of creating the immensity of its spheres? Is there truly the hand of a creator-God behind the reality of nature's wonders that inspired the mind of 'Early Man' in coming to the conclusion that all physical elements of nature are essentially the products of divine creation from On High?

To all believers of the single-God religions, the existence of a creator-God is so obvious and convincing. Theists always assert that their God has left infinite amount of physical evidence of his existence in each and every matter and creature we obviously observe in the structure of the universe; that even a dimly sighted person should be able to examine all of God's work in observable certification. But the questions therefore arise:

- Are Theists really correct to hold this opinion?
- Are they right to ascribe the components of the natural world to a creator they call God?
- How did all believers come to the conclusion that everything we behold in the configuration of the universe is indeed the creation of their God?
- Do the sacred scriptures that inform humans of the existence of God and origin of life on earth contain infallible account, and therefore trustworthy for belief as the word of the creator-God in print?
- Are the accounts of sacred scriptures that narrate the manners in which humankind has populated the earth and lived life in the last six thousand years truly reliable and consistent with the reality of what we behold in nature?

It should be noted that all scientific investigations into the origin of the universe and all the components of the natural world have constantly shown great indication of evolution by means of cumulative natural selection, instead of supernatural creation. Therefore, there's no evidence for the creation account of Genesis. According to Richard Dawkins, *"The theory of evolution by cumulative natural selection is the only theory we know of that is in principle capable of explaining the existence of organized complexity."*

Our earth is manifestly the creator of every element and organism that dwells in it. The wide-ranging clue that cumulative natural selection can in effect design anything, no matter how complex, ranging from the formation of the awesome universe to the smallest atoms and molecules, is largely convincing; and this pointer explicitly discards the need for any imaginary 'God' or 'Creator.' All assortments of life as we find them on our planet apparently have, on the whole, evolved and finely moulded their existence, through millions of years, to fit the distinctive conditions that prevail in their ecosystems.

I once observed indications of this assertion some years in the past whilst I was still a bachelor. I was then away from my apartment in the city of Lagos on a business trip to the city of Port Harcourt, leaving remnants of yam porridge and a basin of water at a corner in my kitchen. Within three weeks of my return to the kitchen, uncountable numbers of organisms have grown out of the remnants of my yam porridge and bucket of water. How do we explain the growth of these uncountable lives in my kitchen? Could it, therefore, be said that the God of religion had then created these countless microorganisms that grew out of the remnants of my yam porridge and unkempt bowl of water? No! This was never an act of God. The very conducive condition that then prevailed in my kitchen naturally made these lives to evolve, rapidly turning the whole kitchen into a breeding ground for bacteria and germs. This is a very simple and cost free experiment that anyone can perform to verify how various lives can evolve out of any appropriate condition; and how these lives can flourish and finely tune their survival to fit the precise conditions that go well with their existence.

Any rational person can just imagine how countless species of life would have infinitely evolved out of the plenteous rivers, ponds, and oceans of the earth; in addition to the fully conducive ecosystems, prevalent all around the rainy environments of the blue planet, from early days through the course of about 4.5 billion years of its existence. The reason why there is no life on planet Mercury, Mars, Jupiter, etc., is simply because the ecosystems that exist in those regions are just not suitable for life to develop, otherwise different species of organisms would have also evolved everywhere on those planets.

The fact of the matter is that, even if the *Argument from Design* effectively proves that the universe is the handiwork of intelligent designer, it will not successfully prove that the intelligent designer is truly the God of religion who, by theists' accounts, authored the grossly unintelligent 'holy books' that are today available on planet earth. The intelligent designer might as well be Nature, or as vast group of scientists had aptly called it, *"Evolution by cumulative natural selection."*

We have clearly seen that the idea of God actually originated from primitive ignorance of 'Early Man,' as it was then the habitual practice of the ancients to ascribe 'God' to each and every thing they did not sensibly understand in nature. Humans' intrinsic mould into this absurd custom actually accounts for why the ancients had invented gods for all the physical elements of nature, including iron, rocks, and trees, etc.

We also have seen that all the holy books popularly known as the 'word of God in print' are fantastic mythology books, not different from any work of fiction. For those who are still confused and unsure of this plain fact that the sacred books available on earth today are altogether a bunch of mythology books, it will only take some attentive efforts of reading and coherent comparison with accepted mythologies of the ancients to confirm the core basis of these holy books as blatant imaginary tales that are of equal status with every literary work of fiction available on earth. How these discrepant, contradictory and false theologies have so terribly conquered the universal intelligence of humankind and surmount it into the path of outrageous folly is extremely the faulty emblem of ignorance that is totally out of order in the human society. It is exceedingly puzzling to imagine how vast population of the human race have continued to rely on fantasy tales, yet in the 21st century civilization, to reveal the unknown to them.

Indeed, the tenet of dogmatic faith is undoubtedly founded upon downright fallacy and deception. I have so far seen nothing that can be more repugnant to reason and common sense than this strange idea of a God fashioned from the imagination of mankind as the creator and governor of the mortal world. In the candid words of Charles Bradlaugh:

> *I have never yet heard living man give me a clear, coherent definition of the word "God," and I have never read any definition from either dead or living man expressing a definite and comprehensible idea of Deity. In fact, it has always appeared to me that men use that word rather to hide their ignorance than to express their knowledge.*

Chapter

4

This Cannot Be True!

*"A miracle is an event described by those to whom it
was told by people who did not see it."*

– Elbert Hubbard

𝒟avid Hume a long time ago wrote in his book, 'An Enquiry Concerning Human Understanding' that, *"No testimony is sufficient to establish a miracle, unless the testimony is of such a kind, that its falsehood would be more miraculous than the fact which it endeavours to establish."* This critical observation undeniably holds true of the preposterous legacy that the Christian religion has oddly bequeathed upon the trusting minds of the entire congregation of those who naively follow the heaps of organized superstitions that this most popular religion of our modern world dutifully promotes all through the length and breadth of the spherical globe.

The Immaculate Conception

The reported miracle of the 'Virgin Mary,' according to the testimonies of Matthew and Luke, published to the world in the New Testament Bible as the amazing conception of Jesus Christ, had always remained an awesome puzzlement that continually poses enigmatic riddle to countless number of discerning minds from ages to ages.

The New Testament publications incredibly reported the miraculous story of what the Christian faith has thus promulgated as the Immaculate Conception — a spotless and pure, stainless and impeccably clean, wholly sinless, and incorrupt fertilization of the Virgin Mary's zygote, without any blemish, by the miraculous union of the Holy Ghost, instead of the male spermatozoa. The gospel accounts described Mary as a young woman who was probably in her teens or a little older; and at that time a virgin under marital engagement to a man whose name was Joseph, who perhaps might as well be in his early to late twenties. The gospel writers thus alleged Mary as having miraculously conceived of a child without any cohabitation with this man, or any other man whosoever on planet earth.

The gospel according to Matthew alleged that, following Joseph's consideration of a secret divorce of his affianced wife, as a consequence of her inexplicable conception, an anonymous angel of God therefore made a revelation known to him in a dream during his night sleep that the Holy Spirit was miraculously responsible for Mary's conception. While the account according to Luke, narrated that Angel Gabriel appeared to Mary during the day to prophesy a divine message to the young woman. Luke 1:31 (NIV) says, *"You will be with child and give birth to a son, and you are to give him the name Jesus."* When Mary questioned the angel in verse 34, *"How will this be... since I am a virgin?"* Angel Gabriel then explained to her in verse 35, *"The Holy Spirit will come upon you, and the power of the Most High will over-shadow you, so the holy one to be born will be called the Son of God."*

The first substance in this case, regardless of its discrepant reporting by the two biographers, made 'God the Father' teleport 'God the Holy Ghost' to the very soil of our spherical globe, wittingly on divine mission to facilitate the fertilization of the ovum of a virgin woman, in order to give birth to 'God the Son' on planet earth. All this in an effort to erect a foundation for the fulfilment of a prophetic sign given by Prophet Isaiah to King Ahaz, as the sign of his victory over the two kings of Israel and Syria in the book of Isaiah 7:14-16 (KJV). *"Therefore the Lord himself shall give you a sign, "Behold a virgin shall conceive, and bear a son;" (verse 16) "For before this child shall know to refuse the evil and choose the good, the land that thou abhorrest shall be forsaken of both her kings."*

Here was a sign, which Prophet Isaiah particularly gave to King Ahaz some seven hundred years before Mary's conception of Jesus. At the time that Isaiah offered this sign to Ahaz, he had equally backed it up with an outline of timetable that would indicate the fulfilment of the sign, which later turned out a fateful sign of false prophecy, lacking the authority of *'God'*. I shall come to that later.

The second substance of the case had consequently put 'God the Father' under the necessity to dispatch two important embassies from his heavenly authority on a diplomatic mission to planet earth—one to Mary, and another to Joseph. The one to Mary would formerly prophesy her miraculous conception through the inexplicable action of God the Holy Ghost. While the other embassy to Joseph would officially make holy appeal and representation to his host for leniency on his betrothed wife— that he might temper justice with mercy and refrain from executing his secret plan of divorce that could put Mary to public ridicule. Nevertheless, this angelic ambassador should expediently pacify Joseph to craft a room of adoption for 'God the Son,' on behalf of 'God the Holy Ghost,' in the lineage of David, under the carpenter's roof. This is incredibly beyond absurd! Many rational readers would agree.

Frankly, I naturally would have no problem believing this exceptional tale of phenomenal miracle, because it is indeed a proclaimed wonder of the almighty creator of the universe. However, in this peculiar matter concerning the Immaculate Conception of Jesus, the simple fact that well clogged my conviction in believing the story is the starting point of the testimony, which had essentially emanated from unrelated people to the miracle, and lacking any iota of endorsement from the direct beneficiary of the miracle. Therefore, the aberrant factor that assigned the dispersal of such weighty testimony through the mouths of strangers who entirely had no link to its occurrence made such testimony a blatant falsehood. This is when in reality, the direct recipient of the divine miracle and her spouse were capable of narrating the tales themselves to the entire world. In consequence, this odd factor of narrating the *Immaculate Conception* through the mouth of strangers, who entirely had no link to the miracle, grossly made the testimony rather a feeble one, wholly lacking the least of any authentic evidence. To all intents and purposes, the oddity of broadcasting this sort of vital miraculous episode through the mouths of those who are totally unrelated to its occurrence made such testimony accurately the type David Hume had then described in his book that, *"...its falsehood would be more miraculous than the fact which it endeavours to establish."* This factor has thus diminished my conviction, much so that it becomes very hard for me to profess a belief in the story.

In plain fact, the whole tale appeared much to me like another piece of fictional saga, utterly without any valid evidence that well supported the miraculous account in any point of fact. It, thus, rendered any reliability upon such testimony resting flimsily on the conclusion of manipulative hearsays and unfounded imports that normally do the rounds in the dome of religion, purposely as a means of imposing fraudulent fantasies and insubstantial fallacies on the gullible minds of dogmatic believers.

It is reasonable that such an amazing miracle that involves an implausible violation of nature's law requires a much stronger proof and attestation to humankind than the mere word of strangers that, in any way, do not have connections to the miracle. Alas, in this case, humankind has neither the words of Mary nor that of Joseph, narrating the circumstances under which the Immaculate Conception had truly occurred. Actual testimonies that ought to produce reliable clues in support of the occurrence of the miraculous conception were either the words of Joseph or Mary or both. But, the religion of Christianity had effectively suppressed the testimonies of Joseph and Mary, and instead subjugated it for the hearsays of Matthew and Luke.

How, therefore, could the Immaculate Conception be a corresponding fulfilment of the prophecy of Isaiah 7:14, as the book of Matthew 1:22 has wrongly claimed, when Prophet Isaiah, on the other hand, had under personal oath confessed the secret mission he undertook to fulfil this particular prophecy by subterfuge? In Isaiah 8:2-4 (NIV), the prophet recounted under oath to the Jews and subsequently the entire world thus:

> *And I will call in Uriah the priest and Zechariah son of Jeberekiah as reliable witnesses for me. Then I went to the prophetess, and she conceived, and gave birth to a son. And the Lord said to me; name him Maher-Shalal-Hash-Baz.*

*Before the boy knows how to say 'My father' or 'My
mother,' the wealth of Damascus and the plunder of
Samaria will be carried off by the king of Assyria*
- (Isaiah 8:2-4, NIV).

Even though bible storytellers had again manufactured another thorny
prophecy of similar character to that of Isaiah 7:14, through Isaiah's
mouth in the fourth verse of the eighth chapter to enfeeble his crucial
confession; it, however, does not require the diligence of a crack detective
of the FBI or the KGB to identify that the ruse of the name change from
Immanuel to Maher-Shalal-Hash-Baz is another tricky distortion to
suppress Prophet Isaiah's confession in the eighth chapter of the book that
carries his name (Isaiah 8:2-3). The devise of an unconnected false
prophecy again from Isaiah's mouth in favour of the King of Assyria,
carrying off the *"wealth and plunder of Damascus and Samaria, before the
boy knows how to say my father or my mother"* is absolutely a latter
deceptive game plan to alter Isaiah's self-fulfilment of the false prophecy
of Isaiah 7:14.

To pick out the pointlessness of the afterwards prophecy as a deceptive
scheme to distort Isaiah's confession, a reasonable reader of the story only
need to scrutinize this second prophecy, which has no particular bearing
and connection to any preceding event. However, the prophecy suddenly
appeared out of the blue, wearing a deceptive mask that bears a misleading
resemblance to the former prophecy to King Ahaz, but without any
authentic validation that truly reveals its fulfilment anywhere in Biblical
record, or whichever historical record. At any rate, the prophecy of Isaiah
7 verse 14 comprises sequels that linked its target to King Ahaz and the
imminent war between the nation of Judah, Israel, and Syria. The abrupt
and incoherent prophecy of Isaiah 8:4 is disapprovingly without the least
of any sequel upheld in any authentic outcome in history. In any event, it
is typically a cunning invention that Bible editors later placed over Isaiah
8:2-3 to overshadow Prophet Isaiah's sworn admission that practically
revealed the cunning plans that fulfilled his bogus prophecy to King Ahaz

in Isaiah 7:14-16. The invention of the subsequent prophecy had afterwards enabled the architects of the Christian system of faith to interchange the Immaculate Conception for the fulfilment of Isaiah 7:14, instead of the actual messy conception of Isaiah's prophetess through Isaiah's spermatozoa.

Assuming the confessions of Prophet Isaiah in the book that bears his name, (Isaiah 8:2-3) were not readily available in the Bible, the entire world would have erroneously believed the fallacy that the 'prophetic virgin' of Isaiah 7:14 had truly conceived of her son by the miraculous means of the Holy Spirit, other than the spermatozoa of Isaiah himself. Unto this day, the church would have possibly outwitted rational minds into believing the fallacy of the Immaculate Conception, save for gullible devotees. They would have forever kept preaching the falsehood that Isaiah's virgin prophetess was the first mother of the first begotten son of God, whose name was Maher-Shalal-Shalal-Hash-Baz, and whose conception was ably under the immaculate union of the Holy Spirit. While, they would on the other hand, twist the status of the Virgin Mary as the second mother of the beloved son of God; thereby, making the Holy Spirit the polygamous father of the triune brothers – Immanuel, Maher-Shalal-Hash-Baz, and later on Jesus.

In the case of the Immaculate Conception, at least the gospel writers should have equally accorded Joseph or Mary a slot in the Bible to narrate to the entire world, some episodes from their courtship. Perhaps their tales would have clarified the gloomy fog that mystified how Joseph had possibly become aware of Mary's Immaculate Conception, even before Mary herself could know of it, to such extent that would compel him to contemplate a secret divorce plan ahead of official declaration from celestial authority. This is because the dialogue that the book of Luke recorded to have taken place between Mary and Angel Gabriel in the first chapter (verses 28 to 35) was strictly a future prophecy, which the Bible had plainly reported in the future tense, and surely not a confirmation of Mary's Immaculate Conception. The account affirmed in verses 31-35 (NIV):

> *"You will be with child and give birth to a son, and you are*
> *to give him the name Jesus ... How will this be ... since I am*
> *a virgin? "The Holy Spirit will come upon you, and the*
> *power of the Most High will over-shadow you, so the holy*
> *one to be born will be called the Son of God."*

Assuming that Mary had, earlier in the day, reported this angelic encounter to Joseph, how then should a divine prophecy of this nature (most especially when it is foretold to an affianced woman) infuriate her betrothed husband to contemplate a secret divorce! Fascinatingly, also, to such an extent that would warrant the Almighty God sending another angelic emissary to Joseph to pacify him to refrain from his planned divorce action; when in actuality, both Mary and Joseph, as a natural rule, should have expressed joyfulness and gratitude for such a divine prophecy in their favour. This is given that the prophecy was wholly in line with their ultimate dream of procreating soon after their marriage. Therefore, the affianced couple should have earnestly looked forward to fulfilment of the prophecy, rather than the reported absurdity of Joseph considering a secret divorce thereafter. Again, this fictionalized theology of Christianity is irrational beyond absurd!

There exists no good premise at all for supposing this unreasonable tale to be true, except on neurotic ground of just wanting to believe what is not true. Dogmatic believers are typical examples of *credulous animals* that must believe something, even when there subsists no good premise at all for supposing the fairy tale to be true.

In any event, if the Immaculate Conception was truly the fulfilment of Isaiah 7:14, what then had prompted Angel Gabriel and the other anonymous angel in Matthew's account to defy the prophetic name of Isaiah 7:14 by naming this child Jesus, instead of Immanuel? (Compare Isaiah 7:14, Matthew 1:21-25 and Luke 1:31). Howbeit, this case has persistently remained a mystery to my keen mind.

Regrettably, no one was able to confirm any particular testimony directly from the mouth of either Joseph or Mary. Religionists had effectively suppressed the gospel that ought to be according to Joseph and

Mary, and patronizingly told it in discrepant manners through the mouths of Matthew and Luke. Disappointingly, also, the two angelic emissaries that officially travelled all the way to earth purposely to testify for the miraculous conception did not put down any particle of corresponding evidence in support of their doubtful revelation. Not a speckle of proof that could bear whatever witness to their testimony did they leave with any inhabitant of Jerusalem, Bethlehem, Bethany, Samaria, Gaza, Galilee, Judea, or Nazareth as to bestow an atom of credible authentication in support of the miraculous account.

Even the product of the Immaculate Conception, Jesus Christ, in all of his numerous teachings, illustrations, parables, and tales during his earthly all over the mounts and streets of Israel, never once uttered a word to describe the circumstance under which he miraculously inhabited the womb of a virgin woman without going through the natural process of human reproduction. I honestly cannot fathom how Jesus' consistent reference to himself in the New Testament as the 'Son of Man,' is in any way related to his being the offspring of a Ghost, or the only begotten Son of God (whatever that means).

Instead of producing valid evidence in support of the Immaculate Conception, the laughable legacies the inventors of the Christian faith had thus bequeathed to their credulous followers were faulty fabrications of some Jewish faceless historians who related the event in discrepant manners several centuries after it had purportedly occurred. While they deceitfully fathered the authorship of their discrepant narration upon Jesus' apostles through the questionable inspiration of *God the Holy Ghost* — the imaginary celestial father of Jesus Christ, who in unswerving point of fact did not directly proclaim himself anywhere in the Bible as the vim and vigour responsible for the Immaculate Conception.

As is usual with religion, the manufacturers of this piece of fictional tale have indeed called upon the whole world to come and buy the product of their hearsays. Moreover, they say it is only by professing faith in the celestially begotten product of the hearsays that the entire world could be born-again (whatever that means), and become saved from eternal damnation their 'God' had decreed for humankind through the sins of Adam and Eve.

"It is wrong always, everywhere, and for anyone, to believe anything upon insufficient evidence," so observed the perceptive mathematician, William Clifford in his book, 'The Ethics of Belief.' How the entire world has given undue credit to these ludicrous hearsays in the first place is what has continuously puzzled my mind. However, what we do know with some degree of certainty is that, it took the pioneers of the absurd tale several centuries of bloody wars and persecutions before they could impose their fabrications upon the gullible minds of mankind. As David Hume had rightfully said, *"the Christian religion was not only at first attended with miracles, but even at this day cannot be believed by any reasonable person without one."*

Now, in our present day, the belief of this preposterous tale is so deep rooted in the heart of man, and more than ever in Africa, that many people cannot sleep peacefully if they have not read the story in one day, most especially for the sake of miracles. I know of some gullible Christian women in my country, who have long been married without conceiving, probably due to one medical problem or another. Instead of seeking medical help for their infertility, they would religiously open the New Testament pages of the Holy Bible that contained the miraculous conception story, place it underneath of their pillows, and sleep with it every night. This is a gullible practice they devotedly observed in vanity, searching for sham miraculous remedy to conceive of a child in the manner of Mary, through the magical wand of the Holy Ghost.

Many other gullible Christians would open the Psalms; others prefer the reported word of Jesus Christ in red-letter prints, and conscientiously sleep with it wide open beneath their pillows every night as protection against any torment of evil spirit and nightmares that might come visiting during their sleeping hours. Imagine the utter lack of caution that religion has forced upon the gullible minds of many people of my homeland! Many of these bizarre and out of the ordinary episodes do not happen within the community of those who exported this strange religion to our own part of the world. People of the black continent have turned everything upside down, adoring even what their religion has not in any sense commanded.

Deceitful Genealogy Account of Jesus

After the fable of the Immaculate Conception of Jesus Christ, follows his genealogy account according to Matthew and Luke. This is a binary account of extreme fabrication, proving absolute falsehood in its entirety, as the two accounts contradict each other in every detail.

If Mathew and Luke had written their genealogy accounts under divine inspiration as the church claimed they did, it is only reasonable that both authors should have detailed their own version in perfect order, devoid of any contradiction, or any trait of irreconcilable differences, as there could only be but one truth in this particular case. On the other hand, if Matthew and Luke had both obtained details of Jesus' genealogy directly from his father or any other source, it equally should be reasonable that the source should have furnished both authors alike with the same genealogical descent. However, the two doubtful genealogies that these two biographers gave of Jesus Christ are of the greatest riddles of all times, which would be perpetually questionable for time everlasting. Any reasonable individual would wonder where the two biographers had both received their information.

Both apostles had offered the same lineal descent facing two opposite directions in their respective books, where the father of Joseph according to one entirely differed from the father of Joseph according to the other. Moreover, the great-grandfather of Jesus according to Matthew disagreed totally with whom Luke listed as the great-grandfather of Jesus. These disparities unconnectedly progressed in conflicting manner throughout the Davidic lineage that the two biographers had enumerated as Jesus' earthly genealogy.

The gospel of Matthew detailed a total of 28 generations from Jesus down to David, while that of Luke enumerated a contradictory list of 43 generations from Jesus down to David. The two versions of Jesus' Jewish ancestors according to the acclaimed inspiration of the Messiah's celestial father—the Holy Spirit— are distinctly listed below for your comparison:

GENEALOGY ACCORDING TO Matthew 1:6-16 (NIV)	GENEALOGY ACCORDING TO Luke 3:23-31(NIV)
1 Jesus	1 Jesus
2 Joseph	2 Joseph
3 Jacob	3 Heli
4 Matthan	4 Matthat
5 Eleazar	5 Levi
6 Eliud	6 Melki
7 Akim	7 Jannai
8 Zadok	8 Joseph
9 Azor	9 Mattathias
10 Eliakim	10 Amos
11 Abiud	11 Nahum
12 Zerubbabel	12 Esli
13 Shealtiel	13 Naggai
14 Jeconiah	14 Maath
15 Josiah	15 Mattathias
16 Amon	16 Semein
17 Manasseh	17 Josech
18 Hezekiah	18 Joda
19 Ahaz	19 Joanan
20 Jotham	20 Rhesa
21 Uzziah	21 Zerubbabel
22 Jehoram	22 Shealtiel
23 Jehoshaphat	23 Neri
24 Asa	24 Melki
25 Abijah	25 Addi
26 Rehoboam	26 Cosam
27 Solomon	27 Elmadam
28 David	28 Er
	29 Joshua
	30 Eliezer
	31 Jorim
	32 Matthat
	33 Levi
	34 Simeon
	35 Judah
	36 Joseph
	37 Jonam

	38 Eliakim
	39 Melea
	40 Menna
	41 Mattatha
	42 Nathan
	43 David

Source: Paine, 1794 ... rpt. 1988.

True to character, Bible storytellers typically adored the narration of their numerous tales in deliberate distortion to confuse the minds of their gullible readers. In enumerating the details of Jesus' ancestors, both Apostles ran their listing in opposite directions, I guess to enfeeble easy detection of their gross errors. At any rate, all the names that Matthew and Luke had distrustfully listed in their enumerations of Jesus' earthly genealogy were gravely in extreme conflict with each other.

The gross contradictions in these two genealogies of Jesus thus revealed two obvious facts to the perception of any logical reader. The first implies that whoever the anonymous authors of the book of Matthew and the book of Luke claimed they were, certainly those persons were not the real Matthew and Luke, the intimate apostles that lived, worked, and dined with Jesus on daily basis for three successive years; but downrightly the impersonators of the genuine Matthew and Luke — that is if both apostles ever existed at all in history.

Secondly, the extreme contradictions between these two genealogies typically proved beyond all reasonable doubts that they were nothing but bare forgeries and wayward assumptions, evident enough to correlate the suspicions that those amazing tales concerning the historical Jesus are of equal fabrications.

As I have earlier stated, if Matthew and Luke had truthfully written their accounts under divine inspiration, it is **impossible** that it could awfully be this contradictory if their very source of divine inspiration is the same Holy Spirit who is the celestial father of their Christ; or Joseph, his earthly dad. For there could only be but only one fact and one truth in this case. Therefore, if the truth is one and we all agree to that fact, the question would then arise as to which of these two genealogy accounts the church officially endorsed as the valid truth. Because, these two conflicting accounts cannot both be the whole truth at the same time, just as it is very impossible for Joseph to be the son of two different fathers. Being Joseph the son of Jacob according to Matthew, and at the same time, Joseph the son of Heli according to Luke. Everyone should agree in this case that it is practically not possible for all of Jesus' ancestors to be the sons of two fathers as Jesus' biographers had incoherently enumerated it in the gospel accounts of Matthew and Luke.

Besides, if one account should pass for the truth, obviously the other account would be utter falsehood. If Matthew had correctly enumerated the genealogy of Jesus, Luke would have detailed outright fallacy in his own genealogical list. On the other hand, if Luke had detailed the truth, Matthew would have wholly itemized falsehood. In any event, as both genealogies had totally disagreed to correspond with each other in every exacting detail, possibility greatly abounds, more than anything else, that both biographers would have altogether written falsehood. Therefore, how these conspicuous frauds have practically become the true word of the creator of the universe is another mystery of the Christian and Jewish religions that humanity owes attentive duty to unmask.

At any rate, since to err and prevaricate are truly of humans, for that reason, the question that here again arises is whether these disconnected reports are truthfully the inspiration of the Holy Spirit or that of mortal men. I elect to leave whatever conclusion at the discretion of the reader.

It is obvious that the anonymous authors of those books have fathered their works upon Matthew and Luke, the apostles of Christ, to garner credibility for their writings as inspired word of the ruler of the universe, as is the case with most books of the Bible. Then again, the conclusion would be that all the stories in the Bible, from Genesis through Revelation, are all concocted fabrications, interlarded with detached fragments of historical facts and personalities, purposely to establish another false religion on earth.

If Matthew and Luke should erect the very foundation of the religion of Christianity upon utter misrepresentation and falsehood, as the two genealogy accounts of Jesus had evidently shown, what validation is there left for believing other subsequent narratives about Jesus in their gospels? If they have falsely invented the genealogy account of their Messiah, how are we sure that fabrications and fibs are not the underlying motives beneath those petty tales of what Jesus spoke to every Patrick, Dikeledi and Themba, and what every Angela, Nichodemus, and Gumede said to him?

- How can we be sure that the narration of all those puissant and incredible miracles of Jesus raising Lazarus from the dead after four days, without a word from Lazarus narrating his ordeal in the great beyond written anywhere in their gospel are not falsehood as well?

- How, again can we believe the spurious stories of the gospellers when they narrate such unconfirmed tales about Jesus walking on water?

- How, yet again, can anyone believe the fallacy of the heavens opening up, with the creator of the universe proclaiming to the nation of Israel in thunderous tone of voice during the Baptismal Service conducted in River Jordan by John the Baptist: *"This is my beloved son, in whom I am well pleased"* Matthew 3:17 (KJV). This is because we now know that the Christian heaven is not anywhere within sphere of the Milky Way Galaxy, and any sound or light from beyond the Milky Way Galaxy takes more than two million light years to reach the earth.

- In addition, how can we ever again believe the specious tale that Jesus fasted forty days and forty nights, neither eating nor drinking? What is more ... that Jesus and Satan had incredibly, soon after the 40th day of the Lenten period, miraculously grown wings and flown away to the very top of an anonymous mountain to view the beauties of world governments and kingdoms. We do not know whether they had both climbed to the very top of Mount Everest or Kilimanjaro; nonetheless, that this fasting and starving

Messiah had climbed such a high mountain alongside his tempter, without the fragment of an effort!

- How can we again believe the discrepant narratives of Jesus' crucifixion, resurrection, and his ascension to heaven through the space, without the need of a spaceship to transport him through the several hundreds of million miles away from the earth?

- How, again, can we believe Matthew's reports about the great earthquake that *"shook the earth and the rock split,"* and this earthquake could not destroy any house or synagogue in Jerusalem, but only rendered the graves opened, and allowed dead bodies of unidentified 'saints' to roam about the streets of Jerusalem in their skeletal nakedness. However, Matthew, in his dry report dismally failed to provide readers the details of how the saints gave up the ghost again on the same day of their resurrection and reburied their resurrected bodies themselves. We are not told if they ascended to heaven (like Jesus) in the full vision of all inhabitants of Jerusalem, Gaza or Bethany. In any event, Matthew could not explicitly give any tangible account of whether the saints had checked into hotel rooms in Jerusalem or gallivanted on its streets with bells in hands, preaching fervently in loud voices to various atheists, sceptics, and freethinkers: *"Ye offspring of vipers! In the days of old, we prophesied to thee of the mighty one who is to come in the name of the Most High God with his gospel of resurrection to final judgment, but ye believeth not, but crucified him. In the mighty name of Jesus, the bones have risen again, as ye behold."*

- How again can any rational mind believe Matthew's narration that another nameless angel had prompted Joseph to flee with Jesus and his mother to Egypt, in order to escape King Herod's mass execution of all male children aged between two years and below in Bethlehem and its districts? However, Matthew could not give explicit detail of how John the Baptist had escaped King Herod's gallows during the genocide; given that John too was also a boy of less than two years of age at that time, but stayed behind in Bethlehem of Judea, with no divine stipulation to flee to Oklahoma or Ukraine.

- How, on earth, can we believe Bible storytellers again when they give their narration of the fierce fighting in the heavenly realms between the Christian God and Satan; that this heavenly warfare had culminated in their God hurling Satan down into our tiny earth, out of all the gigantic cosmic space available in the awesome universe?

Why should I believe these spurious stories, especially when they hold no more substantiation than the Yoruba or Ashanti tales by moonlight do? Indeed, too many unresolved mysteries undeniably exist in the Christian legacy to humanity.

It is quite certain that the person of David Hume would never have professed a belief in these kinds of phoney testimonies, unless the evidence of it be so strong that it would, in reality, become another miracle for him not to believe in it. However, in this case, the baseless testimonies that Matthew and company slyly reported in support of their bogus miracles in the Bible unduly lacked every pinch of credible evidence for any reasonable man to profess a belief in them.

Nonetheless, I am not particularly concerned here with details of evidence in support of Matthew and Luke's testimonies regarding all the miracles they reported in their gospel accounts. What is of utmost concern to me here is whether it is reasonable for any man who is free from the claws of theological programming to trust Matthew and Luke in all the stories they have related to humanity concerning Jesus? At least, not after we have detected the forgery of both men in the genealogy account of Jesus, which the Christian faith regarded as the bedrock upon which the foundation of its religion credibly or incredibly lies. Isn't it incredible that those who still profess belief in several of these absurd stories, despite the proof of modern scientific observations to the contrary, are very much delusional and ignorant in exact manner similar to that of primitive people that lived and believed such stories in the Dark Age?

Fiddling the Davidic Messiah

It is in the light of the promised Davidic Messiah in the ninth chapter of Isaiah verses six and seven that the book of Matthew Chapter 1:6-16 and the book of Luke chapter 3:23-31 have both given ancestral enumeration by name through the line of David to Joseph the father of Jesus. This was done purposely to establish the fact that Jesus was, indeed, a bona-fide descendant of David, in order to lay the fulfilment of the promised 'Davidic Messiah' in him. Another question that here arise, is how Jesus could possibly be a blood descendant of David, when, according to Biblical account, Joseph was not the biological father of Jesus, but only a surrogate father, as he was not the actual person responsible for Mary's conception of Jesus.

If Joseph was of the lineal descent of David, it does not naturally follow, especially in matters of spirituality and mysticism that Jesus would by design become a blood descendant of the house of David, because Joseph was not the natural father of Jesus, but a stepfather. Jesus was only an adopted child of Joseph and therefore should not qualify as a blood descendant of David in a matter that involved sacred spiritual heritage. If the prophecy of the promised Messiah had stipulated, 'from the linage of Holy Ghost;' then, there would be no contention or controversy as to Jesus being the promised Messiah, for humanity has duly conceded the credit of being the only begotten son of a Ghost to His Divine Grace.

Assuming the genealogy of Jesus according to Matthew and Luke were accurate and truthful, Jesus would still not have qualified as a blood descendant in the lineal descent of David, as he does not carry the blood of Joseph flowing in his veins, but that of a ghost. As a prerequisite, there must be a definite bloodline by birth and not by mere adoption, under which anyone could qualify as belonging to a particular lineage. More so, as the glaring disagreements in the two accounts proved against each other that they were no more than mere fabrication and falsehood, clearly devoid of any divine inspiration, it therefore has no authority whatsoever for any rational mind to believe any more than the genealogy of Mongo Park of Great Britain or that of Bashorun Ogunmola of Yorubaland.

As for the gullible man, he is duty-bound, as always, to swallow anything, because his religion has weakened his ability to reason. His religion has taught him from childhood, until the end of time, to be fearful of the mysteries of God that are beyond the comprehension of normal logic and evidence. He must simply believe or face the wraths of God and be condemned to ceaseless damnation in hellfire where his weeping, wailing, and gnashing of teeth abound for life eternal. His fear and his inordinate propensity to adulate becomes the controlling factor that empowers the church to lead him by his nose and push whatever stupid stories down his throat. Of course, he is an ever-ready robot to swallow them as a whole. Meanwhile, he credulously hazards his future hope of everlasting life and happiness dangling on adherence to an extremely doubtful contradiction that the creator of the universe has sent his 'only begotten son' into planet earth to die for his sin (whatever that means). At any rate, he would continue to swim in sin under the pretence that the blood of his Christ should wash him clean of all his wayward iniquities. At the same time, he credulously hopes for the grace of his redeemer to give him everlasting life, simply because he professes blind faith in the name of Jesus, and has accepted Jesus as the only begotten son of the creator of the universe, and as his true Lord and personal saviour. As they proclaimed in their gospel, *"For God so loved the world that he gave his only begotten Son* (to be murdered by the church) *that whosoever believeth in him* (his brutal crucifixion) *should not perish but have everlasting life"* (in an unknown earthly or heavenly paradise) John 3:16.

The gullible man has received brainwashed education through the tutoring of his religion to contemplate his inherited faith as the only one with genuine approval of the creator of the universe. The teachings and creeds of his church he sees as the only truth. He credulously perceived his praise and worship, including his tithes and offerings as the just and true deeds that will admit him into his fantasized heavenly glory. He views the devotional observances of every other religious faith as contemptible and evil, and thus foolishly condemns and calumniates the followers of other sectarian faiths as infidels who have the verdict of everlasting destruction in hellfire awaiting their destinies. What an abject betrayal of human paucity in the arena of religious tolerance and interfaith!

The Failed Prophecies of Jesus

We read in Matthew chapter 24:3, (KJV) *"And as he (Jesus) sat upon the Mount of Olives, the disciples came unto him privately, saying, tell us, when shall these things be? And what shall be the sign of thy coming, and of the end of the world?"*

Responding to questions from his disciples, Jesus reportedly gave various signs, ranging from the emergence of false prophets showing great signs and wonders, to the rumours of war, nations rising against nations, and kingdom against kingdom, famine, and pestilences. He also included the occurrence of earthquakes in diverse places, the spread of the gospel messages across all ends of the earth, and the persecutions of his followers, before the imminent 'great tribulations' should occur.

Verses 29–33 of the 24th chapter of Matthew predicted a very frightening description of supernatural events that would herald the second coming of Jesus Christ, and subsequently, the end of the world. The King James Version reads:

> *Immediately after the great tribulations of those days shall the sun be darkened and the moon shall not give her light and the stars shall fall from heaven...* *"And powers of the heavens shall be shaken; and then shall the tribes of the earth mourn* (whatever that means) *and they shall see the Son of Man coming into the clouds of heaven with power and great glory...*

How our tiny earth would contain each of those gigantic stars, described by astronomers as many times bigger than planet earth, was what the Messiah had failed to tell us in his prophecy.

In addition, Jesus boasted to the Israelites in the 34th and 35th verse of the 24th Chapter of Matthew (KJV):

> *Verily, I say to you, this generation shall not pass, till these things are fulfilled. Heaven and earth shall pass away, but my words shall not pass away.*

Taking the words of Jesus in the gospel of Matthew 16:28 and Matthew 24:34-35 into crucial reckoning, the question then arises: after two millennia, is Jesus still correct concerning the prophecy of his second coming and the end of the world? For me, the answer to this question, with certitude, would be a resounding NO. Jesus was emphatically off the beam, because his prophecies have certainly not achieved the least of any authentic realization unto this day. Although, Jesus gave these end-time prophecies since c.30 CE, which is almost two thousand years ago, but this prophecy of the Christ is yet to come to any reliable fulfilment.

Very disappointingly for this grandeur prophecy of the Messiah, the heavens and the earth have remained firmly established upon their very original details, but the words of the Christ had passed away just like the rushing of the violent winds. In direct opposition to the prophecy of Jesus, not a single day has passed since c.30CE that the Sun and the Moon had not shone their lights unto our planet earth. Moreover, not a single star of heaven has since c.30CE to date fallen unto this earth in fulfilment of the ignoramus prophecy of His Holiness.

What a great disappointment it was for the generation of those living then, and of those standing with Jesus in Matthew 16:28, whom he proudly assured during his prophetic declaration, *"Verily, I say to you, there be some standing here which shall not taste of death, till they see the Son of Man coming in his Kingdom."* Unfortunately disappointing for those generation of Jews, they all have tasted of death, passing away to the great beyond in fatal let-down and failure of hope without the grace to see and applaud the cynosure of the second coming of *"the Son of Man into the clouds of the heavens with power and great glory."* This, of course, includes the visual sighting of the befitting pomp and pageantry that the 24th chapter of Matthew (verses 30-31) had superciliously prophesied would accompany the second coming of His Royal Majesty.

However, the fact of the matter remains that nearly fifty generations of Christ followers who have earnestly awaited the second coming of their Messiah have all passed away in fatal disappointments, as their saviour's second coming has sadly failed them during their lifetime. Only the Christian God knows how many more generations to come would likewise pass away in equal abject disappointments before the reality becomes apparent to many of the so-called Bible defenders, who have persistently faced the greatest embarrassment of their faiths vis-à-vis their numerous failed predictions of the end-time, that Jesus' prophecies according to the New Testament records are downright bogus.

What an inglorious disappointment it has equally been for the congregation of Jehovah's Witnesses in keeping a discreet and diligent watch over the fulfilment of their Christ's prophecy as regards his second coming and the end of the world. Ever since the 19th century when the organization resorted to the trade of gazing into the end-time prophecy of Jesus from their Watchtower, never was there a single time that the 'witnesses' have not faced blatant embarrassments, as their end-time predictions have continuously failed. Instead of owning up to the fallacies of Jesus' prophecies and the nullity of his second coming and the end of the world, and courteously tell the truth to her followers; alternatively, the witnessing sect has dishonestly engaged in camouflaging the fallacy of Jesus' prophecies by inventing volumes of absurd metaphorical interpretations to harmonize away the failed prophecy. Furthermore, they have intensified their deceptive ploy, more than ever before, to confound the credulous minds of their followers, in order to stay tight in business.

It is a ruse and vain subterfuge on the part of Christian apologists in attempting to pervert their Messiah's failed prophecy of the end-time. The preposterous contrivance of the organization of Jehovah's Witnesses to harmonize the fulfilment of Jesus' failed prophecy within the conundrum of esoteric metaphor is very dishonest of a religious faith that pretends to preach the gospel truth. It artfully compresses the whole idea of prophetic accuracy under the vagueness of confusing and crafty manipulations —

suppressing the truth by pillage — where it best complements their pious trade of extortion and mind control.

Wandering outside established course of rational truth, the Jehovah's Witnesses have in deception harmonized the fulfilment of Jesus' second coming to the world to have symbolically occurred in heaven in the year 1914, devoid of all the substance the Messiah had specified in his prophecy, including ocular observation of its fulfilment by all human races.

What a ministry of professional deceivers! And what a deceptive twist the Jehovah's Witnesses had adopted in their attempt to bring, into line, the failed second coming of their Messiah as having occurred in heaven in the year 1914. It is inexplicably deficient in every sense to the fundamentals under which Jesus had specified the end-time prophecy. The approach under which Jesus had expressed his end-time prophecy was practically to prove to his followers the reality that he was indeed their true Messiah who knows the destiny of the cock from its gestation periods inside of the eggshell through the show-glass as Kentucky Fried Chicken.

In fact, no perversion of the church and self-styled prophets can change the actuality of the target motive responsible for the second coming prophecy. The definite motive that informed the prophecy of Jesus' second coming was practically for him to demonstrate to his compatriots, who were then unyielding to his gospel, that he was certainly their true Lord and Messiah — the only begotten son of God who solely possessed celestial mandate from On High — to deliver final judgement upon their destinies. Therefore, Jesus' second coming in the clouds of heaven, which he clearly detailed would be heralded in blaring trumpets of his angelic subjects was practically to corroborate his heavenly kingship to sceptical Israelites that he was indeed their true saviour. Jesus emphatically assured the generation of those standing with him when he rendered the prophecy, that its fulfilment would be in their lifetime in "power and great glory," and clearly visible to their naked eyes. In fact, as visible as the sun in the sky, and not as enigmatic as the imaginary ceremonials, which only the congregations of Jehovah's Witnesses were its sole spectators in their fantasized heavenly kingdom in 1914 C.E, after the utter extirpation of all the generations of Jesus' contemporaries who the messiah prophesied would witness his 'second coming' with their naked eyes.

Actually, Jesus had intended a big show out of his second return to earth, for his sceptics and everyone to see and recognize the reality of his Messiahship; and that he was truly the only begotten son of God, as well as the second in command to God, and ultimately the embodiment of the Almighty God. In that, on his majestic second coming to earth, he could as usual castigate his adamant generation of atheists and nonbelievers thus: *"Whereunto then, shall I liken the men of this generation? And to what are they like? Thou art the wicked and adulterous generation of atheists and unbelievers unto whom I forewarned that the Son of Man shall return again in his heavenly glory before thou taste of death, but ye believeth not, and unto this day thou hast hardened thine wicked heart. Ye generation of viper! Doest thou believeth now that the Son of man hast cometh in glory to deliver his judgment? Go ye into the lake of fire prepareth for thine everlasting torment by my loving father. There shall thine wailing and gnashing of teeth endureth for life eternal."*

Reasoning with New Testament Gospel

If a keen reader should take an analytical study of the testimonies of the New Testament, it would become as plain to him as the nose is noticeable on the face that the four authors of the gospel have, without doubt, contrived the cartloads of cunning predictions and miraculous accounts that covered the entirety of Jesus' ministry. It is evident that these arrays of artificial predictions, most especially the part that preludes Jesus' betrayal by Judas, the Messiah's arrest, his trial by Pilate, and denial by Peter, as well as his tortures, execution, and resurrection are altogether fictionalized fables that were cleverly designed to boost the supernatural status they have packaged for the Christian leader. The plain rationale that simply upheld this fact is that all the purported prophecies of Jesus were narrated by the gospel account writers several years after they've long occurred. It was then easy for these authors to pervert the narration of these events in deceptive manners that portrayed Jesus as precisely foretelling his betrayal by Judas, his denial by Simon Peter, his trials and tortures, and finally his death and resurrection, because they were completely past events. However, the subterfuge of Jesus' predictions regarding these things was to make for its uncanny fulfilment clearly noticeable as corroborating the divine authority of the Christian messiah. Nevertheless, discerning minds could still scan, with utmost interest, the narration of invalid testimonies in the gospels of the New Testament to validate Jesus' predictions; in addition to the recounting of ruse miraculous accounts that they cleverly designed to personify him to the entire world, after his death, as embodiment of omnipotent God.

At any rate, this end-time prophecy of Jesus and his second coming appeared truly to have soared far beyond the frontier of engineering competence of the messiah's biographers and followers. Had Jesus' followers truly possessed the supernatural wherewithal to search out their messiah from the great beyond, they would have superciliously brought him into the world again to dramatize his second coming in the clouds of heaven to the entire world. If they had truly possessed the omnipotent power to put an end to this world, they would have callously done so a long time ago, just to satisfy their wild obsession for the fulfilment of their messiah's bogus prophecies. However, as the fulfilments of Jesus' end-time prophecy had totally failed, and proved beyond the competency of his followers' spiritual prowess, the plot of all colours of symbolic fictions to cover these failures within the shadow of allegory, in order to mystify the understandings of their gullible adherents, now becomes the apparent and the only way out for them.

The Jehovah's Witnesses are very much aware of the extreme folly of the gullibility of man, as they have been around in the churching business for a very long time now. They certainly know that, if they narrate any stupid story to humankind, as long as it is a narration within the ambit of religion, the human mind would surely swallow it in whole. If they had equally told us that our whole world had ended in the year 1914; although humankind still lives in that same world in the 2000 millennium; but for the reason that religion and faith is here concerned, the timid mind of man would credulously believe that his worldly life had truly expired in the year

1914. If he dares doubt it that his world actually terminated in 1914, religionists would pervert the meaning of that 'end,' and twist it around in some repugnant metaphorical interpretation to confound our acceptance and understanding further more.

This is my honest advice for the organization of Jehovah's Witnesses if only they can listen; please go back to your Bible and read the 24th chapter of Matthew again, before you rewrite your numerous publications concerning the prophecy of Jesus' second coming and the end of the world.

It should have occurred to the great multitudes of Christian devotees by now that those spurious deceptions in the 24th chapter of Matthew, which many Bible commentators usually refer to as the prophecies of the end-time, are grossly inconsistent with the concept of what true prophecies really are. In the first place, those bogus signs should never have passed for being tagged prophecies or come anywhere close to being prophetic, as they merely recounted events that have regularly occurred throughout world's history — right from the primeval age up to the time that Jesus lived on earth.

In plain fact, a true and genuine prophecy must be a visionary insight into the hidden and the unknown to humankind. Therefore, such captions as, *"there will be wars and rumours of war"* or *"nations will rise against nations, and kingdom against kingdom"* should not at all qualify as truthful prophecy. This is because of the simple reason that the fact of their regular occurrences abound in world's history before the foretelling of the make-believe prophecy.

History abounds with the fact that there existed numerous rumours of war, before and after Jesus. The waging of wars between nations and kingdoms were very largely in existence before and after the time of Jesus. The nation of Israel had waged countless wars with the nation of Syria, Babylon, Rome, Midian, and Ammon, Moab, ad infinitum, before the birth of the Christian Messiah. In fact, Pontius Pilate, a non-Jew, happened to become the governor of the nation of Israel in Jesus' day due to the conquest of war. So, what then is the significance of Jesus' prophecy if the mongering of war had continued unto this day, as it had been on earth from the dawn of recorded time?

The prophecy of Jesus would have been more of a sincere and candid prophecy if the Messiah had predicted that there would never be war and rumours of war on planet earth anymore until his second coming, and then the end of the world would come. Such prophetic avowals would have been very honest and genuine, because humanity has never known or experienced such peace and tranquillity right from the day of Cain and Abel, throughout the history of the world. Therefore, if war should subsequently cease to occur on earth, it would unquestionably accord the deserving credit to such prophecy as truly logical and foretelling due to its outright fulfilment. Moreover, the need would certainly not have called for religionists resorting to the trick of figurative interpretations as cover up for any downright failures. Therefore, Jesus' prophecy regarding wars and rumours of war, and that of nations rising against nations, and kingdom rising against kingdom are entirely void prophecies, as the waging of wars were then daily occurrence, most especially in biblical lands. The reports of relentless war between nations are mostly the theme of proceedings that continually dominate all the pages of the Old Testament Bible. History abounds with the fact that our ancestors from the Dark Ages, up to the time of Jesus and beyond, enjoyed war mongering so much that they frequently engaged in pillaging one another without any justification, but as a means of livelihood; where then they shared the spoils of war with the priestly class, and even with their *gods*. How then would prophecy become applicable to such a case that was an ardent habit of humankind, and a fervent inclination of the Biblical Jews, of which Jesus himself was a witness?

It is only nowadays in our present civilization that warring between nations has actually been on the decline, and this is in direct opposition to Jesus' prophecy. The incessant warring between kingdoms and nations of the Dark and Middle ages, even without the slightest atom of provocation are no longer in existence in our modern society as in Jesus' day. This is a widespread global development in our modern world that out-rightly exposes the fallacy of Jesus' predictions. Not even in the remotest part of

Africa would a kingdom rise against another kingdom just anyhow, anymore. This is largely due to the efforts of the United Nations at curbing the outbreak of wars amongst member nations.

As for the sign of drought and famine, it also falls within the class of prophecies that are equivocal and ambiguous. It totally failed to specify the exact places, years, and dates where such drought and famine would occur in the future, and for how long it would last. However, Jesus equivocally made his predictions to fit the circumstances of every occurrence of drought and famine that might come up anywhere in the world; as if this has not been the constant occurrence that humankind has witnessed on regular basis ever since existence.

Just as drought has recently ravaged the nation of Zimbabwe; thus it had devastated the Ethiopian nation in the 1980s. So too had drought devastated Israel in the day of Jacob when his children migrated to Egypt in search of food. The nation of Egypt also experienced drought in the day of Joseph when the Egyptians resorted to food rationing to curb acute starvation. Severe drought had also devastated the nation of Judah in the day of Elimelech when he too migrated with his family to the land of the Moabites in search of food. In the same ancient vein, the Chad Republic, Niger, Sudan, Britain, and many other countries had experienced severe droughts at different points in history, to mention but a few. Therefore, what relationship *hath* prophecies with the regular occurrence of natural events in the world, most especially when such prophetic signs have dismally failed to carry specific prognostications as to hit any accurate targets for posterity to ascertain its precise fulfilment?

However, to prognosticate in vague terms, such signs that have largely been a part of humankind's life from the beginning of their existence, and generalize it to go well with all circumstances of future occurrences, in reality does not fit anywhere close to the sense of any true prophetic indication, except in the realms of religious absurdity. This is especially so, when such prophecies are said to hold every positive attribution to the individual who, for that matter, lays the claim to being a supernatural being that equally holds a binary function in heavenly hierarchy as second in authority to the Almighty creator of the universe. Moreover, in most cases, his followers, at different times, have knitted him together as the embodiment of the Almighty God on earth, the one whom Christianity declared as the co-creator of all things, and *"in whom are hidden all the treasures of wisdom and knowledge"* (Colossians 2:3 NIV). In reality, such manners of rendering ambiguous predictions are most commonly consistent with the tricks of false prophets in all ages, even up to this day.

Those signs given as end-time prophecies of Jesus in the book of Matthew do not give a conception of anything consequential of visionary insight that admit a fragment of tangible predictions. They wholly contain questionable vagueness that portrays the character of false prophets, rather than someone who holds divine authority and power. Anyone could as well make such ambiguous predictions to fit into all circumstances in the world. Had earthquakes not occurred in "diverse places" in the world before and during the life of Jesus? Where then is the sense in this pretentious prophecy if the occurrence of earthquakes remained as it was from the beginning of our world to this day?

Some fatal epidemic diseases of past ages have now become minor ailments of today, many of which anyone could get hold of its medications from across the counter of any pharmacy. So too will the fatal diseases that critically afflict humanity today become the minor ailment of our tomorrow. Such epidemic illnesses as the HIV/AIDS, XDR-TB, the Ebola Virus, including Haemorrhagic Viral Fever, Hepatitis, Cancer, and so on will surely become minor ailments of our tomorrow. This is my 'prophecy' and hope for the human race. Please note that my prophecy is not borne out of the most unreasonable prophetic fancies of religious prophets; many of whose characters and feign visionary capabilities are always synonymous with destructions, wars, and total doom for the world that Mother Nature had created for our enjoyment. My prophecy is that of hope for humanity — a reasonable and realistic prophecy — that the empirical evidence of science and our life-long experience of the wonderful, evolutionary law of nature will most surely fulfil.

What then is the momentous of Jesus' prophecies regarding pestilences on earth? As if this has not been the usual occurrence from generation to generation. In the days of my own father who departed this world just in 1981, which was merely some 37 years ago, there was nothing like HIV/AIDS in Nigeria. Nonetheless, malaria fevers, small pox, measles, polio, which have now become minor ailments of our present day, were then endemic and fatal. Today, a single dosage of anti-malaria therapy is all it takes from across the counter of any pharmacy to knock out malaria fever fast from the body. However, this same disease has sent millions of people to their early graves in West Africa during my father's day.

Of all the numerous signs that Jesus predicted in the New Testament gospels as the forewarning of the end-time, including other extras added to it by Paul, Timothy, Peter, and John in their epistles and the book of Revelation, only two predictions could credibly pass the test of being prophetic. However, these signs have barely attained partial fulfilments.

The first of these signs was Jesus' caveat to his followers when he put them on red alert that they would in future face great persecutions. *"Then you will be handed over to be persecuted and put to death, and you will be hated by all nations because of me"* Matthew 24:9 (NIV). All the same, the basis for the fulfilment of this prophetic sign is not far-fetched. Jesus had during his day led a campaign against the corruption and avarice of the prevailing authority of Judaism. Because of Jesus' stern opposition to the popular religious systems of his day, the entirety of the Jewish priesthood then brought severe persecutions upon his head, which subsequently resulted in his fateful crucifixion. The same fate that then befell Jesus had thus come upon his followers, as they adamantly continued to preach against the hypocrisy of the Jewish high priests in the same way as Jesus Christ did during his evangelical ministry (Compare Acts of Apostles 7:51-60).

To some degree of certainty, several historical records have truly confirmed the fulfilment of this particular prophecy. Many facts from past record were actually in agreement with the reports of severe persecutions that the followers of Christ encountered, especially in the hands of the Jewish religious leaders and the Roman Emperors and their cohorts.

On the other hand, this persecution prophecy of Jesus is also bedevilled with half-truth. To put it in plain language, it is a bias prophecy. If Jesus' prophetic revelation was actually true and in good faith, His Holiness should have equally foreseen that his own followers would also engender greater persecution of others. Many historical records have also confirmed the fact that through torturous executions, genocides, and violent force of arms, early Christian crusaders had forcefully employed brutal lines of attack to compel converts into the Christian faith. Why then did Jesus not foretell such an epic catastrophe in the annals of world history — that his own followers would likewise bring about greater persecution of others, in their efforts to spread his gospel to all ends of the earth? If Jesus truly was the supernatural being, or the Deputy God his biographers have elevated him into, he should have precisely proclaimed that, just as his disciples would face great persecution, so also would they bring greater persecution to others, before his second coming, and finally the end of the world. Perhaps this was a case of prophetic omission or prophetic suppression, only the Christian messiah could confirm.

The second of the prophetic signs that also came to partial fulfilment is the prophecy of Matthew 24:14 (NIV):

> *And this gospel of the kingdom will be preached in the whole world as a testimony to all nations and then the end will come.*

To a very reasonable extent, this prophecy has equally come to a partial fulfilment, because the gospel of the kingdom has been preached, even more than being a mere testimony, but as a means of livelihood to clergy and professional preachers throughout the entire world; other than that, the end of the world has refused to come. After those who make ostentatious livelihood from preaching the gospels of Jesus' kingdom to the dull ears of others have consistently preached it with colossal intensity to all corners of the earth, of course the end of the world has practically refused to come.

It is a fact on record that the Bible is the most widely translated, the most widely read, and the most widely distributed book on planet earth. Likewise, its gospels are the most widely preached in all corners of the earth. What then is more, except a fatal let-down for those who have been feeding fat by preaching the end of the world as a means of affluent livelihood! The irony of this case is that, even those hypocrite preachers who have continually made a racket of noise preaching the end of the world into the dull ears of gullible congregation do not truly desire for the end of the world to come, because they would consequently crash out of being proprietors of the most lucrative trade in the world.

Even though, Jesus had conceitedly made this bogus prediction in Matthew 24:22, (NIV) *"If those days had not been cut short, no one will survive, but for the sake of the elect those days will be shortened."* For real, how shortened are these days since c.30 CE? It is almost two thousand years now, but those days are still growing longer with each passing minute, incapable of becoming shortened by the spurious authority of the second in command to God. What an illusory pledge of the fictionalized Deputy God to cut short the days of humankind on earth, and relocate them to his fantasized heavenly mansions and torment theatres in an unknown extra-terrestrial location.

As I have already pointed out, a true prophecy must be able to see clearly into the future and foretell with accuracy those things which are hidden and unknown to human knowledge. During the time of Jesus, many of our New Age discoveries were entirely unknown to humankind. It would have been more of an honest prophecy if Jesus had foreseen and foretold these New Age Discoveries for his biographers to publish them among the official list of their Messiah's composite signs in the gospel of Matthew, Luke, Mark, or John; or in the epistles of Paul, Peter, James, Timothy, or Jude.

Why then did Jesus not prophesy that humankind would in future invent such scientific marvels like the radio, telephone, motorcar, airplane, computer, television, and many more? Why had the Messiah not predicted the invention of the telescope to observe heavenly bodies, spaceship to explore the extra-terrestrials, submarines to investigate the world beneath the seas, and the internet services that carry all the information of this world in their domains? How had it happened then that Jesus never predicted that man would walk on the moon, and would accurately forecast the weather in all corners of the earth before his second coming, and subsequently the end of the world?

The simple reason for this failure is that Jesus did not at all know these things, as they were not yet in existence in his day. Because Jesus had no knowledge of these things, and did not truly possess those paranormal powers that his religion has falsely arrogated to him, he most surely could not pretend to have foreseen them at all.

In plain fact, it would very much be difficult for any man of artificial visionary skill to describe the unknown in significant terms. Here lies the exact problem which the faceless author of the book of Matthew truly encountered whilst he fabricated the prophecies of the end-time, and spoke them through the mouth of Jesus.

False prophecies in the vein of warmongerings, destructions, and doom, including natural disasters, diseases, pestilences, and the emergence of false prophets that were then the order of the faceless writer's day were the things they could possibly recount, re-caption, and pretend to foretell; and thereafter bequeath as prophetic legacy to gullible devotees.

Soon after I had concluded the writing of this subheading, one Bible defender brought forward an argument in absurdity, narrating that the Bible foretold that, *"In the last days, the knowledge of man shall increase."* He proposed this vague statement as enough visionary insight of Jesus predicting the inventions of our modern progress. More often than not, I have always known religious dogmatists for their extravagant penchant for distorting Biblical fairy-tales, and wilfully concocting their invented theories in obstinate support of the numerous fallacies in the alleged holy book. I therefore demanded the confirmation of this particular prophecy from the pages of the Bible with him. However, unto this day, we both have searched in futility for this statement from all the passages of the Bible. On the other hand, if such prediction truly existed in the Bible, but escaped our detection, the problem of the vague prediction would confine alongside those indistinct tricks of all biblical prophets and their usual manners of hiding under the veil of prophetic ambiguity to sustain their religious prophecies, rather than using the means of realistic and analytical communication.

Ever since man's origin on earth, his knowledge has progressed in consistent evolution through the ages, until his gradual advancement to this present state of civilization. For example, the knowledge that man possessed during the day of Moses far out-weighed the knowledge that existed in Abraham's day. During the day of Moses, man possessed writing techniques and the skill to build magnificent pyramids, whereas the age of Adam or Noah knew nothing of such. Furthermore, the quality of the writing skills available in the world about one thousand years after Moses' day far surpasses the quality of the pioneering invention. In this sense, the knowledge of man has notably increased down the line of history from generation to generation. Nonetheless, they were evidently not the signs of the last days as wrongly claimed by dogmatic Bible defenders.

From ages to ages, humankind has consistently built knowledge upon existing knowledge. The ground-breaking knowledge of Pythagoras, Euclid, Plato, Socrates, *etc.*, was what great minds like Isaac Newton, Albert Einstein, and Alexandra Bell built upon for their striking scientific inventions. Likewise, Edwin Hubble improved on the pioneering knowledge of Galileo to invent telescopes that are more powerful. How then should religionists pervert the progressive increase in human knowledge to stand for a sign of the end-time or of the last days? Whereas, human progressive knowledge has constantly opened up from the primordial age into our modern civilization. In a nutshell, the knowledge of man has increasingly evolved into different stages of development from the beginning.

Furthermore, if we should consider for the sake of a case, the Mosaic account of Genesis, human knowledge has essentially resumed its increase from the very moment the serpent opened his eyes to discernment in the Garden of Eden, because, there and then, Adam and Eve sewed fig leaves together to make coverings for their nakedness. What then is the prophetic insight, discernible in this vague statement: *"In the last days, the knowledge of man shall increase?"* It describes nothing perceptible to the mind, except the imprudence of befogged vagueness.

The honest fact of this matter, if we could boldly tell it with certainty to the very face of our gullible advocates, implies that Jesus has written no book or gospel. As a result, Jesus never foretold any end-time prophecy to anyone. The falsehood of the prophecies in the four gospels, including the epistles of Paul, Timothy, Peter, James and John are, beyond doubt, the works of faceless impersonators. Very frankly, they are blatant forgeries of those who had no knowledge of future inventions at the time they wrote the New Testament; therefore, they could not pretend to have foreseen them, as those primitive authors would have surely encountered the limitations of how to describe the future inventions of what, in fact, they did not truly foresee.

If anything like prophecy truly exists, Michel de Nostradamus was the actual person we could consider as having in some way foreseen future events; not Jesus, not Paul, neither was it Timothy, Peter, James, nor John. Even though some prospective inventions, which Nostradamus had far-sightedly predicted were never in physical existence in his day, he could still describe them with logical accuracy to the grasp and clear perception of posterity. This, of course, was truly indicative of his authentic visionary capability into the future. Over four hundred years ago, Nostradamus predicted that man would invent a *flying steel wing bird,* which precisely described the airplane. Not even David Hume could contest the fact that Nostradamus distinctly foresaw this future discovery right from his day, and gave its precise description for future generation to validate its certainty. However, Nostradamus had never claimed to be another paranormal son of a ghost. Religious gurus never elevated him to the fictitious position of an executive member of the God's triune head in different versions of their 'sacred' books. Nevertheless, Nostradamus' foretelling had evidently remained more logical in meaning than those of Jesus'. For the most part, any rational mind could accurately relate to the prophecies of Nostradamus as more truly coherent in conclusive exactitude and precision than those ambiguous prophecies of Jesus. To the knowledge of all and sundry of diverse religious and irreligious convictions, the prophecies of Nostradamus were much more consistent and reliable. What rationalism do we then hold responsible for this plain fact, except to assign the bogus prophecies of Jesus, as contained in the New Testament Bible to the manipulations and fallacies of religion manufacturers.

Biblical Fraud Prophecies

Another phoney prophecy of Jesus as recorded in the book of Matthew 24:11(KJV) declared that, *"And many false prophets shall rise, and shall deceive many."* This verse also has the same problem of not meeting the requirements to enter into the records of anything called prophecy, as it barely correlated the common occurrence of the lifestyle of most Biblical lands before, during, and after the time of Jesus.

From the time of Moses — Israelites' first prophet — up to the time that Jesus walked on earth, humankind has repeatedly witnessed ceaseless upsurge of false prophets and their false predictions. Nearly all the pages of the Bible books ascribed to the writings of the prophets of Old Testament are populated with bogus prophecies of artificial prophets who have relentlessly deceived many.

False prophets like Samuel, Isaiah, Jeremiah, Ezekiel, Daniel, Malachi, and so on and so forth, have deceptively made it their regular stock in trade to attribute the wicked actions of humankind to the directives of God. It was then the usual trademark of these biblical prophets to initiate their prophetic falsehood by reciting their deceptive phrase of *"thus saith the Lord"* as a prefix to every of their false prophecy.

In ancient Israel, it was the common practice of the Jews, firstly to seek the counsel of the Lord before they do anything; therefore, this custom had encouraged the upsurge of false prophets in several biblical lands. Just as it is the widespread practice of most businesspersons to diversify into booming trade, considerable number of Israelites took to the trade of prophesying, as there were great demands for soothsaying among ancient Jews – See 1Kings 22:6-23 for details of this fact.

In the Bible book of Ezekiel, Prophet Ezekiel falsely predicted the utter destruction of Egypt thus:

> *Therefore thus saith the Lord, Behold I will bring a sword upon thee, and cut off man and beast out of thee. And the land of Egypt shall be desolate and waste; and they shall know that I am the Lord, because he hath said, the river is mine and I have made it ... No foot of man shall pass through, neither shall it be inhabited for forty years. And I will make the land of Egypt desolate and her city among the cities that are desolate for forty years. And I will scatter the Egyptians among the nations, and I will disperse them through the countries. Yet thus saith the Lord* – Ezekiel 29:8-12 KJV.

From the evidence of recorded and unrecorded history, never once was the history of Egypt told as a desolate nation, or known to be a wasteland for any period. From the day of Egypt's foundation until this present day, there has never been one single day that the Egyptians have not inhabited their land, much less forty successive years. Never in world's history were the Egyptians ever on any compulsory Diasporas for any given time. Has anyone of you heard of the history of Egypt being a desolate land in the past?

Therefore, this prophecy of Ezekiel has proven absolute falsehood, imposed upon the order of the creator of the universe by an impostor who called himself his prophet. The passage of time has absolutely done justice to the prophecy of Ezekiel by exposing its falsehood, just as the passage of time has also done justice to Jesus' prophecies by exposing the fallacy of his second coming and the end of the world.

Furthermore, Prophet Jeremiah was another expert in the act of deceit and false predictions. However, the Bible has attributed this peculiar syndrome of conspicuous lying and rendering of false prophecy to the operation of God's command when it states in the book of 1Kings 22:23 (NIV), *"So now the Lord has put a lying spirit in the mouths of all these prophets of yours."* Consequently, all the Jewish prophets had duly adopted these lying skills. What a degrading portrayal of the character of the Christian God as a Liar-in-Chief of the Jewish Council of Prophets!

In one of Prophet Jeremiah's many sham prophecies, the habitual lying prophet predicted in the book named after him (Jeremiah 36:30 KJV), *"Therefore thus saith the Lord of Jehoiackim the king of Judah, he shall have none to sit upon the throne of David."* Very unfortunately, for this lying Prophet, the book of 2Kings chapter 24 verse six plainly detected his falsehood and proved him another fake prophet like several of his predecessors in the Bible. *"So Jehoiackim slept with his fathers and Jehoiachin his son reign in his stead."* Compare also Prophet Jeremiah's prophecy to King Zedekiah in the book of Jeremiah 34:4-5, and the revelation of its falsehood in the tenth verse of the 52nd chapter of the same book.

Another one of those con prophets of the Bible that I quickly like to mention before I put this chapter to a close is Prophet Isaiah. The seventh chapter of the Book of Isaiah told the story of the King of Syria and the King of Israel's alliance to match their armies to Jerusalem to make war against Ahaz, the King of Judah. On hearing the rumours of war that was looming in his nation, the account reported King Ahaz thus became beleaguered with great fears that he might possibly lose the impending battle against the two kings of Syria and Israel. The story declared in the third verse of the seventh chapter that the Lord therefore commanded Prophet Isaiah to go unto King Ahaz to assure him that the two kings of Israel and Syria would not succeed in their plot against the nation of Judah.

Furthermore, to satisfy King Ahaz that the Lord had actually spoken these words out of the mouth of Prophet Isaiah, the account affirmed in the tenth verse, *"Again the Lord spoke to Ahaz, ask the Lord your God for a sign, whether in the deepest depths or in the highest heights."* This request, the report narrated, King Ahaz rejected by asserting, *"I will not put the Lord to the test."* However, Isaiah bluntly refused to accept 'NO' for an answer. Therefore, he desperately compelled a sign upon King Ahaz by himself. The fourteenth verse states, *"Therefore the Lord himself will give you a sign: Behold a virgin shall conceive, and bear a son, and shall call his name Immanuel," verse 16 "for before the child shall know to refuse the evil and choose the good, the land that thou abhorest shall be forsaken of both her kings."*

After Isaiah had thus compulsorily imposed a counterfeit sign of the Lord upon King Ahaz, and the period for the fulfilment of the sign, which he sets to be *"before the child shall know to refuse the evil and choose the good;"* that is, before the child should become wise as to comprehend things. It therefore became of necessity for the cunning Prophet, as the South Africans would say, to "make a plan" for the fulfilment of this false sign of the Lord into which he had terribly committed himself.

Consequently, Prophet Isaiah thus revealed the sneaky plan he had designed for the fulfilment of his prophetic sign. *"And I went unto the Prophetess and she conceived and bares a son"* (Isaiah 8:3 KJV). Here lays the trick and swindle of a false Prophet of God. He goes to his king as a pretended emissary of God, and impose a false prophecy and sign upon him; and through the back door, he again contrived his machinery to stage-manage a hanky-panky fulfilment of the false prophecy.

Could anyone of rational mind imagine that this false prophecy of the cunning Prophet Isaiah to King Ahaz of Judah, which Isaiah on his own had fulfilled by trick was exactly what the inventors of Christianity have distorted and fast-forwarded to their gospel in the New Testament? Dogmatists of the Christian faith have continuously misrepresented this sign to stand for the prophecy of the Virgin Mary's Immaculate Conception of Jesus Christ. As well, they have fanatically misapplied Isaiah's mendacity as the cornerstone of their incredible system of religious faith. The totality of their followers have thus credulously believed this falsehood as the only true way to attain holiness in order to gain entrance into the kingdom of heaven. The calamitous consequence of Isaiah's misleading prophecy to King Ahaz and the entire nation of Judah, we shall later see.

Overall, the Christian system of faith encompasses extreme absurdity. How possibly might Isaiah's concubine, who was another sham prophetess, still be a virgin? When Isaiah on his own account had revealed to the world that he went unto the prophetess and she conceived and bares a son for him. This was a revelation, which clearly signified Isaiah to have engaged himself in sexual intimacy with this nameless prophetess that culminated into her conception and bearing of a son. Is this adulterous custom not the common practice of promiscuous men generally all around the world, to sleep about secretly with women who are not their wives. What was the certainty that Isaiah had not even impregnated his prophetess 'virgin' concubine before giving his deceptive prediction to King Ahaz? When a virgin woman had engaged herself in sexual intercourse with a man and thus become pregnant through the intercourse, what then still makes that woman a virgin? Hadn't her virginity in effect been conked out due to the sexual activity that resulted in the eventual conception of the child?

What special relevance or exception does the case of Isaiah hold vis-à-vis the customary practice of natural reproduction all over the world? If religion dogmatists regard the degree of promiscuity as an exceptional thriller in this case, Isaiah's show might not have conceivably surpassed that of Eleazar the priest who had a free share of thirty-two Midianites virgin prisoners of war all to himself to bear sons and daughters. Why should Christianity feign this sham prophecy of Isaiah as if it holds any noteworthy importance; and thereafter feature it as an express prophecy of the Virgin Mary's conception of Jesus?

In ancient Yorubaland where tradition was especially strong, my people regarded it a taboo for any man to marry a woman who is not a virgin. On the first night of the newly wedded couple, the groom's parent would traditionally lay a pure white cloth on top of the couple's bed as a virginity check for their son's wife. They would naturally expect the white cloth to carry a mark of bloodstain the following morning when their son returned it to them, indicating a pass mark for the virginity check. Customary rituals to commemorate the virginity loss of their daughter-in-law through this proper manner would then commence. Consequently, the groom's family would carry, in trumpet blast and fanfare, additional valuables to the bride's family, which would include tubers of yam, one goat, palm oil, salt, kolanuts, natural honey, and many other treasures as bonus bride price for the proper upkeep of their daughter. This is a particular tradition we held in high esteem in our culture before the invasion of western civilization into our land. Later, the beauty of this custom has permanently eroded from our community for good. Therefore, if Isaiah's self-fulfilled prophecy is anything to be reckoned with, nearly all the first-borns in our village in the ancient times are equally born of virgin mothers. Perhaps, as the first child of my mother, I too might be a product of a virgin Josephine, who knows?

The manufacturers of Christianity have deceitfully perverted the 'virgin birth' of Jesus to stand for the fulfilment of Isaiah's prophecy, *"Behold a virgin shall conceive and bear a son."* However, they have failed to apply Isaiah's self-fulfilment of this prophecy (Isaiah 8:3) *"I went unto the prophetess, and she conceive, and bare a son,"* to suite any secret actions of Joseph. It is conversely disappointing to note that nowhere in the entire passages of the Bible did biblical authors allow Joseph a slot to narrate his own part of the story.

Moreover, the name that the false Prophet Isaiah predicted to King Ahaz in Isaiah 7:14 for the child was Immanuel. However, in the book of Matthew, this name had swiftly changed from Immanuel to Jesus to convey another unconnected prophecy. Furthermore, no passage in the book of Isaiah or the entire Bible precisely confirmed which one of this duplicity of prophetic names Isaiah had eventually given to his child, begotten of his virgin prophetess. We sincerely do not know whether Isaiah had truly fathered any child in history whose name was Maher-Shalal-Hash-Baz that honestly fulfilled the prophecy of Isaiah 8:4. In the same way Joseph and Mary did not have a son in history by the name Immanuel that truly corresponds with the fulfilment of Isaiah 7:14.

These usual traits of illogical inconsistencies and discrepancies are routinely synonymous with absurd contrivance of scripture writers to fill the pages of the Bible with fragments of fabricated anecdotes that harmonize Old Testament tales with chips and scraps of New Testament histories in whatever state of disorderliness. Unto this day, I still cannot figure out the connection and logicality of this particular name change around from Immanuel to Maher-Shalal-Hash-Baz to Jesus.

Noteworthy is the misapplication of the Immaculate Conception of Jesus Christ by Virgin Mary to stand as the fulfilment of Isaiah 7:14 by the Christian religion. Whilst in reality, the prediction, assuming it a true prophecy has no iota of any sensible allusion suggesting the future conception of Jesus by the Virgin Mary or any other virgin woman. The fraud of this prophecy, in all ramifications, strictly confined to the trick of Isaiah, who employed the service of a fellow con prophetess to stage-manage a swindle on king Ahaz by imposing a false sign upon the king as an indication that pointed to King Ahaz's victory over the two kings of Syria and Israel.

It is, therefore, curious to note that Prophet Isaiah questionably left out the fulfilment or errors of his prediction to King Ahaz in the book that bears his name. Unless a reader should flip the Bible pages backward to jump over another eight long books (the Songs of Solomon, Ecclesiastes, Proverbs, Psalms, Job, Esther, Nehemiah, and Ezra) before the reader can detect the falsehood of Isaiah's prophecy to King Ahaz. For instance, in the standard size of the New International Version of the Bible, it would take a reader to flip backwards, another 266 pages, before the reader could reach the conclusion of Isaiah's prophecy to King Ahaz in the 28th chapter of 2Chronicles verses 1-8. It reads:

> *Wherefore the Lord his God delivered him* (Ahaz) *into the hand of the king of Syria; and they smote him, and carried away a great multitude of them captive and brought them to Damascus. And he* (Ahaz) *was also delivered into the hand of the king of Israel, who smote him with a great slaughter... and the children of Israel carried away captive of their brethrens two hundred thousand, women, sons, and daughters, and took also away much spoil from them, and brought the spoil to Samaria* – 2Chronicles 28:5-8 KJV.

Instead of the two kings of Syria and Israel to "be forsaken" (that is, killed) in fulfilment of Isaiah's prophecy, which he pretended the Lord had published through his own mouth; on the contrary, they triumphed over

King Ahaz. The calamitous consequences of the outcome of the war were extremely shocking and outrageous. If the story is true, the joint armies of Syria and Israel overwhelmed Jerusalem with brutal mass executions of King Ahaz and one hundred and twenty thousand of his armies in just one day (I do not know how possible that was, especially without the weapons of mass destruction). In addition, two hundred thousand women, sons and daughters of Judah, with several spoils of war were reportedly taken into captivity to Damascus and Samaria.

Not contented with his false prophecy to King Ahaz, Prophet Isaiah tried his luck yet again on another one. In the first verse of the 17ᵗʰ chapter of the book of Isaiah, Prophet Isaiah predicted, once more, the complete destruction of the city of Damascus. Probably, because Isaiah was angry with the King of Syria for killing his king and taking into captive, a staggering two hundred thousand women, sons, and daughters of Judah, along with many spoils of war to Damascus, no one can tell (I wonder why the king of Syria had not seized Isaiah among the two hundred thousand prisoners of war taken captive to Damascus). However, Isaiah seemed very angry when he voiced out his prediction and imposed it upon the Lord by deceit, *"See, Damascus will no longer be a city but will become a heap of ruins… declares the Lord Almighty"* Isaiah 17:1-3 (NIV).

Posterity has proven this prophecy of doom complete falsehood in its entirety. It is almost two thousand eight hundred years since Isaiah foretold his prophecy, yet the city of Damascus has continued to thrive vibrantly unto this day. Here ends the story of Prophet Isaiah and his false prophecy, which the church has compulsorily burdened upon humanity as the word of God.

What a book of rambling fact the Bible is! A false prophecy of over seven hundred years is fast tracked to lay the foundation for another false religion. Most of its history starts and ends abruptly without any sequence and consistency; with readers left in the dark to search effortlessly for conclusions. Only through the mercy of sheer luck and probability would readers accidentally come across conclusions in another book written entirely by a different author. Moreover, one would never find conclusion anywhere at all to several other stories.

Thomas Paine (1794) once wrote in his book, The Age of Reason, concerning the book of Isaiah:

> *Whoever will take the trouble of reading the book ascribed to Isaiah will find it one of the most wild and disorderly composition ever put together; it has neither beginning, middle nor end; and, except for a short historical part and a few sketches of history in two or three of the first chapters, is one continued, incoherent, bombastical rant, full of extravagant metaphor, without application and destitute of meaning; a school boy would scarcely have been excusable for writing such stuff; it is (at least in the translation) that kind of composition and false taste that is properly called prose run mad.*

As we can see so far, the Bible is a ludicrous collection of lavish prophetic failures, comprising the typical trait of telling the bulk of its stories in extreme distortion of analytical communication and deliberate disorderliness of writing styles. The consequence of which hangs on the proverbial neck of the church, and unto eternity would continue to hunt her pending when she truthfully reveals to humanity, the source of those blasphemously obscene prophecies and fallacies they have fathered on divine inspiration. This in sharp contrast to the evidence of perfect orderliness, great wisdom, and truthfulness that the laws of nature have constantly revealed in practical demonstrations to the perceptive knowledge of man through the excellent qualities of the glory of Mother Nature that humankind remarkably beholds in the universe.

The fact that those excessive failures of Bible prophecies, and the recurrent contradictions and discrepancies in the Christian holy book did not seem in any way to affect the reputation of the Bible, and that of the church that has encouraged the propagation of these absurd stories, as is evident in the remarkable growth of evangelism at very explosive rates worldwide, is a conclusion that is not far-fetched. I shall touch on a few issues in the next chapter.

*****

*"Doth someone say that there be
gods above?
There are not; no, there are not.
Let no fool, led by the old false
fable, thus deceive you."*

– Euripides (480–406 BCE)

*****

Chapter

5

The Gullibility of Man

*"A donkey is a simple creature, it would follow a carrot on a stick,
but it is still capable, even with its most basic of intellect of
determining when there is no carrot."*

– John Kelly Ireland

History of fatal consequences, stirring time after time, in the religious annals of all human civilization had been the widespread results of the gullibility of man. This is the grave outcome of man's acute failure to apply insightful valuation and reasoning, as it should be, to assess any claim or idea put forward to him. As a result, humankind has dearly paid for their irrational errors of gullible mindset.

According to the fourth edition of American Heritage Dictionary of English Language, gullibility is the *"tendency to believe too readily and therefore to be easily deceived."* Many charlatans parading as prophets of God, and con men posing as genuine investors have repeatedly duped and preyed upon man's gullible attitudes by means of giving false prophecies and fraudulent malpractices.

The learned lawyer, Gerry Spence wrote in his book, How to Argue and Win Every Time, *"I would rather have a mind opened by wonder than one closed by belief."* To the contrary, the customary attitude of humankind has gullibly chosen to close their perceptive minds through misapplication of faith and belief systems which their religions patently promote. Thus, the tradition of man has developed a habit of accepting every piece of fictional claim that comes his way exactly like the robotic belief machine that his religion has programmed and finely tuned him to become. Without any recourse to reason, logic, and scepticism to analyse whatever claim, the gullible man would credulously subscribe to whatever scheme, plot, or swindle that any con artist might entrap on his path; be it the plot of commercial evangelism, legal or illegal trade, or that of advance fee fraud, or the imposition of false prophecy upon his head.

Whatever dubious schemes that any impostor might introduce to the society of gullible majority would generally thrive into overwhelming booms like wildfire in the veld. The success of one impostor or of one evangelist or priest, alongside another con man or scammer would immediately render effective encouragements to others to establish their own evangelical ministries, trade, or schemes. With the able support of the legendary narrative process — that of one gullible person telling the story to another, and another to another, and so on and so forth, their illicit trades would bloom into mega success. In no time, the avarice of that con man of God is perpetually entrenched in that society of gullible populace. No sooner had the fame of this man of God spread through the narrative efforts of his credulous followers, than he begins to live a life of ostentation, panache, affluence, and glamour under the pretence of God's blessings.

The Ascension Robes

History has it that American self-styled prophet and founder of the Millerites Movement, William Miller, proclaimed *'end of the world'* predictions to his American parishioners on the 21st day of March 1843. We gathered from historical accounts that Prophet Miller claimed he derived his prophecy from the Bible books of Daniel and Revelation, predicting that the whole world would end on the 22nd day of October 1844. Great number of followers, including many Christians outside of Prophet Miller's church had accepted his prophecy without any question. All the followers of Prophet Miller had terribly failed to apply their minds to their leader's claim, as they paid no attention to their responsibility to demand certain evidence from Miller in support of his end-time forecast.

The American Christian followers had erringly behaved like the robotic machine that routinely performs all functions programmed for it to execute without any question. All the followers of Prophet Miller had totally stuck to a sticky end of not utilizing the most precious gift of nature to man — the natural gift of reason — to subject their leader's prediction to logical evaluation, so they might detect his prophetic fallacy of doom, right from the passages of the same Bible of the Prophet. Instead of taking to the path of logic and common sense, man in his ever-gullible character, decided to take the part of credulity, and opted to accept Prophet Miller's false prophecy hook, line and sinker. Conversely, several of Miller's gullible followers had then become blind to some basic biblical assertions, whilst they fell heads-down for his bogus prophecy.

As Miller's appointed doomsday approached, history recounted that many devotees abandoned their farms out of harvest, others reportedly closed shops for business, while several of them gave up their jobs and freely gave away their possessions. Please don't ask me if the possessions were given to American atheists and pagans whom they regarded as not worthy of being partakers in the end-time raptures. I sincerely could not fathom to whom these possessions were given and why. I could not deduce if they were given to adherents of Jehovah's Witnesses whom they perceived would not be destroyed in the end-time apocalypse, but possessed the destiny to inherit the earth forever. However, what we do know from history is that, prior to Prophet Miller's Day of Atonement, the preacher had kept his diary full of actions, as he was busy fleecing and reaping-off his gullible converts, peddling 'Special White Robe for Ascension' to them. Several of whom history affirmed, awaited either their death or their raptures on the appointed doomsday in "freshly dug graves."

From the Millerites' story, one could truly discern the extreme folly to which the human stupidity could go, where dogmatic faith is concerned. In the first place, the Bible is supposed to be the last authority for Christian devotees. And, clearly written in several passages of the Bible (Matthew 24:36; Matthew 25:13; Mark13: 32; Acts 1:7 etc.,) were several warnings of the Christian Messiah and leader, indicating that no man knows the 'Day and Hour' of the end of the world. Jesus Christ had earlier forewarned his followers in Matthew 24:36 (KJV), *"But for that day and hour knoweth no man, no, not the angels of heaven, but my father only."* The Christian holy book had very strongly emphasized it in several of its passages, numerous times, that the only one who knows the day and hour of the end-time is *'God the Father.'* Nevertheless, in outrageous defiance, contrary to Jesus' written command, man, in his emblematic character had credulously awaited the fulfilment of the false prophecy of a con man. At the end of the day, the gullible devotees paid dearly for their errors when the false prophecy woefully failed.

What on earth had transformed William Miller to *'God the Father,'* that he should know the day and hour? If Miller was not 'God the Father,' what then had compelled man to believe him when he piously claimed to know the day and hour, and proclaimed such date as the 22nd day of October 1844; perhaps 12h00 GMT or 10h30 CAT, my history source did not give the time detail. However, why should these devotees believe the American preacher, if it were not for their outrageous gullibility? Instead of taking the trouble to consult their Bible and dig deeper in search of rational truth concerning their faith, the passion of these gullible devotees had credulously opted for digging their own graves. Oh ye gullible men! Why then hast thou forsaken the voice of thy Messiah, but gullibly harkened the voice of a con man, when thy Lord and thy saviour assertively saith — *no man knoweth the day and hour?*

Again, the Christian Bible declared, the day and hour of the end-time would come like a "thief;" that is, the day and hour would appear on earth without any preceding notice. On the contrary, from the 21st day of March 1843 to the 22nd day of October of 1844 offered a clear 580 days or nineteen months advance notice; directly contradicting several warnings of the Bible in its various books (1Thessalonians 5:2; 2Peters 3:10; and Revelation 3:3) that emphasized the day would come to humans like a thief without prior notice. If not for man's chronic absurdity and his emblematic gullibility, why, for god's sake, should he choose to uphold the phoney advance notice of Prophet Miller, which stood in direct conflict with the several affirmations of his professed sacred scriptures?

Thirdly, we also gathered from history that many Christians in America freely gave away their possessions; the purpose why they did that, we really do not know. If the Millerites had actually believed the whole world would end on the 22nd day of October 1844, what sensible reasons were therein to give possessions away? Since, of course, the whole world, including all the souls that lived in it would expectedly grind to a total halt in apocalyptic catastrophe; in which case, all those possessions would perish, and all believers would rapture to a heavenly paradise, while all unbelievers are delivered to hellfire, leaving this world without a soul. How then would those possessions be useful to any recipient?

Besides, dogmatic believers have totally failed to disclose through the inspiration of their fictionalized Holy Spirit, the exact venue of their heaven and hell. In absolute confusion, some sectarian faiths proclaimed it would be here on earth, while others constantly maintained the location would be in heaven. Whether in planet Jupiter, Uranus, or Neptune, they actually do not know. In any event, if any rational man is not ready for every marathon of illogical and speculative confusion, he should not attempt to inquire from our faithful Christians where precisely the location of their future heaven actually is. Ever since the past two millennia of the existence of the Christian faith, gullible followers of Christ possessed not the slightest idea of the location of their hopeful heavenly abode, except that these credulous devotees would indicate straight to the starry skies, and gullibly substitute the galactic cosmic space as the venue of their paradisiacal heaven. Notwithstanding, they have credulously hung their hope of everlasting life on the belief of this unknown heavenly paradise. Curious, as this matter might be, all the Christian priests have oddly classified the location of this paradise and torment amphitheatre as an inexplicable mystery of their God, while they deceitfully encourage the persistence of their devotees in the practice of blind faith.

It is incredibly amusing, as I imagine the different scenes of attendance drama, all over the streets of America, which must have followed the failed prophecy of Miller. Imagine the jostles and mad rush to regain employment back into the jobs the Millerites had foolishly abandoned due to their inanity to rapture to heaven! Anyone could imagine the different colours of ejectment summons and legal actions that must have flooded American law courts for the recovery of those precious possessions the Millerites had foolishly given away after Miller's prophecy had miserably failed.

On doomsday, history told us that many of the Millerites gracefully adorned their special ascension robes—specially procured from the con Prophet for their epic ascension to heaven. Very trustingly, they awaited their death or raptures inside the fresh graves they had credulously dug for themselves.

Hum! Just imagine the peak of man's outrageous folly in the arena of dogmatic faith! Oh gullible men of little faith, what fellowship hast the graves with raptures? Doest Miller, thy Prophet of Doom, prophesied to thee that thou shall be caught up with thy Christ in the skies, and thence sold he ye special white robes for thy ascension to heaven to meet thy God! What a fool has these professional preachers made of man through this absurd religion called Christianity! Just imagine how over-zealous gullibility had totally befogged the Millerites' common sense of reckoning, to an appalling extent that they could no more perceive the reality of their credulous religious hope.

If one should ask, what actually was the hope of the Millerites in this circumstance that illustrates any cogency to the rational mind? Was their hope truly apropos to their raptures to heaven, or in relations to dying in their respective graves? Perhaps, their hope was truly to die in their graves and, thereafter, spiritually rapture to heaven, as one pastor analyst had considered it. Either way, this matter is typically puzzling. For real, if the Millerites had truly believed in their raptures to heaven and, because of their faith, they suitably purchased special ascension robes from their prophet, what then were the factors that again put them under the necessity to dig graves for their own burial? This is considering the fact that they were practically looking ahead to be caught in the air with their Christ; hence the purchase of *Ascension Robes*. If, on the other hand, they truthfully had the faith of dying here on earth and, as a result, had committed time to dig their personal burial graves, why then the purchase of ascension robes? Assuming the conviction of the Millerites was truly to die in their graves and, subsequently rapture in the spirit to heaven; of what use would a material or physical robe serve a non-physical, but spiritual rhapsody? Again, the question arises as to why the purchase of ascension robes? According to Albert Einstein, *"Two things are infinite: the universe and human stupidity."* These are the plain examples of the numerous crises that the accommodation of dogmatic faith had burdened upon humanity from the dawn of recorded time unto this day—heaps upon heaps of ridiculous devout madness!

The absurdity of pious gullibility had incredibly blocked the perceptive minds of the Millerites to the basic reality that no one would remain on earth to give proper burial to their corpses in the graves they dug for themselves should the entire world abruptly come to an end, as their leader had prophesied. Had these gullible devotees chosen to die in the comfort of their beds and beautiful homes, would it not be better than giving them away to die inside of those shallow holes they dug as burial graves? Perhaps, Prophet Miller had subtly brainwashed his credulous followers through the means of another false prophecy that his exclusive 'Ascension Robes' would provide his credulous devotees the resurrecting powers to rapture from their graves to heaven. While, at the same time, he decreed anyone who failed to purchase the special ascension robes would never be resurrected for heavenly raptures, even though a faithful disciple. Indeed, religion was invented when the first con man met the first fool, as Albert Einstein has aptly observed.

The Prophetess' Voice

In 1856, twelve years after the disaster that greeted the failure of Prophet Miller's end-time prophecy in America, history was all over again repeated in South Africa, as the Xhosa tribes in the then Transkei region, now the Province of Eastern Cape, were entirely misled into a very terrible national disaster as a result of dogmatic belief systems. This horrible tragedy occurred when a great number of the Xhosa population committed suicide by naively starving to death, while they obeyed the prophecy of a fourteen-year-old girl named Nongqawuse. Here is a summary of the story as history has related it to us.

Reportedly, in the month of April 1856, a fourteen-year-old farm labourer by the name Nongqawuse became an overnight Prophetess, whose prophetic voice her people hearkened throughout her entire homeland. On this fateful day in April 1856, history has it that little Nongqawuse went to the farm, as usual, to chase birds away from millet fields. While she was on break to drink water from the nearby Gxara River, she allegedly claimed to have seen two mysterious figures that miraculously appeared on the surface of the river, and becoming visible to her vision like the manifestation of the Xhosa ancestors. These two supposedly ancestral figures had apparently prophesied to the little girl, revealing the divine resolution of the Xhosa ancestors to chase all the white settlers away from Xhosaland through their supernatural powers. Prophetess Nongqawuse consequently received directives from these divine spirits for onward communication to the entire Xhosa nation, asserting the eruption of a paranormal whirlwind on the 18th day of February 1857 that would sweep all the white settlers into the sea.

As sacrificial obeisance that would dependably guarantee supernatural victory for the mystical forces of the Xhosa ancestors in their spiritual warfare to flush out all the white settlers from their homeland, all the Xhosas had then received divine directives through their fourteen-year-old Prophetess' voice, to kill each and every of their livestock. They must, in addition, destroy all their crops and cultivate no more until after doomsday. Those who refuse to heed the Prophetess' voice and decline to partake in the great sacrifice would equally face the wrath of the ancestors. They would alongside the white settlers be turned into frogs, mice, and ants, and blown into the sea.

For ten consecutive months, from April 1856 to February 1857, the entire Xhosa people devotedly obeyed their teenage Prophetess to the letter, as they conscientiously observed every bit of the commandments contained in her prognostications. They accordingly slaughtered all their livestock, with estimates standing at over three hundred thousand; some account put the figure at over four hundred thousand livestock. They also destroyed all their crops, until they had nothing left to eat. The Xhosas had practically refused to cultivate their fields anymore; instead, they dug grain pits in anticipation that their ancestors would miraculously fill those pits with abundant foodstuffs after the doomsday apocalypse, as the juvenile Prophetess Nongqawuse had duly prophesied.

Some of the catastrophic disasters that little Prophetess Nongqawuse had reportedly predicted for the day of reckoning included the rising of two blood-red suns that would collide in the sky and plunged the entire Xhosaland into total darkness. Then, a great whirlwind would erupt and sweep all the white settlers into the sea. Subsequently, a new sun would rise in the sky, with the grain pits of the Xhosas overflowing in abundant foodstuffs. New crops would then cover their land, and every dead person would be resurrected through the supernatural wand of their ancestors.

On doomsday — the 18th day of February 1857 — the sun luminously rose in her radiant routine, and shone brilliantly through the course of the day, unperturbed by the prophecy of our diminutive Prophetess of doom. With absolute peace and serenity, the sun customarily sets on its horizon as any other normal day. Extremely disappointing yet again, the Nongqawuse prophecy of doom, reminiscent of the likes of her numerous predecessors from c.1800 BCE through c.30CE to date, had woefully failed. A nation at peace with herself had consequently come under very heavy ruins, gloom, and misery. This shocking disaster allegedly recorded the premature death of over one hundred thousand people, including children and infants. As several Xhosas had trustingly refused to cultivate and plant any crop during the preceding planting seasons, several hundred thousands more had subsequently lived at the mercy of impending menace of severe hunger and starvation, years after.

Once again, man had foolishly succumbed to the fantasies of a charlatan. As a result, he had very regrettably received great measures of ruthless penalty another time for his gullible errors of failing to use nature's gift of reason that costs him nothing. This precious gift of inestimable value that Mother Nature had specially endowed upon him, he credulously discarded at the crucial time that he mostly required it.

After reading through the little Prophetess Nongqawuse story, I have no difficulties in concluding that this unfortunate disaster was the outcome of a grand plot by some unscrupulous white settlers then in Xhosaland. Prior to the unfortunate disaster, we gathered from oral history that the Xhosas had previously resisted attempts by those white settlers to coerce them into providing cheap labour in their farms. Therefore, my Ouija Board had divined some unscrupulous white settlers as the callous culprits, who, in all probability, would have designed the plot with devilish ulterior motives to enslave the Xhosas at all costs, in order to acquire cheap labour for their commercial farming activities. Before the great disaster, majority of the Xhosas were reportedly self-sustained with enough food and livestock to live on; therefore, a good number of them had bluntly refused to work for paltry wages in commercial farm plantations. As a result, commercial farming had then become a lot more difficult in Xhosaland. However, after the disaster of Nongqawuse's prophecy of doom, the menace of severe starvation that then loomed in Xhosaland had consequently become the inevitable factor that compelled the survival of the Xhosas on working for those 'peanut' wages they formerly abhorred.

It is, however, curious to observe how the designers of this callous plot had coerced the Xhosas under the duress of overhanging lack of food, into accepting appalling conditions they had previously resisted. The knock-effect of the plotters' blow had practically hit hard on the Xhosa nation through the deficiencies that abound in their superstitious beliefs. One of such beliefs is the superstitious reverence that the entire Xhosa nation had credulously developed for the spirit of the dead, which they always relate to as the influence of the ancestors in their everyday life. The dubious plotters had practically manipulated this porous superstition to con the Xhosas out-rightly into the snare of the fateful disaster. The plan to succumb the Xhosas into credulously forfeiting their powerbase had greatly succeeded because the plotters, on one hand, craftily exploited the illogical superstitious beliefs of the Xhosa nation. Similarly, on the other hand, these plotters cleverly manipulated the emotional need of the Xhosa people, which was then to chase the white settlers out of their land, to rip them off their powerbase through the mysteries of phoney prophecy. The powerbase of the Xhosas then were their enormous livestock possessions and other agricultural produce; and all these they credulously forfeited to the Nongqawuse disaster.

How come in those days that there were no radical like-minds in the homeland of Msanzi revolutionary base like the Nelson Mandelas, the Steve Bikos, the Chris Hanis, including the likes of Archbishop Emeritus Desmond Tutu, the Thabo Mbekis, the Oliver Tambos, and so on. I mean, where then were those critically minded Xhosas, who should have troubleshot a resistant movement similar to African National Congress to guard against the nuisance of the Nongqawuse's prophecy of doom upon their people by discrediting such paltry blunder of a teenage-farm-labourer. The mystery of the lack of any decisive resistance crusade to the Nongqawuse's saga is what still baffles my sense of imagination unto this day.

Once again, with us the black race, history has repeated itself another time on our shore. Through the handiwork of a few white exploiters, we have gullibly allowed ruinous consequences to befall our nation the second time again. On the first mission of the white people to Africa in the 16th and 17th centuries, a handful of ruthless mercenaries amongst them had meted out deadly blows upon our ancestors. At that time, only very few of these mercenaries had rounded up over 30 million of our ancestors, and traded them off into captivity as slave labourers in various farm plantations, under some miserable conditions that have dishonoured humanity so terribly to this day. What a humiliating cruelty that the lips of fellow humans were pierced with hot iron rods and securely padlocked to prohibit them from eating and talking at will on the very same farm plantation where they constituted the entire labour force!

We gathered from history that more than half of the staggering number of our black African ancestors who the slave traders had packaged away like sardines, in chains and cuffs, did actually die in the Trans-Atlantic crossings and their bodies were thrown into the oceans to feed marine creatures. It is disheartening to note that the campaign for reparation to

Africa, for the indescribable atrocities of slavery had virtually died with Chief Moshood Abiola, the man who initiated the reparation crusade in Nigeria in the 1980s.

Then again, in the 19th century, another handful of exploiters had once more succumbed Africans to slavery; and this time around on their very own land under the mask of spurious prognostication. When then shall the black race wake up from their slumbering stupor, and very respectably become masters of their destinies.

The Gospel According to 419

In the late 1980s, a number of notorious syndicate fraudsters illicitly emerged under cover in Africa's most populous city of Lagos. These underworld syndicates largely specialized, with matchless finesse, in worldwide duping of foreign nationals. The scam of the syndicates, which has its nickname coined after the Nigerian criminal code that deals with the cases of "obtaining of properties under false pretences," is renowned in Nigeria as 419 — pronounced, four-one-nine — and famously known in the United States and other parts of the world as 'Advance Fee Fraud.'

Many of these Nigerian fraud syndicates usually hit upon their foreign victims by sourcing most of their contact addresses through international telephone directories, foreign business catalogues, and international yellow pages. They also catch in on their victims through the membership directories of foreign Chambers of Commerce and Industries, internet search engines, and the business sections of High Commissions and Embassies. As well, they obtain foreign contacts through large number of relatives and friends that are resident all over the globe due to the severe economic recessions that emanated from the long years of military misrule in that country.

As soon as anyone of these 419 scammers laid his hands on some foreign addresses, he would immediately forward his 419 sermons to potential targets at their respective addresses through the traditional post, e-mail, or facsimile. The bait is at that moment laid and, patiently, he awaits responses from interested targets in due course.

In due course, converts from overseas would begin to flock into the 419 fold in droves. Nearly everyone that received a copy of this sermon had shown remarkable interest in the gospel. Countless people all over the word had readily accepted this bogus proposal with pleasure, and gladly offered themselves as loyal comrades-in-crime to faceless crooks in Nigeria; pledging their eagerness and unflinching support to the priesthoods of the nefarious syndicate of 419 scammers.

A new convert would quickly forward all documentations and information required of him to his newly found Nigerian partners in crime — the illicit business associates he had never seen or known anywhere from Adam. Nevertheless, their sermon sounded too good to be ignored, and he could not afford to miss the tantalizing booty. A whooping thirty-five and a half million American dollars! No, not in this world could any son of Adam afford to miss such largesse!

From then onwards, he begins to live in the frenzy and euphoria of hallelujah, my millions have come! He kicks the air out of excitement and credulously says, "Oh! Yes, I have arrived! Even though I have constantly failed every week to win the lotto jackpot of my home country, at least I could hit it big on the Nigerian oil wealth. After all, my partners in crime have assured me that this manna from the Central Bank of Nigeria is risk free on both sides, and I could eat my God sent manna, not only for forty years like the Jews did in the wilderness, but for as long as I live. I could as well bequeath it to my children, and this colossal wealth would run in my family to life eternal. Come what may, I am on standby to swindle the Nigerian government of several millions of U.S dollars." The following Sunday, he goes to his local church to tender a meagre offering of $10 (ten dollars) or £10 (ten pounds) to the church's coffer as his gesture of thanksgiving for the goodness of the Lord.

LAGOS
NIGERIA

ATTENTION: PRESIDENT / CEO

DEAR SIR/Madam,

CONFIDENTIAL BUSINESS PROPOSAL

HAVING CONSULTED WITH MY COLLEAGUES, AND BASED ON THE INFORMATION GATHERED FROM THE NIGERIAN CHAMBER OF COMMERCE AND INDUSTRY, I HAVE THE PRIVILEGE TO REQUEST FOR YOUR ASSISTANCE TO TRANSFER THE SUM OF US$35,500,000 (THIRTY-FIVE MILLION, FIVE HUNDRED THOUSAND U.S DOLLARS) INTO YOUR ACCOUNTS.

THE ABOVE SUM RESULTED FROM AN OVER-INVOICED CONTRACT, EXECUTED, COMMISSIONED, AND PAID FOR ABOUT FIVE YEARS AGO BY A FOREIGN CONTRACTOR. THIS ACTION WAS HOWEVER INTENTIONAL AND SINCE THEN, THE FUND HAD BEEN IN A SUSPENSE ACCOUNT AT THE CENTRAL BANK OF NIGERIA.

WE ARE NOW READY TO TRANSFER THE FUND OVERSEAS AND THAT IS WHERE YOU COME IN. THE TOTAL SUM WILL BE SHARED AS FOLLOWS: 70% FOR US, THE OFFICIALS, 25% FOR YOU AND 5% FOR LOCAL AND INTERNATIONAL EXPENSES INCIDENT TO THE TRANSFER.

PLEASE BE ASSURED THAT THE TRANSFER IS RISK FREE ON BOTH SIDES. IF YOU FIND THIS PROPOSAL ACCEPTABLE, WE SHALL REQUIRE THE FOLLOWING DOCUMENTS FROM YOU AS SOON AS POSSIBLE.

A)   YOUR BANKING DETAILS.
B)   YOUR PRIVATE TELEPHONE AND FAX NUMBERS FOR CONFIDENTIALITY AND EASY COMMUNICATION.
C)   YOUR COMPANY'S BLANK LETTER-HEADED PAPER, DULY STAMPED, AND SIGNED. ALTERNATIVELY, WE WILL FURNISH YOU WITH WHAT TO WRITE INTO YOUR LETTER-HEADED PAPER, ALONG WITH INSTRUCTIONS EXPLAINING COMPREHENSIVELY, WHAT WE REQUIRE OF YOU.

THE BUSINESS WILL TAKE US THIRTY WORKING DAYS TO ACCOMPLISH.

PLEASE, REPLY URGENTLY.

YOURS' FAITHFULLY,

 DR. SO AND SO

From that moment, a victim foolishly succumbs to the swindle of charlatans; and very easily he becomes a target upon which unscrupulous tricksters continually preyed. As a futile lead up to obtaining his enticing booty from Nigeria, he would make advance payments upon payments until he runs out of money. Without asking his business gangsters any sceptical questions as to why he should be under the prerequisite to advance money several times into unknown accounts, he would credulously continue to deposit large sums of money to several fraudulent bank accounts in different parts of the world, until he becomes stark broke. He either quits his dubious business adventures frustrated with nothing, or else he runs deeper and deeper into debts. What a fool do the gospels according to 419 make of our honourable colonial masters!

From Lagos via London to Paris, Las Vegas, Toronto, Tokyo, and Sydney through Madagascar back to Lagos through Timbuktu. All around the globe, Nigerian tricksters have continuously duped targets from every corner of our planet earth. As at 1997, the Nigerian fraud industry had reportedly become the country's fourth largest industry. Allegedly raking into the coffers of scammers, well over five billion US dollars — all profit without tax — with about ninety percent of those staggering amounts coming from the pockets of their white victims. At the start of the 2000 millennium, the figures had virtually tripled.

From one end of the earth to the other, no prophet or seer could have possibly foreseen with accuracy that this tersely worded one page Nigerian 419 letter (customarily written in capital letters as reproduced in previous page) could perform such a magical swindle of unbelievable magnitude on the entire human race. The stupendous success of this modest piece of miraculous letter had taken Nostradamus by awesome shock and surprise. In fact, David Hume would have been totally thrown into absolute scepticism and disbelief, hearing the reports and testimonies of his descendants naively loosing such a breath-taking amount of money to faceless black African crooks. Had it been possible for the late Mr Hume to visit our world once again, the testimony of the efficacy of this Nigerian 419 letter, as supernatural multi-billion dollar conjurer would become the number one testimony, credible enough for him to establish a genuine miracle of clear conviction. This is purely on the straightforward reason that the evidence of the efficacy of this scam letter abounds overwhelmingly everywhere in the world. It is an empirical fact, which anyone could certainly verify from bank account balances of numerous victims; over and above the various streets of Nigerian towns and cities that, of course, adorn and titivate with state-of-the-art mansions and multibillion dollars' worth of flashy cars purchased with fraud money, dubiously extorted from their white victims.

Of all the evils that the 419 scourge has brought upon the entire world, coupled with the stinking image of unlimited disrepute into which the cankerworm has dragged Nigeria and her good people; even to such extremity that compelled the listing of my own dear motherland as a *"Rogue State"* in the official administrative gazettes of the American government. In the midst of all these unspeakable adversities, one good benefit still stood in favour of the emergence of the scourge called 419. I think for this purpose, the Omniscient God of religion has allowed it to spread and flourish to all ends of the earth.

The 419 plague has largely assisted humanity in concretizing the assertion that denotes gullibility as a dangerous affliction and appalling misery, which is no respecter of class and race, age or gender. Sincerely, the entire human race should admit the plain fact that the scourge of the notorious 419 scam has helped in no little way to expose the dangerous level of the gullibility of man. Again, as Albert Einstein has very candidly observed, *"Two things are infinite: the universe and human stupidity."*

Prior to the emergence of 419 on our continent, many of us black Africans have always posited that we were the only gullible race in the world. We never had it even near to our wildest dreams and thoughts that numerous Asians and plentiful descendants of our honourable colonial masters are equally such a character of gullible take in; even to the despicable excesses of becoming more or less like a platter of buffet upon which the descendants of their former slaves fete. What an abject betrayal of intellectual intrepidity bequeathed to you by your famous ancestors, whose excellent works of invention and ingenuity opened the entire world to great technological marvels that humanity enjoys today!

Ye masters of honour and integrity! Why hast thou cast into the winds, thy pretended honour and integrity, in the face of unholy wealth coming from the land of thy former slaves — the land which thou *abhorrest* and *referreth* to as under-developed and the Third World? Why hast thou permitted the Nigeria 419 scourge to drag thine reputation mockingly into the mud, and subject the legacy of incorruptible honour and logical insight of thine ancestors into abject ridicule? Why hast thou allowed an authority of astute nobility and credence that once upon a time utterly commanded eminent esteem over all human race, to become sullied with greed and proclivity to steal from the habitually perceived corruptible, dishonest, and backward black race?

To paraphrase the Yoruba famous saying, if you see a man in swindle, he too is another dishonest party to the scam. How much truly has this popular aphorism become in this case of the Nigerian 419ers and their foreign victims? No snare or disguise existed under the sun, in which any crook could cheat an honest man, because he would certainly weigh his judgment on the standard scale of honesty and candour. Using the gift of reason, which Mother Nature has freely endowed upon him, the honest man would most surely subject such 419 snares that have swindled the greed and the gullible all around the globe, to rational evaluation and assessment.

In every uncertain business circumstance that might confront the man of integrity, no matter how juicy and attractive the proposal might be, before the man of nobility and honour should make his decision, either to proceed with transactions, if such dealings conform to his laid down standards, or to decline if otherwise; he would definitely raise ethical questions. A true man of sincerity would certainly probe his inner conscience with such moral questions as to why he should connive with crooks to steal other people's money. Therefore, the honest answer to this frank question would be satisfactory enough to assist any honourable man overpower the temptation that abounds in accepting the bogus Nigerian 419 proposals.

Ever since the operations of the Nigerian 419 syndicates became public knowledge, every national government of the world has mounted intensive media campaign on radio, television, the print media, and internet websites against it. Local and international law enforcement agencies all around the world have embarked upon very drastic measures in conjunction with the banks, other credit finance institutions, High Commissions and Embassies, Immigration officials, and so on, at exposing the tricks regularly used by the 419 syndicates that predominantly target the white race. Probably because they are the richer race rather than the most gullible, I am not sure of that fact. However, it has become a popular boulevard aphorism on the streets of Lagos that, *"Oyinbo people Na big muumuu, dem too dey trust"* (meaning White people are the biggest take in; they are too gullible, because they trust too readily). It is, however, disheartening to note that many of these gullible white targets still fall heads deep for the 419 snares, which on daily basis metamorphose into different pigments of criminal sophistications. The urge to loot from the Nigerian oil treasury, or as the case might be, to double-cross those presumed to have looted from the Nigerian oil prosperity is still uppermost in their gullible heart.

I could not imagine what in this world would have become of my dear native land, supposing this money transfer swindles were actually true. By now, imperialists from abroad must have milked a nation of vast human and natural resources dry to their very last penny and their last drop of blood. My motherland must have become extirpated from planet earth a long time ago, either out of scarcity of funds and starvation, or taken into captivity on a second slavery due to over-indebtedness. Hysteria might possibly have become the order of the day in the land of immense greatness in the act of churching.

Having thus shown the unrestrained excesses of the gullibility of man, especially where it concerns religion, faith, tradition, and money. Having as well shown the extreme folly to which the gullibility of man could swallow, without any recourse to divine gift of reason, which the creative process of nature has specially endowed upon humankind to argue firmly for the virtues of common sense and rationalism over the belief of bogus claims for which there exists no empirical evidence. Having thus itemised the series of heavy penalties that such gullible recklessness have at different points in history inflicted upon the human race, most especially during the course of their numerous years, walking under the hag of superstitions and false religious beliefs. Having so exposed the unrestrained obsession of man to cling on to uncanny conjectures and fantasies of self-style prophets and professional preachers in relations to imaginary gods and other mystical elements; pertinently, it is curious, furthermore, to observe how man's propensity to believe too readily has continued to advance the growth of false religions all over the world.

The Moronic Plates

Several years ago, I hosted two young white lads who had then paid an unscheduled visit to my apartment in Pretoria. The two young men wore black and white uniforms and badges with the inscription 'ELDER' tagged to their chests. The visitors introduced themselves, with utmost courtesy, as missionaries of the Church of Jesus Christ of Latter-day Saints. Before they commenced the theme of their theological preaching, they likewise introduced the Book of Mormon, which they described as the sacred book of their church. That day happened to be my first day of seeing the Book of Mormon; although I had earlier seen their church building around Sunnyside, the suburb in which I then lived in Pretoria. However, I was unfamiliar with any of their teachings and religious ways of life, until this beautiful evening in Sunnyside, when these two young looking 'ELDERS' came to increase my knowledge of 'God' with the fullness of their sectarian glad tidings to the world.

After I had listened very attentively to the ministrations of these two visiting evangelizers, which purposely narrated the restoration of another everlasting gospel through the Book of Mormon to the entire world, I then proceeded to question the two missionaries. I simply prompted a query into how their church came about having another set of Holy Scriptures, which is entirely different from the universal Holy Bible that is common to every Christian's household, and with which I have been familiar since the days of my childhood. In their response, the two evangelists narrated a very brief history of how a spectral angel by the name *Moroni* had paid several amazing visits to their church founder, Prophet Joseph Smith, in the 19th century. They recounted how the angel guided Prophet Smith to a spot near a Mountainside of New York, where he miraculously dug up ancient spiritual accounts of the people of Nephi and the Lamanites who had emigrated from Jerusalem in 600 BCE to the Americas. The evangelizers further explained that the manuscripts of the Book of Mormon were originally written in ancient language known as the Reformed Egyptian Language, and its texts were engraved on some golden plates, which Prophet Smith was able to translate into the English language under divine guide of the Holy Spirit.

After the two visiting 'elders' had concluded their explanations, I then proceeded to enquire of the present whereabouts of the original golden plates. In a response that very much portrayed the impression of being like an already rehearsed answer, the evangelizers enlightened me that, after the publication of the Book of Mormon, Angel Moroni inexplicably reappeared from his celestial abode to recover the original golden plates from the custody of Prophet Joseph Smith.

Eish! My inner intuition received the answer with great suspicion and scepticism, as it revolted in the quietness of its personal thoughts, and whispered calmly within, *"What a ministry of professional liars!* "*...How could the centrepiece of the Mormon's religion, the only object imbued with empirical evidence of divinity simply vanish into thin air?"* Unfortunately, my visiting evangelists had dismally failed in encouraging my faith to grow into the level of joining their religious fold, as they could not deduce cogent and coherent reasons as to what iniquity would befall humanity, had Angel Moroni allowed the original golden plates in the custody of Prophet Smith's church, or in a National museum in America.

Assuming this very weighty evidence, upon which the devotees of Joseph Smith's church professed their religious faith had been preserved sacred in a holy place within the sanctuary of their church, what iniquity would it have called upon humanity? Alternatively, had these golden plates been securely kept in the National Library or the National Archive of the United States of America, where all the doubting Thomas of this world like me would see it, and read from it, undoubtedly the outcome of everyone's approach to the Mormon's religion would have been entirely positive today. Moreover, had Prophet Smith allowed the experts in ancient Reformed Egyptian Texts the prospect of verifying and endorsing the validity of the alleged divine originality for these golden plates, together with the accuracy of his translations, not a single soul would have breathed peacefully on the surface of planet earth un-repented to the Mormon faith. Furthermore, the necessity would never have called for those young looking 'elders' gallivanting about the streets from house to house, clad in their black and white uniforms like corporate sales representatives, in search of gullible converts to join their religious fold. Assuming the original Plates of Mormon were available to support the Book of Mormon, it would most surely be enough preaching for the entire world to convert to Mormonism. From the native hometown of Prophet Smith in New York to Adelaide in Australia, through Punjab in India, to the Cape Peninsula in South Africa, the whole world would have unquestionably regarded Prophet Smith as the true *"revelator and prophet of these last days."*

Instead of leaving the physical evidence to speak for itself, Prophet Smith had then contrived to enlist the service of eleven compatriots to speak for the plates, and act as proxies for the entire world. Furthermore, these solicited surrogates of the Prophet had later endorsed attestations that they were the preferred few that divine authority had elected to see and handle the sacred golden plates on behalf of humankind. Thereafter, their church envoys would go from door to door preaching their fictionalized gospels to the entire neighbourhood, and asking their district residents to read the Book of Mormon and pray in their heart for divine revelation of the Holy Spirit to reveal the truthfulness of the book to their understanding.

It is an absolute gullibility for anyone to believe this kind of paltry testimony in the 21st century civilization. More so, it is totally a mockery of man's ability to exercise firmly, the power of his reason, and argue for the virtue of logic over bogus claims, because religion and faith is here concerned. What a despicable foolery does the Mormonism system of faith make of man by calling upon the whole world to accept as true, the hearsays of nineteenth century American businesspersons! An entity that required the belief of all demanded that the evidence of it be equal to all.

Otherwise, the whole story ought to receive the blunt aspersion of having every identity of profane fraud and imposition hidden beneath the cornerstone of its foundation.

Why for God's sake must Angel Moroni transport the original golden plates to heaven? Did he intend preaching man's ancient doctrines to fellow angels in the celestial realms, of which they knoweth not before hand? Howbeit, are golden plates of earthling source yielding the highest dividends of spiritual or pecuniary values in the heavenly kingdom that should warrant the angel to airlift them for auctions up there? These golden plates according to Mormonism were human made. Its texts were also written on earth, and containing the ancient spiritual and secular accounts of mortal men whose descendants remained here on earth. Why hide the unchangeable originals away from man, if truly it does exist? Why must angel Moroni leave man with copies, which are subject to the errors of translation, and of copyists? Why leave humankind with artificial reproduction that any man may well counterfeit, subvert, or pervert, and even alter at will? This footnote extract from the year 2000 edition of the Book of Mormon, under the subheading – 'About this edition', correlates my argument:

> *Some minor errors in the text have been perpetuated in past editions of the Book of Mormon. This edition contains corrections that seem appropriate to bring the material into conformity with prepublication manuscripts and early editions edited by the Prophet Joseph Smith.*

Just imagine the fraud of religionists! How did those errors find their ways into the book in the first place? Indeed, the new millennium edition could only contain *"corrections that seem appropriate,"* especially when those corrections are not coming from the original **golden texts**. If at all, Angel Moroni must hide these plates away from Prophet Smith for whatever reason known to him, at least he ought to have re-buried the plates elsewhere in another spot beneath our planet earth. This would enable our earthly archaeologists, someday in future, excavate them for scientific investigations into the Moronic handwritings, in order that a credible live broadcast of the result of their findings might beam to the entire world via satellite television on CNN or the National Geographic Channels.

Holy Moroni! Why not alternatively leave the plates in the custody of the translator's church, so that it would be beneficial to mankind in accordance with the apostolic sermons of 2Timothy 3:16-17 (KJV), *"For doctrine, for reproof, for correction, for instruction in righteousness that the man of God may be perfect, thoroughly furnished unto all good works."*

The fact of the case, however, is that Prophet Smith could not afford committing such enormous mistake by leaving his plates behind, lest discerning minds of his native America strip naked his piece of fallacious evidence. Most especially, when they call such spurious evidence to question in the public tribunal of insight and reality, in their quest to investigate and ascertain the evidence of its divine originality. Hence, the miraculous disappearance of the original texts of Mormon as the ancient Nephi and Lamanites had engraved it in the Mormonism mysterious golden plates.

As I have earlier mentioned, the fact that those excessive failures of Bible prophecies, and the recurrent contradictions and discrepancies in the Christian holy book did not seem in any way to affect the reputation of the Bible, and that of the church that has encouraged the propagation of these absurd stories, as is evident in the remarkable growth of evangelism at very explosive rates worldwide, is a conclusion that is not far-fetched. When humankind has become like the robotic belief machine and has developed the habit of accepting any piece of claim that comes his way without any recourse to logic, reason, and scepticism to access such claim; as such, whatever disguise of religious schemes or irreligious schisms, superstitious beliefs, or fraudulent prophecies, which any person might introduce to that society where gullibility rules, will forever flourish like wildfire in a dry tropical forest. This will be easily achieved with the general assistance of story-telling, and man's inordinate search for security and perverted spiritual enlightenments and his unrestrained dependency on fabulous spiritual authority (either of the church, or of mystical elements). All these factors, with the assistance of man's obsessed love for religious frenzies and fallacies are what had greatly fanned the flames of the advancement of counterfeit evangelism at a very alarming rate.

The success of one evangelist, priest, or pastor would immediately encourage another to establish his own ministry. Consequently, the spread of commercial evangelism would progress at a very staggering speed. Every jobless man would metamorphose overnight into being anointed man of God, to join the bandwagon of proprietors of an exceptionally lucrative trade; where devotees who deposited their tithes and generous offerings certainly never come calling again for withdrawals. All the same, the only qualification required of anyone to join the ranks of counterfeit men of God is a pretentious attitude to Divine Calling. If this man of God intended being a prolific preacher, he would hurriedly undertake a six-month crash course or a one-year certificate course in Systematic Theology and the art of churching.

To God be the glory, the business of churching has now become easier. With the advent of very wonderful and efficient modern technologies, a new pastor can now buy the CDs and DVDs containing the recorded sermons and gesticulations of other veteran pastors, and easily preach them up every Sunday to the little congregation of his own church at the other side of the country.

It was exactly so in Nigeria, in the hey days of the 419 scam, where many graduates and school dropouts who had been jobless for years would just wake up one morning to see one equally jobless Patrick like them, a co-inhabitant in the neighbourhood, becoming an overnight millionaire. On investigation, they would get to know that Patrick had received his first millions, somewhere from Europe through a gullible white man, just on the mere efforts of sending his Caucasian victim a few line of letter that contained bogus proposals for the remittance of some fictitious amount of money to the white man's account overseas. Whereas, the only qualification obligatory of others to join the bandwagon of scammers, and begin the swindle of millions of hard currencies from overseas was to be able to send bogus proposals to white men via the Nigerian Postal Service, a service that then costs a paltry 30 US cents per letter, or via e-mail, which costs far less. Somehow, they fabricate some white lies to their targets, requesting their assistance to bankroll counterfeit expenses that would facilitate the transfer of millions of stolen dollars from the Nigerian government, which stashed away in their possessions in the Central Bank of Nigeria to their foreign accounts. Thereafter, the transaction is a done deal! The money would start rolling in non-stop from overseas. Nearly all Nigerian youths, including several professionals – lawyers, accountants, doctors, engineers, economist, etc., became overnight scammers because of the vast successes of those who pioneered Nigeria's fraud industry.

It is also in this same vein that many Nigerians are presently turning into overnight pastors, with lots of commercial ministries in London, Johannesburg, Pretoria, Accra, Zambia, Kenya, etc., and their ultimate centre of operations in Nigeria. The huge successes of the pioneers of commercial evangelism in Nigeria gave tremendous encouragements to others to set up their own evangelical trade as a means of livelihood.

It reminds me of the first Pentecostal church I ever attended in Nigeria in the 1980s. The church, which has a retired pop star as its founding pastor was then the only Pentecostal church liberal enough in the city of Lagos to permit women to wear glitzy cosmetic make-ups, jerry-curled hairstyles, and ostentatious dresses that so pleased them to church. For that reason, the church teemed with youngsters.

Not long after the establishment of the church, the pastor upgraded his car from the modest Honda Prelude 3 doors, which he drove throughout his career as a singer to the latest model of Mercedes Benz E230. At the same time, the pastor and his wife adorned themselves in different styles of comfortable designers' outfits, after being a pastor for a short while.

Soon after the pastor had upgraded his car, a division erupted in the church. The second in command to the flamboyant pop star cum preacher also wanted his own autonomy. As a result, he seceded with some members loyal to him, to establish his own church. Shortly after the breakaway pastor had established his own church, his assistant on the other side also pulled out from the church to establish his own church. The chain of breakaway pastors progressed in that order until I departed the city of Lagos. To cut my long story short, the terrific successes of the pioneering pastors of commercial evangelism offered great inspirations to several others, until the whole country of Nigeria has now become flooded with church operators.

In Africa, people are ever ready to believe anything, therefore the continent is a fertile ground for the rapid spread and growth of everything cogent and bogus; be it sectarian faith or scam. There are many spurious beliefs that are widespread in various countries of Africa, too shameful to disclose to the outside world that such beliefs could ever be contemplated by any normal human mind. For instance, many African countries hold the widespread beliefs that having sex with a psychotic person makes one to become super wealthy and sexually potent. When Mr Amadu tells the story to Mr Ibu of what he overheard in a pub about becoming an instant millionaire after having sexual intercourse with a mad woman, Mr Ibu would immediately fall head down for this spurious tale. Without asking any further question, Mr Ibu would secretly search after a psychotic woman to sleep with, in order to become super rich or sexually potent.

As soon as Zanele receives unfounded information through brother Kilo that Angelina became pregnant after starting to attend Pastor Silas church, then the whole family of Zanele, including her mother-in-law and her great grandfather-in-law would become overnight members of Pastor Silas church in search of bogus miracles, because of the unfounded rumour that comes from the mouth of brother Kilo.

In the same vein, if Mr Okonta should give a credulous testimony that he acquired his car after he started to attend Faith Miracle Healing Church, consequently every one of his relatives and friends, including the parents-in-law to all his church members who heard him give the credulous testimony would become overnight member of Faith Miracle Healing Church in search of bogus miracles. Without any pinch of enquiry into how Mr Okonta had saved his money to purchase his car, and for how long he has worked with Aba Petroleum Company; however, Faith Miracle Healing Church would teem endlessly with crowds because of

Okonta's credulous testimony. To those gullible followers, Mr Okonta's car was a miracle borne out of the prayers of his church Pastor.

Good heavens, gullibility surely rules in Africa! It's hard to imagine that some of our people still hold such unfounded belief that having sex with an infant is a cure or another form of antiretroviral pills for HIV/AIDS! Hard to believe that many superstitious Africans still hold the credulous belief that the drinking of Albinos blood is a veritable way for them to acquire bogus supernatural powers. In some parts of Kenya, the inclined belief that having sex with aged women (grandmothers and great-grandmothers) as a way of attaining supernatural powers is still to this day very widespread. Furthermore, it is prevalent for Nigerians to hold solidarity rallies in support of their corrupt leaders.

Eish! I have a 33-year-old cousin who is a graduate of Mechanical Engineering and a High School teacher, who calls himself a born-again Christian. Up until year 2009, he was never aware that Jerusalem and Damascus are cities of this world, and that River Jordan is a river on planet earth. At the age of thirty-three, he is virtually oblivious of the fact that the city of Damascus is situated on planet earth in the Islamic nation of Syria, while the Jordan River runs across the earthling nations of Israel and Jordan in the Middle East, the same way as the Niger River runs across the country of Nigeria. To him the Jordan River, Damascus, and Jerusalem are spiritually of the heavenly realms as his religion had fictitiously represented it to him. It's totally unbelievable how the gullibility of man could draw out to such extreme folly.

How would a nation of people that hold this sort of susceptible belief not gullibly swallow whatever fallacious story that any deceitful priest or cleric might push down their throats? In short, they would passionately believe any spurious story that comes their path, including the outrageous audacity and extreme trumpery that sprang out of the mouth of a 33-year-old son of man, who imposed himself as 'universal light of the world' and the only true way to attain heavenly kingdom. With utmost fervour, the spread of whatever fallacious tale or scheme would greatly advance in any community that teems with countless ignorant souls. Because, such a gullible populace utterly lacked the orientation to establish with certainty, any evidential fact that concerns the truthfulness of whatever pious story or chain of simulated claims imposed upon their lives.

Sometimes ago, I watched the motion picture of a DVD that offered a very impressive presentation of *'The Indescribable Universe'* to the congregation of Christian faithfuls. The question that readily came to my mind at the end of the features of the DVD was how the brilliant 'God' of Christianity who allegedly created this flawless and amazing universe in uttermost exactitude of mathematical firmness could possibly be the author of the several faulty books of the Holy Scriptures. Certainly, there must be a misleading claim somewhere in this case that is entirely out of order. For, it was very certain to me that the theme of the DVD did not in any sense agree with the faulty contents of the Bible, which it was deceptively designed to promote. The bottom line, however, is that countless numbers of Christian devotees all over the world have trustingly bought millions of copies of the DVD; and millions of hard currencies from all corners of the world have over flown into the coffers of the producers under the banner of religion. This is a typical example of how the proponents of religion have regularly exploited and perverted all kinds of invented stories as to portray the picture of reality, in desperate attempts to sustain the falsehood of their sacred books for selfish aims. As a result, every Lucas, Amanda, Sipho, and Margaret of this world have credulously believed such stupid fallacy denoting the picture of the ancient cross that crucified their redeemer alongside several other Jewish criminals, as truly showing on exhibition in the galactic heavenly realms.

Lately, the high levels of unemployment, poverty, and diseases that are intolerably spoiling the continent of Africa day by day have become other major factors that have ceaselessly drawn great crowds to religious devotion. Many Africans are in search of miraculous succours and bogus hopes to alleviating their social and health problems. Thus, the diverse religious organizations that are operational in the continent have greatly enjoyed phenomenal patronage because of these factors.

The fear of the unknown has attained bizarre levels in the black continent to such a degree that many gullible Africans can no longer do anything on their own, unless they seek untrue protection and security from false prophets in religious institutions, and from witchdoctors in oracle shrines. Countless numbers of people have credulously regarded their pastors, their native doctors, their priests, oracles, and idols as direct proxies and representatives of divine authority on earth. As a result, these factors had led several Africans to the extreme point of superfluous dependency on those that claimed to be custodians of divine authority on earth; culminating in the spiralling growth of churches and different manners of spiritual houses all over Africa.

Chapter

6

Man's Word Fathered on God

"Our remedies oft in ourselves to lie, which we ascribe to heaven."

– William Shakespeare

Hardly there exists anyone on earth today, who in fact has not heard or read about the Bible — the sacred book of the Jewish and Christian religion — that claims to contain the word of the creator of the universe in print. From the remotest villages of the world, to the heart of its vibrant towns and cities, missionaries of the Christian religion have preached the words of the Bible to nearly all inhabitants of the earth, in their efforts to woo converts into their devout faith.

The Bible is a large collection of sixty-six books, which divides into two parts namely — the Old Testament, Genesis to Malachi, with 39 books; and the New Testament, containing four different biographies of Jesus Christ, the Acts of Apostles, twenty-one epistolary correspondences, and the book of Revelation. The conviction prevails in the world today that forty different authors wrote the Bible through a period of one thousand, five hundred years. Some accounts estimated the period to one thousand, six hundred years; purportedly from the time of Moses to the time of John — the last surviving apostle of Jesus Christ — whom the church reckoned with as the author of Revelation, the last book of the Bible.

Ever since the Bible attained the prominence of its present status, holding a library collection of sixty-six books, the Christian holy book has subsequently undergone over 1,800 translations from its original texts of

Hebrew and Aramaic languages into almost all the different languages and dialects available in the world. This amazing record of huge translations thus made the Holy Bible the most popular book ever in print in the history of humankind; with more than 2.5 billion copies sold and freely distributed all around the globe.

Throughout the ages, clerics and Bible advocates have conscientiously sermonized to us that the various collections of histories of ancient Jews that we read today in the scriptures are the words of a supernatural god, revealed to humankind by means of the Holy Spirit. These divine revelations include the warmongering adventures of the Israelites with the different nations in their vicinity, as well as the inconsequential and despicable tales narrating the lives and times of many of their prophets, leaders, kings, and people. Even so, Bible adherents have deepened their affirmation that these tales are unquestionably the word of the creator of the universe.

Nevertheless, how might anyone possibly be sure of the certainty that those bounteous tales that glorified the pages of this famous book are the actual word of the maker of our world, and are of the true inspiration of an invisible Holy Spirit, particularly in the face of blatant contradictions, discrepancies, and deceptive notions that abundantly enclosed therein?

How, out of the blue, could the proceedings of human history authoritatively become the word of the gods, and not the word of those people whose thoughts, actions, and dialogues these historians had related in the passages of the book? In other words, why are the expressions in Bible passages simply not the words and fancies of those historians who took the trouble to narrate these tales? Seeing that many of their stories could only thrive in the realms of fictions and imaginary tales, but would by no means have a place in the domain where truth and certainty resides, except for having a predominant position in the kingdom of fabrications and downright fibs.

When Judah gave commandment to Onan, his son, in Genesis 38:8-9 (NIV) *"Lie with your brother's wife and fulfil your duty to her as a brother-in-law to produce offspring for your brother."* What then has twisted this directive into the word of the creator of the universe, if there exists any? Weren't Judah, Onan, and Tamar capable of narrating these conversations themselves to other parties, from the first person to the second, to the third, and so on, until the story had subsequently become an appendage of the oral tradition of the Jews, up through the line to the generation of Moses? And, following when the Jews had then acquired documentation skills, they afterwards compiled these tales into a library of books. Therefore, if either of Judah, Onan, and Tamar were capable of narrating their stories by words of mouth to others, and afterwards, the story found its way into the pages of a book, what then had transformed this narration into divinely inspired word of the creator of the universe?

The ninth verse of the 38th chapter of Genesis reads, *"But Onan knew that the offspring would not be his; so whenever he lay with his brother's wife, he spilled his semen on the ground to keep from producing offspring for his (deceased) brother."* Although, this action was a secret affair, known only to Onan and his widowed sister-in-law, Tamar; however, it does not in any way require exclusive revelation of the divine to make the affair a public tale, as both or any of the parties involved could as well reveal this secret to community knowledge, if it was their wish to do so. Why then must it take special revelation from a god, through the aid of unseen *Ghost* to narrate this paltry tale to humankind? Couldn't Onan have revealed it directly if asked by his father or anyone else in the family and neighbourhood, the reason why he had not impregnated his sister-in-law after a long period of sleeping together? In the same vein, Tamar could reveal the secret too, in an effort to explain the reason why she had not been pregnant for Onan, as to produce offspring for her deceased husband. She might well let the cat out of the bag to reveal that Onan was the culprit who habitually poured out his semen to the ground whenever he slept with her, instead of depositing the semen into its rightful spot. How then does this inconsequential tale require special revelation from a supernatural god or the Holy Spirit, when the direct actions and dialogues of man were actually what those historians have recorded in the Bible, but cunningly tagged the *'word of God?'*

The actors involved in this case, Onan and Tamar were not deaf and dumb; even Judah, their father, who instigated the show could as well release the tale into public domain, as it was directly in point to the Jewish custom and tradition. Then, after the Jews had acquired writing skills, these oral stories, subsequently, became the various chapters and verses of scriptural compilations that you and I today read as the Holy Bible.

Let there be Light

The first book of the Bible—the Book of Genesis— allegedly written over four thousand years ago by Moses, under the divine inspiration of God's Holy Spirit, opens the bounteous tales of the Bible. The book of Genesis begins with the account of how a supernatural god created the universe and all that fills it in just six days, or one hundred and forty-four literal hours.

Several Biblical dogmatists, such as the Jehovah's Witnesses argue that the creative days that Moses reported in Genesis account were not just a 24-hour literal day, but figuratively a thousand years. Through the design of fabulous allegorical analysis, the witnesses have thus twisted the six creative days in the first chapter of Genesis as a period of six thousand years in their own metaphorical arithmetic. Thus they have invented their interpretation to harmonize the Genesis creative day with the empirical evidence of science and nature, which out-rightly disproves the Genesis six literal days as baseless. Moses thus narrated in the first chapter of Genesis:

> *And God said, let there be light and there was light. And God saw that the light was good, and he separated the light from the darkness. God called the light "day" and the darkness he called "night." And there was evening and there was morning – the first day. –* Genesis 1: 3-5 (NIV)

Perhaps it would have been more accurate for Jehovah's Witnesses to re-translate their own version of the Holy Bible (New World Translation of the Holy Scriptures) by making the last sentence of the fifth verse to read thus: "And there came to be evening of five hundred years, and there came to be morning of another five hundred years – a first day of one thousand years." Probably this suggested retranslation would have made the interpretation of the Genesis creative days a lot clearer to the understanding of their numerous readers and followers.

However, one would have expected the Holy Spirit that inspired Moses to elucidate, in clearer details to humankind, what light it was that came into existence on the first day, and from which source shone that light onto earth? As the only known sources of light into this earth, from the dawn of time through all ages unto this day, remained the Sun, the Moon, and the Stars, the luminaries that Moses had only made God create on the fourth day in his Genesis account, perhaps on the fourth millennia according to the figurative interpretation of the Jehovah's Witnesses.

How Moses had fashioned his first three mornings and evenings, and his first three days and nights before the creation of the Sun, the Moon, and the Stars on the fourth day, ridiculously, had unto this day become another hag of mystery in the Genesis creation history. The earthlings know it with absolute certainty that nothing more than the appearance of the sun in the skies brings 'morning' and 'day' on earth, while the setting of the sun ushers in the evening; and the dearth of the sun consequently produces the night.

The riddle of the first three mornings and evenings, and the first three days and nights in the book of Genesis indeed requires the paranormal insight of the Mosaic magical power that far supersedes the quality of human intellectual ability to unravel.

It has become very difficult for me to admit it as my rule of faith that Moses and the Holy Spirit would have elected to leave the explanatory part of this noteworthy riddle in the hands of Jehovah's Witnesses — an organization that seems the ultimate father of all Biblical dogmatists in the act of reasoning from the scriptures. Directly in their attempt to harmonize the absurdity of the creative tale of Genesis in every particular with the empirical evidence of science, the witnesses have indeed reasoned from their scriptures. They absurdly posit that the light, which Moses made God create on the first day, was 'light diffused' from the sun, the moon, and the stars, which had long been in existence in outer space before the Genesis God had created them on the first day and again on the fourth day. Ah! This ludicrous submission is typically amusing.

> *And God made two great lights – the greater light to govern the day and the lesser light to govern the night. He also made the stars… and God saw that it was good. And there was evening, and there was morning – the fourth day –* Genesis 1:16-19.

Of course, this account did not say, 'And God made two great lights – the greater light to govern five hundred years to make the first day and the lesser light to govern another five hundred years to make the first night, making a total of one thousand years of the first creative day.'

The witnesses have expressed a contrary view in their book (Life - How did it get here—By Creation or Evolution) to the Genesis 1:16-19 assertion. They therein submit that the sun, the moon, and the stars had long been in existence in outer space, but God only made their light *"visible to earthly observer to see"* on the first day, and again on the fourth day.

The fact of this matter is that, it is a scientific conclusion that the universe has long been in existence for billions of years; contrary to the younger age of about six thousand years the Mosaic accounts of creation had fabricated for its existence in the book of Genesis. The Jehovah's Witnesses have here chosen to adjust the Genesis creative days to harmonize with scientific conclusions, possibly to avoid the aspersion of the Genesis tale suffering relegation into the ranks of abject supposition and baseless myth. This sect of Christian believers had apparently foreseen the implication of the scientific conclusion upon their trade as a thorn in the flesh, which might possibly bring the Genesis tale to a demotion on an equal level with any of its mythical equivalent in several other cultures. Hence, the inexplicable twist to the millennium-day arithmetic, purposely to down-tone the farce of Genesis 24-hour creative day.

If the sun, the moon, and the stars had long been in existence in outer space before the Mosaic creation, which light then did the Mosaic God of

Genesis create on the first day and again on the fourth day. Why then did the Holy Spirit not inspire Moses to write thus in Genesis that the Sun, the Moon, and the Stars had long been in existence in outer space for billions of years, before their recreation for the second time in Genesis? Instead, Moses had deceptively related speculative lies in the book of Genesis; writing pretentiously as if under divine command of the creator of the universe, whilst in actual fact, he fed the human civilization with invalid reports. Why should it take man, through the evidence of science to detect the fact of this matter, which grossly exposes the fallacy of the Mosaic account? Perhaps, it might as well be correct for me to uphold my strong suspicion as a fact beyond doubt that, everything which Moses had made God create from day one to six in Genesis had long been in existence before the Genesis creative days.

Furthermore, the second chapter of Genesis, verses two to three (NIV) affirmed, *"By the seventh day God had finished the work he had been doing; so on the seventh day he rested from all his work. And God blessed the seventh day and made it holy..."*

The two important questions that here arise, particularly, for the attention of the Jehovah's Witnesses are: Firstly, does this 'seventh day' break, as written in Genesis 2:2, essentially translates to the fact that the God of Genesis had taken a vacation for a period of one thousand years, after he had finished creating the universe? Secondly, one would need to know if the Christian God had also blessed and made sacred, a period of one thousand years for himself in Genesis 2:3; and subsequently the Jewish Sabbath, which was a consequence of the 'seventh day' rest.

> *For in six days the Lord made the heavens and the earth, the sea, and all that is in them, but he rested on the seventh day. Therefore, the Lord blessed the Sabbath day and made it holy* – Exodus 20:11 (NIV).

If the answer from the Jehovah's Witnesses is yes, that the 'seventh day' break the Genesis God had allotted himself was truly a sabbatical vacation of one thousand years, it therefore means that this God must have rested throughout the lifetime of the first human couple. For Genesis 5:5 (NIV) says, *"Altogether, Adam lived 930 years, and then he died."* Therefore, the Jehovah's Witnesses' construal of the creative day would surmise that their God was still at rest the whole lifetime of Adam and Eve, and only returned to active duty seventy years after the death of Adam. As a result, the truth of God's alleged coming down to the Garden of Eden after the serpent's mischief, to engage in another work of hunting for animals' skin to make coverings for Adam and Eve whilst still on sabbatical leave would consequently come into grave questioning. In the same vein, the truth of the curses that God placed upon the serpent, Adam and Eve, and later Cain their first son, would equally come under the hammer of critical questioning. This is for the reason that God should still be on sabbatical leave for a period of one thousand years that spans over these periods.

Perhaps the standpoint of the witnesses might be valid in another sense, as it would be totally unfair for me to rule their viewpoint entirely out of context. For, the perception of Jehovah's Witnesses seems rather to explain the reason why the serpent had easily succeeded in the *coup d'état* he staged against the government of the Genesis God in the Garden of Eden. Of course, this God must have truly been fast asleep for an ordinary animal of his creation to, as simple as ABC, overturn his spiritual arrangements on earth. From this viewpoint, the 'Witnesses' might probably be right.

The Nephilim Conflict

In the sixth chapter of Genesis, we read the story of how some 'angelic sons of God' had abandoned their original positions in heaven after they noticed that the 'daughters of men' were beautiful on earth. The account told us that the angels descended to the earth, materialized into fleshly bodies, and married any of the daughters of men they chose. "*Nephilim were on the earth in those days – and also afterwards – when the sons of God went to the daughters of men and had children by them. They were the heroes of old, men of renown*" (Genesis 6:4 NIV).

Taking a careful look at Genesis 6:4, one would notice a very superfluous phrase in the verse, *"and also afterwards."* Some Bible translations rendered it *"and after that."* If one should ask, what exactly was the message the author of Genesis 6:4 had intended putting across to the reader by expressing this statement? *"Nephilim were on earth in those days – and also afterwards."* To all accepted clues steered by the wheel of common sense, excepting the absurdity of religious belief, this statement simply means *Nephilim* were here on earth prior to Noah's day, during Noah's day, *"and also afterwards;"* that is, after the day of Noah.

If we take the words of Genesis 7:21-23 unerringly to mean what Moses had recorded in those verses, devoid of any ulterior and misleading symbolic interpretation of Bible commentators and self-styled prophets and priests, the conclusion would, in that case, translate to the fact that all men, including each and every one of those *Nephilim* (giant offspring of the angelic sons of God with daughters of men) had been cut-off in their entirety from the surface of the earth, leaving only the family of Noah and select living creatures to repopulate the earth. The Genesis account also narrated the story to us that *Nephilim* were chiefly the blameworthy culprits that frustrated the Genesis God to express regret that he ever created man, thus his decision to terminate their existence alongside that of humans from the surface of the earth through the Noah's flood – Genesis 6: 5-7.

If the information in Genesis 7: 21-23 is truly correct; what, for God's sake had informed Moses to give another off-beam detailing in the 33rd verse of the thirteenth chapter of the book of Numbers, where he all over again narrated the drama of how the Israelites had seen the Nephilim yet again on the surface of the earth? According to Moses' account in the seventh chapter of Genesis, the Noah's flood had totally wiped off the Nephilim from the very face of the earth. Suddenly again, in the thirteenth chapter of the book of Numbers, Moses wrote: *"We saw the Nephilim there (the descendants of Anak came from the Nephilim). We seemed like grasshoppers in our own eyes, and we looked the same to them"* Numbers 13:33 (NIV). I strongly suspect that Bible editors must have incorporated this phrase *"and also afterwards"* into Genesis 6:4 as a deceptive ploy to bring into line, the conflicting blunders of the Israelites sighting of the Nephilim again in the book of Numbers 13:33. This after Genesis 7:21-23

(NIV) had several centuries in the past, mixed up the confirmation that, *"Men and animals, the creatures that move along the ground and the birds of the air were wiped from the earth. Only Noah was left and those with him in the ark."*

Hmm! I remember when I used to reside in the bustling city of Lagos. Every time I raised the issues of Biblical contradictions with friends, who then were mostly church pastors and avid Christians; whenever they got dormant and could not again continue with prettify rationalization of the unending irregularities and outrageous flaws I have opened up to them, of which details they were very much ignorant prior to our discourse; they would largely dismiss the argument in their usual conceit with phrases of this nature: *"You cannot understand the scriptures, because you do not have the Holy Spirit in you; when you become born-again and you receive the Holy Spirit, it will minister to your understanding."*

To majority of my pastor friends, being born-again is simply for Christian devotees to believe whatever the church pushes down their throat without questions. For them, it is only within that context that one could possibly possess the Holy Spirit and properly understand the scriptures. Meanwhile, they have evidently betrayed their total lack of indulgent and understanding of these scriptures, as they could not proceed with any lucid explanation in their attempt to offer convincing argument in harmonizing the numerous contradictions that emblazon the entire pages of the Bible, which they daily preached up to the dull ears of several gullible church congregants. Instead of them owning up to their ignorance, they would fanatically affirm, you do not know as they utterly do under divine inspiration of the Holy Spirit. Perhaps, in this case too, I could not perceptibly understand the scriptures, because I do not possess the Holy Spirit that Moses possessed inside of him when he wrote both the book of Genesis and Numbers, the two scriptures that narrated the contradictory tales of the Nephilim.

The book of Genesis, under the authorship of Moses, detailed the origin of the Nephilim and their total extirpation from the surface of the earth by the global deluge of Noah. Yet again, the book of Numbers under the same sacred authorship of Moses narrated another striking conflict that totally nullified the Genesis narration regarding the complete annihilation of the Nephilim. In downright error, Moses again reported the drama of the Israelites seeing the Nephilim another time in the book of Numbers. This after the same Moses had written in the book of Genesis that these Nephilim had completely been *"wiped off from the face of the earth."* How can any sensible person reconcile two conflicting reports, originating from the same author? And, without any evidence, countless number of Bible adherents had gullibly affirmed these fictionalize tales as being of divine inspiration of the creator of the universe. Hmmm, the gullibility of man is exceedingly sickening!

Furthermore, the sentence written in bracket in the 33rd verse of the 13th chapter of the book of Numbers (*the descendants of Anak came from the Nephilim*) is another redundancy that Bible editors have annexed in a cunning manner to the verse, to misrepresent *Nephilim* for the *Anakites* or the descendants of Anak. Therefore, the onus comes to bear upon the heads of those that contrived the planting of these words inserted in bracket in the 33rd verse of Numbers Chapter 13 to explain how the 'descendants of Anak' might possibly have come from the Nephilim, which Genesis 7:21-23 had reportedly wiped off the surface of the earth with no survivor.

If we believe the seventh chapter of Genesis, all humans after the global deluge should have descended directly from Noah and his three children — Japheth, Ham, and Shem. Therefore, if Anak happened to be a descendant of Noah's lineage, then the claim of him being a descendant of the Nephilim would be a downright fabrication, except Noah was also a descendant of the Nephilim. However, if the explanation posits that Anak was **not** a descendant of Noah, but was with Noah inside the ark, and therefore survived the global flood with Noah's family, as to repopulate the earth with giant offspring that the Bible had christened the *Anakites* who made the Israelites seemed like grasshoppers in their own eyes; in that case, their explanation should have totally subverted Genesis 7:21-23 by turning everything upside down. Consequently, the only way for things to look upright again would be to rewrite the entire stories in the book of Genesis.

COMPARISON OF GENESIS AND EPIC OF GILGAMESH		
	GENESIS	GILGAMESH
Extent of flood	Global	Global
Cause	Man's wickedness	Man's sins
Intended for whom?	All mankind	One city & all mankind
Sender	Yahweh	Assembly of "gods"
Name of hero	Noah	Utnapishtim
Hero's character	Righteous	Righteous
Means of announcement	Direct from God	In a dream
Ordered to build boat?	Yes	Yes
Did hero complain?	Yes	Yes
Height of boat	Several stories (3)	Several stories (6)
Compartments inside?	Many	Many
Doors	One	One
Windows	At least one	At least one
Outside coating	Pitch	Pitch
Shape of boat	Rectangular	Square
Human passengers	Family members only	Family & few others
Other passengers	All species of animals	All species of animals
Means of flood	Ground water & heavy rain	Heavy rain
Duration of flood	Long (40 days & nights plus)	Short (6 days & nights)
Test to find land	Release of birds	Release of birds
Types of birds	Raven & three doves	Dove, swallow, raven
Ark landing spot	Mountain -- Mt. Ararat	Mountain -- Mt. Nisir
Sacrificed after flood?	Yes, by Noah	Yes, by Utnapishtim

Blessed after flood?	Yes	Yes

Source: Institute for Creation Research. Frank Lorey (1997).

According to their Kinds

The seventh chapter of Genesis recounted in its 23ʳᵈ verse that all men perished out of the face of the earth and only Noah's family survived the global deluge to repopulate the earth as we know it today. *"Then God blessed Noah and his sons saying to them, "Be fruitful and increase in number and fill the earth"* (Genesis 9:1 NIV). The matter-of-fact implication of Genesis 7:23 and Genesis 9:1 is that the biblical Noah was the sole progenitor of all races of humankind that recurrently repopulate every corner of the entire world to this day.

If Noah was the natural or biological father of Japheth, Ham, and Shem as the Genesis account has indicated, it logically becomes reasonable for us to believe that Noah's three sons would have all possessed striking resemblance of their father's physical appearance. That is, they would all have shared great similarities with their parents as per the colour of their skin, the texture of hair, facial features, including the timbre of voice, and other physical identity through Noah's DNA traits — the hereditary component in humans that transfers the genetic details of parents into their offspring from generation to generation.

If we agree to this fact, which science and the ever-consistent law of nature have both proven as empirical reality, the question then arises as to how the different races of humankind have come into existence in our world as we see them today. If we believe this particular story of Genesis, there exists no empirical way on earth that science or anyone could account for the glaring disparity between the human races on our planet. This observed fact should therefore hoist the deep question on whether the evidential truth really exists for humankind to believe the creation account in Genesis.

If Noah and his wife were of the white race, it should automatically follow that all their three children, Japheth, Ham, and Shem, as a natural rule, would most certainly be white or pink skinned. They would have positively taken their physical resemblance after the colour of their parents' skin, including any offspring descending from generation through generation in their particular lineal order. We have intrinsically witnessed this natural fact from the distinct order of lineal descent within the white race anywhere they have inhabited in the world. The Afrikaner whites of European ancestry that came to settle in Africa over the centuries have continued to reproduce from generations through generations in their distinctive breeds, through several centuries, inside the sunny continent of Africa, without any derailment whatsoever. Of course, this particular 'white skinned' populace known as the Afrikaner have steadily reproduced according to their exacting kinds in Zimbabwe, Namibia, South Africa, etc. How then, would I, as a black man, be able to account for my very own existence in this world through the lineal genealogy of Noah? This is supposing Noah and his wife were purely of the white race. Holy Moses! Whence then cometh the different races of the world?

On the other hand, if Noah and his wife also happened to be of the Black Race, it would naturally follow that all their offspring would be black people too; just as we have evidently witnessed the distinct order of lineal descent within the Black Race in any region they found themselves in the world. The totality of all the black people of African ancestry that settled in Europe, the Americas, Canada, and the Caribbean ever since their ancestors departed their land into slavery in the 1600s, have consistently reproduced according to their kinds. In totality, the brown or dark skinned people of African ancestry have consistently bred their own offspring abroad, on top of the white man's native land from generations through generations, according to their exacting breeds. Similarly, unto this day, the Indians that resettled in Southern Africa many centuries ago have consistently reproduced from generation through generation in their own distinctive order, according to their unique kind.

In the assumption that Noah and his wife were black people, the white race and the Indians would not be able to account for their very own existence in the world should they chose to believe the Mosaic narratives in Genesis. If Noah and his wife also happen to be Indians, there is no way the Caucasians, the Black Race, or any other different race could work out how they came into existence on planet earth.

It is a known fact that the human genetic materials — the DNA and RNA factor — which store and copy the genetic data of humans from parents to progeny do not copy incorrectly. The case of Albino is not DNA error, but pigmentation defect (the congenital lack of melanin pigment in the skins, eyes, and the hairs of a person). According to medical scientists, the chances of an Albino giving birth to another Albino of his kind are extremely low, if not completely zero. Therefore, Albinism is not a race, as they have never been regularly descended from one generation to another. Definitely, the white race could never have stemmed from Albinism, if Noah and his wife were supposedly of the black race.

If the argument should arise that any of Noah's daughters-in-law might well have originated from another race; thereby explaining the origin of the different races of humans that are available in the world today. The question would therefore remain, at which point in the lineal genealogy of Adam and Eve down to Noah's daughters-in-law did the human genes derail to reproduce other kinds of human races, which were entirely different in skin colours and other physical compositions to Adam and Eve? The other question is how could any derailment have occurred without the least of crossbreeding from another race? If the disparities that exist in the physical composition of the different races of people had truly emanated from crossbreeding, when and how did other races, different from the lineage of biblical Adam and Eve, evolve on planet earth that utterly escaped the detailing of the Holy Spirit through Moses? The only positive option would be to look into evolutionary theory, which I perceptibly think would not count in this case, because the human life-span, from biblical Adam to the present generation, is too short for any evolutionary string to have a significant change in its basic type. Here lies the several questions and mysteries that require cogent answers to the Genesis account of creation as narrated to humankind by the sacred scriptures of the Abrahamic religions.

If any person should take the effort to study the physical composition of a Blackman and a Whiteman; say for example, ex-president Olusegun Obasanjo of Nigeria and the topflight artiste Rod Stewart; even on television, it would not be difficult to see the distinct difference between the Blackman and the Whiteman. The observable differences in some physical compositions between these two people would clearly reveal the evidential fact to every discerning mind that they both have not descended from the same progenitor, Adam or Noah, in some six or four thousand years ago, as the case might be. From the colour of their skin, the texture of their hair, their facial features, up to the pencil nose identity — the difference is exceedingly clear.

Had the popular music megastar, Michael Jackson, been alive today, he would have attested to this plain fact that, the difference between the Blackman and the Whiteman is very clear. As a Blackman, the late King of Pop had employed all the technologies known to modern science to attain the exterior look of a Whiteman; regrettably, he had wasted huge amount of money in futility.

According to Wikipedia, the free encyclopaedia online, the human race is defined as, *"a group of people with certain common inherited features that distinguished them from other people."* This candid definition simply explains the reason why today, the Chinese are very different in appearance to the Indians, and the Caucasians different to the Black Africans, and so on. Therefore, the Genesis account of creation and destruction and the subsequent repopulation fairy tale as narrated in the Jewish and Christian Bible could certainly not be close to any correctly inspired word of the creator of the universe, if there exists any, but undoubtedly that of the primordial men.

My opinion would have wholly agreed with the first chapter of Genesis verses 21 and 24 (NIV) if the verses could be properly rewritten thus:

> *So (the evolutionary process) created the great creatures of the sea and every living and moving thing with which the water teems, according to their kinds, and every winged birds according to its kind. (Verse 24) And ... the land produce living creatures according to their kinds:*

livestock, creatures that move along the ground, and wild animals, each according to its kind." And it was so.

However, my other point of disagreement with these two verses (Genesis 1:21 &24) is that, the natural order of creation detailed therein did not include humans. Why exempt humans? Is it because humans were the authors of this story of creation in Genesis, and therefore had decided to distinguish his case chiefly apart from that of animals, winged birds, the great creatures of the sea, and even the serpents and worms? It is a plain fact, which the practical laws of nature have predominantly endorsed from the beginning of existence that the evolutionary process had equally produced humans through the creative order of nature, according to their distinct kinds. For this reason, the different races of human, just like every other animal and vegetation life have commonly reproduced according to their exacting kinds.

The natural process of creation has constantly fixed the genetic code into the operating systems of all species of humans, animals, plants, and every other living creature. The purpose of this is to create certain regulatory measures for their reproductive routine in a distinctive trait to guard against any future mutation of these creatures from their original forms; so that every individual living thing on earth might facilitate its reproductive process, strictly according to its basic kind. In other words, Mother Nature has uniquely set the genetic code similar to the distinctive Personal Identification Number (PIN code) to keep the reproduction of all living creatures according to their precise kinds in a distinct line of original natural selection. This natural statute has pragmatically been the creative rule from the beginning of existence, unto this day.

Of Saul and David

A further conflicting narrative that the confused passion of religion has again imposed upon humankind as inspired word of the creator of the universe is the ambiguous description of how David first became an acquaintance of King Saul. Both the sixteenth and seventeenth chapters of the first book of Samuel recounted very conflicting versions of the first acquaintance of these two persons with each other.

The sixteenth chapter plainly attributed the familiarity of David and King Saul to the recommendation given of David to Saul by one of the King's attendants. The story essentially described the commendation of David's exceptional dexterity in the art of playing the musical instrument of harp, as the credentials that brought him for the first time from Bethlehem to King Saul's palace in Jerusalem, as a chartered harp player. While, on the next page, the 17th chapter told another spurious story that totally contradict the one the 16th chapter had given as the way in which David and Saul first came to know each other.

In the usual inconsistent character of Biblical biographers, the two stories virtually portrayed the impression of having two different authors, as they totally belie each other like chalk and cheese.

Here lies the falsehood of these two contradictions, as Prophet Samuel has presented it to the world in the book that bears his name; where he alleged the acquaintance of two people for the first time under two different circumstances. The first of Samuel Chapter 16:14-23(NIV) narrates its own version of the story thus:

> *Now the spirit of the Lord had departed from Saul, and an evil spirit from the Lord tormented him. Saul's attendants said to him, see an evil spirit from God is tormenting you. Let our Lord command his attendants to find someone who can play the harp. He will play when the evil spirit from God comes upon you, and you will feel better...* (Verse 18) *One of the servants answered, I have seen a son of Jesse of Bethlehem who knows how to play the harp. He is a brave man and a warrior... Then Saul sent messengers to Jesse and said send me your son David, who is with the sheep, so Jesse took a donkey, loaded with bread, a skin of wine and a young goat and sent them with his son David to Saul...* (Verse 22) *Then Saul sent words to Jesse saying, allow David to remain in my service, for I am pleased with him. Whenever the spirit of God came upon Saul, David*

would take his harp and play. Then relief would come to
Saul, he would feel better and the evil spirit would leave
him.

This, again, is how the 17th chapter of Samuel had incompatibly narrated the first meeting of David and King Saul in a description that appeared immediately on the next page to the version stated above. It is scandalous how these two narratives, purportedly written under divine guide, stood poles apart. 1Samuel 17:31-58 to 1Samuel 18:1-2 (NIV):

What David said was overheard and reported to Saul, and
Saul sent for him. David said to Saul, let no one loose heart
on account of this Philistine; your servant will go and fight
him; you are only a boy, and he had been fighting from his
youth (1Samuel 17:31-33 NIV).

After further deliberations between Saul and David as reported in verses 34 to 37, the King then appeared to be positive that, after all, David might be capable of facing up to Goliath. Then, the story continued:

Saul said to David, Go and the Lord be with you. Then Saul
dressed David in his own tunic. He puts a coat of amour on
him and a bronze helmet on his head… (Verse 55) As Saul
watched David going out to meet the Philistine, he said to
Abner, commander of the Army, Abner, whose son is that
young man? Abner replied, as surely as you live, o king, I
do not know. Find out whose son this young man is. (Verse
57) As soon as David returned from killing the Philistine,
Abner took him and brought him before Saul, with David
still holding the Philistine's head. Whose son are you young
man? Saul asked him. David said; I am the son of your
servant Jesse of Bethlehem. After David had finished
talking with Saul… from that day, Saul kept David with him
and did not let him return to his father's house.

The 16th chapter affirmed on the previous page that Saul met David for the first time and retained him in his palace, the very day the king offered David employment in his service as a harp player. Verses 21 and 22 of the 16th chapter (NIV) said, "*David came to Saul and entered his service. Saul liked him very much and David became one of his armoured bearers. Then Saul sent words to Jesse saying, Allow David to remain in my service, for I am pleased with him.*" While, on the contrary, the 17th chapter narrated another opposing tale, alleging that Saul had met David for the first time and retained him in his house, the very day that David slaughtered Goliath. How possibly could two people have met for the first time under two very different circumstances? To all intents and purposes, this is only possible with religion, as the Bible had effectively attributed this peculiar syndrome of conspicuous lying of all the Israelites prophets to the operation of God's command in 1 Kings 22:23.

If the two stories in both chapters 16 and 17 are true-life stories, and not a fable or fiction, but I strongly suspect them to be fictional; quite clearly the author of these two chapters must have been under the very torment of "evil spirit from God" that equally tormented Saul in that book of his.

If David had been in the service of King Saul as a harp player cum amour-bearer, whom the Biblical account indicated the king loved very much; then it would be foolhardy for anyone to believe that this king should not have recognized his beloved David at all. Here was a king whose amour David borne, and in whose private sprawl this wizardry harp player played his musical instrument of harp with exceptional dexterity. How possible is it that Saul might possibly not recognise David; the brave, little boy who came to his palace with *a donkey, loaded with bread, a skin of wine and a young goat*, with his harp hung to his back. It would be downright idiotism of Saul not to have recognized David, mainly, during the course of their one-to-one dialogue that subsequently convinced the king of little David's capability to face up to Goliath in the crucial fight (see 1 Sam 17:31-38). The tale specified that Saul had personally dressed David in his royal tunic and other military apparels to prepare him for the all-important battle against Goliath. How reasonable is it that throughout the close encounter between these two men, Saul could not recognize David, his beloved harp entertainer and amour-bearer, whom 1Sam 16:21 (NIV) said, *"Saul liked very much."*

The only reasonable insight that the stories in these two chapters have perhaps suggested of King Saul is his being such a dumb headed leader. King Saul must therefore be an unintelligent king that could not discern his left from right, let alone having the brainpower to inquire directly from David of his personal identity before departing for the battlefield against the legendary Goliath. The story had typically portrayed King Saul as a naïve leader who could not realize the worth of the national sacrifice that the patriotic David had volunteered to do his nation from an impending national disgrace in the hands of the celebrated Philistine war veteran, who, according to the account, had defied Israel forty days.

On the other hand, if King Saul had truly employed the service of David in his palace, as the account in 1Samuel 16:21-22 had stated, why then did David not introduce himself to Saul as such? How should Abner, the commander of King Saul's army, not know David who is the amour-bearer for the king he had a professional duty to protect?

Moreover, why did David's eldest brother, Eliab, burn with anger at the sight of David in the battle camp by posing accusation to David thus: *"Why have you come down here? And with whom did you leave those few sheep in the desert"* (1Sam 17:28 NIV). This statement of Eliab had clearly depicted David not to be in Saul's service, but a shepherd boy who assisted his father in the desert of Bethlehem, keeping the family herds of sheep.

Earlier on the very day that David slew Goliath (1sam 17:20) says, *"Early in the morning David left the flock with a shepherd, loaded up and set out, as Jesse had directed."* This is another revealing proof that signified David a shepherd boy, still under the guidance of Jesse, his father, instead of the falsehood of him being a professional harp player and armoured-bearer in the service of King Saul. Even in verses 34 and 35 of the 17th chapter, while David impressed his physical credentials upon Saul, he (David) equally referred to himself as a shepherd; *"Your servant has been keeping his father's sheep...*" Nowhere in the chapter did David indicate to Saul, ever to be in his employment as an entertainer cum amour-bearer.

Prophet Samuel had earlier narrated in the sixteenth chapter, the special reference and introduction of David to King Saul as the son of Jesse. According to Samuel's report, Saul had twice sent emissaries to Jesse in the sixteenth chapter in relations to David. At first, he sent his messengers to fetch David, "*Then Saul sent messengers to Jesse and said send me your son David, who is with the sheep.*" Soon after, the king sent his envoys again to obtain Jesse's permission to keep David in his service, "*Then Saul sent words to Jesse saying, allow David to remain in my service, for I am pleased with him.*" How again should Samuel narrate another kind of conflicting story on the next page of the same book, which completely pretended Saul to be seeing David for the first time?

> *As Saul watched David going out to meet the Philistine, he said to Abner, commander of the Army, Abner, whose son is that young man? Abner replied, as surely as you live, o king, I do not know. Find out whose son this young man is... As soon as David returned from the killing the Philistine, Abner took him and brought him before Saul, with David still holding the Philistine's head. Whose son are you young man? Saul asked him.*

Anyone can just imagine the catalogue of stupid stories that have sold over two and a half billion copies all over the world. It's very baffling to imagine how great multitude of dogmatic believers are so out-of-touch with the truth. True to the words of Desiderius Erasmus, "*Man's mind is so formed that it is far more susceptible to falsehood than to truth.*" Hmm, it is undeniably true that where religion or faith is concerned, the feral excesses of the gullibility of man ridiculously blossom into very silly galore!

In the assumption that the account in the 17th chapter was the first to occur, one of the rewards of the heroic achievement would have bestowed the king's daughter in marriage to David (1Sam 17:25). On top of this, David's fame should have spread across all households throughout

Jerusalem, Bethlehem, and beyond. For that reason, when King Saul dispatched his emissaries to Jesse (David's father) to fetch David for the harp-playing job, why then did King Saul not refer to David, either as his *son-in-law* or the *Giant Killer*, instead of referring to him as, *"your son who is with the sheep?"*

However, if the description in the 16th chapter happened to be the first episode, the story of David and Goliath in the seventeenth chapter of the first book of Samuel is, without doubt, a downright fabrication. On the other hand, if the 17th chapter's report turned out to be the first occurrence, it therefore brands the tale of David and his harp, Saul and the torment of evil spirit from God, a cock-and-bull story. Nevertheless, whichever came first of the two accounts, they have both belied and contradicted each other in all ramifications, as both accounts portrayed David and Saul, knowing each other for the first time under two contradictory circumstances.

Extreme Discrepancies

The tenth chapter of Genesis enlightened us as to how the antediluvian humans have spread out over the surface of the earth, forming their nations in their own territories, and speaking different languages before the confusion of the tower of Babel. The account is thus narrated:

> *From these the maritime people spread out into their territories by their clans with their nations, each with its own languages* (Genesis 10:5 NIV). *These are the sons of Ham by their clans and languages in their territories and nations* (Genesis 10:20 NIV). *These are the sons of Shem by their clans and languages in their territories and nations... From these the nation spread out over the earth after the flood* (Genesis 10:31-32 NIV).

One good thing that Prophet Moses should have done as he inscribed the tenth chapter of Genesis on scrolls under divine inspiration would have been to write the script of the fifth verse in the original language that the Maritime nation then spoke. As well, he should have endeavour to pen down the 20th verse in the unique language spoken by the nation of Ham; and the 31st verse in the particular language that the Shemites nation originally spoke. In so doing, the grounds on which to suspect Prophet Moses of blatant conjecture and topsy-turvy confusion would certainly not have arisen when he opened the next chapter of the same book of Genesis, speaking entirely from another side of the mouth.

If Moses had provided humanity with the different versions of these original ancient languages, definitely his tales in the 10th and 11th chapters of the book of Genesis would have unquestionably received convincing appraisal from sensible readers, as truly valid. Thus, the basis would not have arisen under which to classify Moses inconsistent tales among the category that fits exactly into the description of the erudite writer, Isaac Asimov, when he wrote, *"Creationists make it sound as though a 'theory' is something you dreamt up after being drunk all night."*

After telling us, in the tenth chapter of Genesis, how the people had spread out over the surface of the earth, forming their nations in their own territories, and speaking different languages, Moses had inconsistently stated thus all over again in the eleventh chapter of Genesis, verses one to nine (NIV):

> *Now the whole world had one language and a common speech. As men moved eastward, they found a plain in Shimar and settled there…* (verse 4) *Then they said come let us build ourselves a city, with a tower that reaches to the heavens, so that we may make a name for ourselves and not be scattered over the face of the earth.* Verses 5-9 state, *"But the Lord came down to see the city and the tower that men were building, the Lord said, "if as one people speaking the same language they have begun to do this; then nothing they plan to do will be impossible for them. Come let us go down and confuse their language so that they will not understand each other."* (Verses 8-9) *So the Lord scattered them from there over all the*

> *earth ... That is why it was called Babel – because there the*
> *Lord scattered them over the face of the earth.*

Which one of these two conflicting accounts should we believe as the truth? Moses, in the 10th chapter of Genesis gave the account of how the earliest people of the world had spread out over the earth after the flood, in their various clans and nations, into the territories of their choice, *"each with its own language."* Immediately at the head of the 11th chapter of the same book of Genesis, Moses invented another sleazy tale that totally ran down the version he related in the tenth chapter. Thus rendering it puzzling for anyone free of theological prejudice and programming to know which one of these two opposing tales actually told the truth.

In the NIV edition of the 'Holy Bible' which I had with me when I wrote this chapter, the last part of the 10th chapter, and the first part of the 11th chapter that recorded these two contradictory accounts are directly on the same page — just imagine!

As Neil Hurle has frankly observed, *"If the Bible is the word of God, then I for one would be very worried about the mental state of the author."* I sincerely believe the age has now come for humanity to commission a thorough probe into the absurdities of religious falsehood.

The 10th chapter, under the authorship of Moses relates the story that men had spread out into various territories of their choice, speaking different languages without the enforced confusion of Babel, but out of their own volition. Conversely, the 11th chapter, under the same authorship of Moses narrates a different story that the entire world were altogether, *"speaking one language and a common speech."* The account in the 11th chapter reiterates that all the people elect to stay together in the plain of Shimar, under one tower that reaches to heaven, *"and not be scattered over the face of the earth."*

For God's sake, is it really possible that a lone author could have single-handedly committed these sorts of incoherent contradictions that adorn the entire pages of Genesis! Is it truly possible for anyone who is free from theological indoctrination of the church to believe these sorts of erratic tales without having the deepest confusion and the most intense crack explosion right inside of his/her brain? Besides, this twaddle is exactly what the confused passion of Christianity has attributed to the inspiration and revelation of an all-wise, all-knowing, and all-intelligent creator of the universe. Good heavens, the mystery of the Christian religion stringently leaves so much to be desired in the minds of perceptive individuals!

If we truly desire to face the truth, is it sane for anyone to believe that an intelligent, all-knowing creator could possibly have inspired these sorts of irreconcilable inconsistencies, even on the same page?

Exceptionally depicting the wild excesses of man's silly obsession for telling the most absurd lies in the realms of religion were such eccentric and derogatory allusions that the author of Genesis 11:5-7 expressed in downright ignorance, portraying God's fear at the possibility of humans, building a heaven-high tower that would reach his heavenly abode through their concerted efforts. This typically revealed nothing sensible to the logical mind, but a wretched betrayal of the primitive ignorance of man. It's an abject betrayal of the downright reasoning of primitive men, who during the early age (the age of Biblical authors) had wholly believed that the heaven was just within the clouds of the blue skies they see right atop of their heads in some little distance away from the earth. This account in Genesis 11:5-7, most surely betrays the timid ignorance of man, rather than any insightful inspiration of a supernatural god. Of course, the gods must be incredibly stupid to inspire this kind of appalling nonsense!

For goodness sake, what a contemptible belittling of the character of the Jewish/Christian God! Prophet Moses had oddly portrayed Him as becoming jittery at the possibility of man's concerted efforts to build a heaven high tower. Therefore, the Genesis God had quickly rushed down to earth from his magnificent throne to destroy the ambitious project.

How firmly could this silly allusion subsist with the rational mind as the ultimate truth of God's inspiration before its foundation falls to the ground as the utter fabrication of man! Of course, if the Jehovah of the Jews is truly the omniscient (all-knowing) creator of the universe, shouldn't he have known the precise proximity he situated the earth away from the heavens, and that it is practically not within man's possibility to build *"a tower that reaches the heaven?"*

With the greatest technologies known to man from the beginning of recorded time through our modern civilization, the tallest tower (the Burj Dubai Tower) that humankind is still capable of erecting on planet earth is far below a thousand metres (1kilometre) high.

Another of such similar betrayal of ignorance and utter naivety is the sham statement that the book of Joshua expressed in its tenth chapter, verses 12 and 13. It declared that the sun and the moon stood still at the command of Joshua, in order to give Israelite's army divine illumination to carry on the slaughter of other fellow humans. And this in direct contrast to the commandment of "thou shall not kill," which the Israelites claimed their God had specified for their nation. What a humorous statement!

"O sun, stand still over Gibeon,

O moon, over the valley of Aijalon,

So the sun stood still and the moon stopped till the nation avenged itself on its enemies" (Joshua 10:12-13 NIV).

You and I today know, through the evidence of science that the sun and the moon are fixed in their permanent positions, but it is the earth that moves round the sun, which the ignoramus author of the book of Joshua should have rightly commanded to stand still. How then should any realistic mind regard the cant phrase, *"O sun, stand still over Gibeon,"* as if the sun is a balloon flying over the top of Mount Gibeon, as an inspiration of the true creator of the universe? Is it not to be believed that the creator-God should, of course, know more than mortal men, the fixed position of this great luminary is in the universe.

From the above extract of Joshua 10:12-13, is it correct to believe that divine authority had erred by inspiring the wrong fixation, or man had patently lied through his fraudulent substitution of human ignorance for divine inspiration? I once again leave the answer to this question at the discretion of the reader.

No logical reader of the Bible would know exactly what and who to believe amongst the false prophets of the bible and their irreconcilable contradictions. Prophet Moses' depiction of God in the book of Numbers 23:19 (NIV) affirmed that, *"God is not a man, that he should lie, nor a son of man, that he should change his mind."* However, the opposing depiction of the character of God is what Prophet Jeremiah penned down in the book that bears his name. Jeremiah 18:8 (KJV) asserts, *"If that nation, against whom I have pronounced, turn from their evil, I will repent of the evil that I thought to do unto them."*

In a nutshell, humankind had told loads upon loads of falsehood in relations to God through several narrations that emblazon their artificial sacred scriptures. The results of these outrageous lies are the glaring contradictions and discrepancies that spread across the entire pages of these sacred books. The revelation of these despicable lies about the creator of the universe (if there exists any) are tangible clues indicating the certainty that the words of the so-called religious Holy Scriptures cannot be anything more than man's word, deceptively fathered on divine inspiration of a fictionalized God. It is indisputably a stack of imposition upon humanity under the subterfuge of religion, in addition to being a lucrative means of wealth for those who make a trade and affluent livelihood, preaching those words to the dull ears of others.

If at all, man should father the inspiration or authorship of any work on the Almighty creator of the universe, if there exists any; at least such work ought to reflect every attribute of the perfect wisdom that the intelligent creator truly possessed; many of which are abundantly evident to our naked eyes in those amazing things we behold in every passing minute of our daily lives. Holy Scriptures should be edifying text, and not the mirage of spurious tales and frivolous contradictions that's a mockery of human ignorance.

Further, the styles of Biblical narrative expressions are deliberately occulted in mysteries to puzzle the understanding of numerous devotees, in order to establish a channel of profession for theological ministers and priests. This is in exact manner as many professional practitioners such as the pharmacists, medical doctors, chemical scientists, and so on would do to conceal the secrets of their professional practice under technical terms that confound the perception and understanding of the public.

Why should the true word of the creator of the universe be deliberately muddled and cluttered amidst the confusion of spurious interpretations, which are susceptible to wilful misapplication of the clerics and priestly class where and when it best suited the purpose of their trade? If God be for us all as a father, his word ought to open equally to the grasp of every man alike, without any hitch and complication, but free on equal level to the discernment of all, regardless of one's cultural or religious faith.

Never in humankind's history exists any book in this world that contains such a record of confusion, extravagant lies, and irreconcilable contradictions as the Bible does. It is only on the pages of this book called the Holy Scriptures that one would find the mystery of concerted falsehood being deceitfully glued with encumbered truth of human histories, altogether to represent revealed word of the creator of the universe. Under the mist of fabulous contradictions, every atrocious and profane deed that the cruelty of man had committed in ages past, the authors of the numerous Biblical stories have piously camouflaged and upraised into divine holy acts at the express command of God.

What fellowship hast divine revelation with the actions and false prophecies of man on earth? When Moses gave his evil command for the total annihilation of the Midianites in the 31st chapter of the book of Numbers, religionists had staunchly fathered such atrocity on the express command of God. Numbers 31:1-41 (NIV) stated:

> *The LORD said to Moses, take vengeance on the Midianites for the Israelites. After that, you will be gathered to your people. So Moses said to the people, Arm some of your men to go to war against the Midianites and carry out the LORD'S vengeance on them...* (Verse 15) *"Have you allowed all the women to live? He (Moses) asked them... Now kill all the boys. And kill every woman who had slept with a man, but save for you every girl who had never slept with a man."* (Verse 31-41) *So, Moses and*

> *Eleazer the priest did as the Lord commanded Moses. The plunder remaining from the spoils that the soldiers took was 675,000 sheep... and 16,000 people (women who have never slept with a man) of which the tribute for the LORD was 32. Moses gave the tribute to Eleazer the priest as the LORD'S part, as the LORD had commanded Moses.*

Just imagine the degree of flippant sacrilege that religious dogmatists have impiously fathered on the express command of their God. *"Take vengeance on the Midianites for the Israelites."* Is this detestable and profane declaration not derogatory to the character of the creator of the universe, if there exists any; supposing *him/her/it* to think of violent vengeance like mortal men? This is together with the pointless extremism that presented the Biblical God to the world as such a brutal character that would command Moses to order the total extermination of a whole nation of men, women, and infants, save for sparing the lives of 32,000 virgin girls for the enjoyment of his soldiers and fellow citizens. Then, a meagre portion of 32 virgins (0.001%) was allotted as the Lord's portion, in direct contravention of the 10% tithing decree of their God.

Just imagine such heretical degree of irreverent taboo that the gullible fanaticism of Christianity had spiritually sanctioned as the express command of a merciful God!

With what I have constantly observed from childhood regarding the love and benevolence of humanity to humanity, the above story is by all standards abominable, horrendous, abhorrent, and in breach of every aspect of moral justice that every nation of the world upholds. How these abominable actions have consequently become the command of the creator of the universe is another hag of religion mysteries to the entire world.

Simply by reciting the cant phrase of *"thus saith the Lord,"* every profane word of ancient savages were incorporated into the bible as true revelation of God by deceit. In Deuteronomy 18:20-22 (NIV) it is written:

> *But a prophet presumes to speak in my name anything I have not commanded him to say, or a prophet who speaks*

*in the name of other gods, must be put to death. You may
say to yourselves, how can we know when a message has
not been spoken by the LORD? If what a prophet
proclaims in the name of the LORD does not take place or
come true, that is a message the LORD had not spoken.
That prophet had spoken presumptuously. Do not be
afraid of him.*

Why then were the Israelites afraid of Prophet Isaiah, when he
prophesied falsehood to King Ahaz in the name of the Lord in the seventh
chapter of the book ascribed to his writing? Why did the nation of Judah
not execute the decree of their Lord as written in Deuteronomy 18:20
upon the prophet's head and put him to death, after his prophecies had
terribly failed? In the same vein, when Prophet Jeremiah predicted
falsehoods to Zedekiah and Jehoiackim both kings of Judah in the book
named after him, Jeremiah 34:4-5 and Jeremiah 36:30, what then had
refrained the people of Judah from summarily executing Jeremiah
according to their God's command when his false prophecy in the name
of the Lord had miserably failed? If the Israelites had earnestly
implemented the decree of Deuteronomy 18:20 upon all those lying
prophets of the Bible, most possibly all of them would have faced
summary executions on the streets of Israel and Judah without any
exception, as not a soul amongst these so-called prophets ever prophesied
anything that truly came to any reasonable fulfilment.

The Ruse of Daniel's Prophecies

What about Daniel, whose prophecy accurately seemed to predict future
events? In truth, investigations of Biblical scholars detected the fact that
the book of Daniel was actually written long after those events it
pretended to prophesy had occurred. In other words, the book of Daniel
fraudulently correlated past history as against prophesying future events.
According to Encyclopaedia Britannica online, *"The Book of Daniel was
written during the persecutions of Israel by the Syrian King Antiochus IV*

Epiphanes." Many historical records have duly confirmed the fact that King Antiochus Epiphanes reigned over Syria between 175 to 164 BCE, which truly revealed the falsehood of Daniel's prophecies.

What business hath the Holy Spirit in inspiring past events, when their original actors could write them down for posterity? How would the falsehood of dubbed revelation entwine the Genesis creation account into wholesome truth or certainty, if actually they were unfounded and baseless? How would divine revelation twist the fallacy of Isaiah's prophecies into reality or truth, if in actual sense, they were fabrications and deceit? All the same, if Matthew and Luke had fabricated the genealogy of Jesus, slyly dubbing them 'divine revelation' would not turn them into certainty, if they were unreal and bogus. What sense is there to report the actions and discourse of man in a book and christen it a revelation of God? How could such a profane tale as that of David peeping at the nakedness of Uriah's wife from his balcony whilst she took her bath be God's revelation? What meaningful lesson is there in King David's action that exemplifies any virtuous morality to humankind that the creator of the universe might possibly want his people to emulate by inspiring the writing of such profane action in his holy book?

Conversely, these pious men have conceitedly imposed the profane word of man upon humankind as divine revelation. Why must it take the revelation of the Holy Spirit to report the impious actions and trivial discourse of humans to the human race in their own world? Whence abided the logic in dubbing the recount of ancient deeds and histories as the word of God?

If Jesus had told numerous illustrations and parables to great multitudes on Mount Olives, or any other mounts in Gaza, Judea, and Nazareth, how should it become the business of the Holy Spirit to inspire the reporting of these dialogues in discrepant manners to the inhabitants of Nazareth, Gaza, or Judea? Should it not be incumbent upon Jesus, or any of the congregation of his great multitudes who witnessed or partook in the discourse to tell or record these stories for posterity?

If Peter and Paul, Timothy, James and Jude had written volumes of epistolary correspondences to several congregations in Joppa, Rome,

Macedonia, including Galatia, Ephesus, and Corinth, encouraging their converts' faith in their newly found religion, how should these letters become the word of God to their respective addressees, and subsequently the entire world?

Forty Faceless Authors

Without a doubt, it is under the face of artificial authors that the architects of the Jewish and Christian religions had cleverly compiled their so-called Holy Scriptures. This conspiracy was the deceitful imposition of Biblical prophets and apostles as falsified authors of the various Bible books. The engineers of the Christian faith covertly converted the writings of various anonymous authors into the works of Bible prophets and Christ apostles. I will analyse a few of these case as we progress with this chapter.

The first case in point is the counterfeit imposition of Moses as the author of the first five books of the Bible namely, Genesis, Exodus, Numbers,, Leviticus, and Deuteronomy, popularly known as the Pentateuch. However, several investigations of Biblical scholars, researchers, and critics into the contents of those books had clearly exposed irrefutable reality that reckoned very grave evidence against Moses as the true author of the Pentateuch.

Countless evidence factually dispute Moses as the authentic author of the first five books of the Bible. Some of these facts include the verification of chronological detail of events that the books of the Bible relate. Also, the input of grammatical substantiations were very much descriptive of the fact that another person was, in reality, writing about the life and time of Moses in those books, and are very clear evidence that exposed Moses as its falsified author. Several scholars and critics have detected the fact that a number of specific events, which the first five books of the Bible recorded in their various verses were not even available in the world during the lifetime of Moses, let alone his penning the fact of these events on the scrolls.

One obvious example of this is the account of Genesis 14:14 (NIV) *"When Abram heard that his relative had been taken captive, he called out the 318 trained men born in his household and went in pursuit as far as Dan.* " The mention of Dan in the book of Genesis had logically raised very strong suspicion against Genesis being as old as the church asserted it to be, as no such city or town by the name of Dan during the lifetime of Abraham, Lot, and Moses.

The paraphrase of a Yoruba adage says: A child that treasures the growth of protruding teeth is at liberty to do so, as long as he can grow commensurate lips to cover his abnormal teeth from causing him public embarrassment. When a religion that pretends to preach the gospel truth, on the contrary prefers to paint the picture of incredible lies to the world, it should equally develop the thick skin to accept the turbulence of discrediting that, of necessity, would attend the unravelling of its peculiar lies. Here lies the blatancy of this incredible fairy-tale of Abram pursuing the captors of Lot, *"as far as Dan."*

If the story is true, the two cities that the entire Bible books had simply referred to as *'Dan'* were the cities formerly known as Leshem in the 19th chapter of Joshua, and the one formerly known as Laish in the 18th chapter of the book of Judges.

Abram's grandson, Jacob (reportedly renamed Israel by God) had twelve sons born to him. The seventh of Jacob's sons, Dan, was one of the eleven sons of Jacob that immigrated with their father and fifty-eight other grandchildren of Jacob to meet Joseph in Egypt (Exodus 1: 1-5).

After four hundred years of their resettlement in Egypt, the descendants of Dan were among the totality of the twelve tribes of Israel that wandered with Moses in the wilderness for another forty years, until they afterwards obtained their own allotment of the Promised Land (Joshua 19: 40-46).

The nineteenth chapter of Joshua verses 47-48 (NIV) states,

> *But the Danites had difficulty taking possession of their territory, so they went up and attacked Leshem, and took it, put it to the sword and occupied it. They settled in Leshem and named it Dan after their forefather.*

The eighteenth chapter of Judges recounted a similar story, but the name of its own city had changed from Leshem to Laish. The account in the book of Judges 18:28-29 (NIV) narrated the story thus:

> *The Danites rebuilt the city and settled there. They named it Dan after their forefather Dan, who was born to Israel – though the city used to be called Laish.*

The nineteenth chapter of Joshua verses 40-48 and the whole of Judges Chapter 18 plainly recounted the story of how the **Danites** had conquered Leshem and/or Laish, and subsequently renamed the cities' previous names to Dan after their ancestor.

Following when the descendants of Dan returned from the land of Egypt, after nearly half a millennium sojourns, they consequently conquered the gentile city of Leshem and/or Laish and settled in it. Afterwards, they renamed the city *'Dan'* in memory of their primary ancestor in Egypt. For heaven's sake, the descendants of Dan that returned from Egypt were more than ten-generation gaps apart from Abram, their foremost ancestor! How, on earth might Abram, the great grandfather of *Dan*, have possibly pursued the captors of Lot as far as to a city named after his own great grandson by descendants of over ten-generation gaps apart, to be modest.

According to the chronological arrangements in the Bible, as chaotic and uncertain as it might be, the conquest of Leshem and Laish (that is if these two cities are truly different from each other) and its subsequent renaming to **Dan** did not happen until several centuries after the death of Abraham, Lot, and Moses. The Bible detailed the conquest of Leshem, and her renaming to Dan, to occur shortly after the allotment of the Promised Land to the twelve tribes of Israel by Joshua. While, on the other hand, the conquest of Laish and its renaming to *Dan* occurred shortly after the death of Samson — the powerful Israelite Judge — who reigned many years after the death of Moses.

These incontrovertible details have consequently detected the author of this particular 14th chapter of Genesis as a mysterious biographer who lived after the 'Danites' had sacked the cities of Leshem and/or Laish and changed its former name(s) to *Dan*. Definitely, the faceless author that detailed this particular account in the book of Genesis could never have been Moses.

Moreover, this anonymous author of the 14ᵗʰ chapter of Genesis has failed to clarify to numerous promoters of his outrageous story, how and where he had seen Abram, the great grandfather of Dan in hot pursuit of Lot's captors, *'as far as Dan.'* This faceless author has also failed to shed light on how Lot had resurrected from his grave as to be taken captive by enemy combatant, together with how Abram had possibly resurrected from his grave, as to lead a troop of "318 trained men" in military combat in pursuit of Lot's captors to 'Dan.' Perhaps, another city exists in heaven named Dan in commemoration of this great-grandson of Abram, where Moses had sighted this incredible drama of Abram in hot pursuit of the captors of Lot *'as far as Dan.'*

In any event, Abram, Lot, and Moses were all long dead before any city by the name **'Dan'** had come into any existence in Biblical lands. Just imagine a bunch of naked lies that biblical story tellers have ascribed to divine revelations of the creator of the universe!

How possible is it that Prophet Moses could ever pass a polygraph test—the lie detector trial—if one were to be conducted for him on this subject by a panel of investigators? Of course, there is no way he could ever pass the test. I particularly find it very puzzling to imagine how this type of disjointed story still, unto this day, mesmerizes the passion of well over two billion devotees across the world. It is certainly true that people of this world fanatically love the lie and hate the truth.

Considering the lavish contradiction and incomparable confusions that abound chapter by chapter in the book of Genesis, the book gives the impression of having numerous faceless authors, as it is not possible that any one person could commit the huge errors and contradictions that Genesis contains. As Thomas Paine has aptly observe, *"it is practically not possible that a lone author could have committed these discrepant errors, and not have at all perceived them."* The human mental machinery and psychology of intelligence analysis would not allow for that; especially for someone in an erudite position that Biblical historians had apportioned to

Moses. A man who was raised under the tutelage of the Egyptian Pharaoh, and as an Egyptian prince would have been accorded the royal privilege of attending the best schools in the land of Egypt — the then superpower of the world.

In the usual practice of most Biblical advocates, they have readily advanced their metaphorical abracadabra in support of Moses conjuring up these details, posthumously under divine inspiration from his unknown grave. Perhaps, that was probably why Moses could write down the details of his funeral long after his death, and posthumously uploaded his information via spiritual telepathic communication, or via spiritual internet website to the Jewish priests for publication on planet earth, one can never tell. Anything is possible with religionists and their mysterious hey presto!

Another case in point is the inventory of the descendants of Esau, the less favoured son of Isaac, whom the Bible called the *'Edomites.'* The book of Genesis 36:1-30 recorded the monarchs of Edom in a particular order by name. Immediately after the listing, Genesis 36:31(NIV) stated, *"These were the kings who reigned in Edom before any Israelite king reigned."* This particular phrase found in Genesis 36:31 gives a direct clue to the fraudulent authorship ascribed to the book of Genesis. It's also a direct indication that Genesis is not as old as the church assert it to be. To detect the fraud of the authorship of this passage in the book of Genesis, one only needed to focus the lens on the time when the first king began his reign in Israel.

In detecting the approximate date of any historical account that does not carry an internal date, records of true-life events which the author detailed in such account, becomes the focal point that should supply tangible clues to the approximate date of writing the account. The particular reference to such true-life event should plainly serve as a direct clue that the author is trying to connect a significant occurrence that held true correlation and endorsement to his report. Therefore, such factual and true-life expression as, **"before any Israelite king reigned,"** is an **underlined fact** which the writer clearly intends to relate to the reader.

The underlined fact is that a **'King'** was at that moment on the throne in Israel when the author penned down his story. Observably, the writer could never have supported his enumeration with such true-life expression, *"these were the kings who reigned in Edom before any Israelite king reigned,"* if at least a king was not on the throne in Israel at the time the author penned down his report in Genesis 36:31. Without any doubt, the statistics of the reign of a king in Israel was among the definite information the author intended to reveal to his readers.

If I should give some details herein in this book that, *"Nelson Mandela, Thabo Mbeki, and Kgalema Motlanthe were the black presidents who ruled South Africa before the reign of any black president in America, "*and fail to affix a date to the publication, it is obvious that my readers would get hold of two specific facts from my report. Firstly – the reader would unmistakably discern the fact that either a black president had reigned past in America, or there presently is a black president ruling the nation of America as at the time I penned down my report. Secondly – whoever reads the detailing of my account should unquestionably discern the fact that I could never have written my book before the inauguration of the first black president in America. Of course, we all know that Barack Obama is America's first black president, whose reign commenced in the United States of America on the 20th day of January 2009; for that reason, I could never have written the account before 2009, because there were no black presidents in America prior to this date. Therefore, if any institution should come up with misleading impositions that I had truly written the account in whichever century BCE, what then should we call that? Of course, it would be blatant falsehood!

We are all familiar with the history of how the nation of Israel began from Abraham through his grandson Jacob. The book of Genesis narrated the story of how God had changed Jacob's name to Israel, together with the account of how he immigrated with his entire nation to Egypt. In addition to how his descendants had later returned from Egypt to settle on the 'Promised Land' through several battles, under the leadership of Moses, Joshua, and Deborah, including Samson, Gideon, and other Judges, before they finally got their first king, whose name was Saul. It is therefore evident from Biblical accounts and other secular histories that the nation of Israel had never installed anyone as their king prior to the time of Saul. Without any doubt, the author of this passage must have written his narrative at some point during or after the rule of the first Israelite king, which carries the time that the book of Genesis was written to sometime during or after the reign of King Saul.

Therefore, the content of Genesis 36:31, *"These were the kings who reigned in Edom before any Israelite king reigned"* should never have entered anywhere inside the book of Judges, let alone the book of Genesis. It is undoubtedly evident, particularly from the expression, **"before any Israelite king reigned,"** that the author of this passage intends for his readers to grab hold of the explicit detail that the Jewish kingship has been instituted as at the time he penned down his report in Genesis 36:31. Under no circumstances could the author of Genesis 36:31 have possibly detailed this particular expression before the reign of the first king of Israel. As a result, the faceless author of the passage must have evidently written his account of the succession of the Edomites kings during or after the reign of King Saul — the first Israelite king.

If the author of the book of Judges should close his tales in the last chapter of his book with this statement, *"In those days Israel had no king; everyone did as he saw fit,"* Judges 21:25(NIV). How then could Moses, the man who departed this earthly life more than three centuries before the reign of any king in Israel receive credit for the authorship of this kind of statement in the book of Genesis, *"these were the kings who reigned in Edom before any Israelite king reigned?"* We all know that Moses died before the reign of any Israelite Judges, let alone any of its kings. It is therefore illogical to ascribe the authorship of the book of Genesis to Prophet Moses.

It is also pertinent to note that Genesis 36 (verses 31 to the end) are exactly word for word with the first book of Chronicles verses 43 to the end. However, the church has never accredited Moses with the authorship of the first book of Chronicles. If there is no controversy that the author of the monarchical enumerations in the first chapter of First Chronicles had written his story after the establishment of the Jewish monarchy (the era where it closely stood in ideal agreement with the order of Biblical history); it then means that these same passages, written word for word in the 36th chapter of Genesis verses 31 to 40, were altogether written after the establishment of the Jewish monarchy by one and the same author.

It is undeniable that Genesis 36:31-40 and 1Chronicles 1:43-54 are altogether doctored jobs (cut and pasted verbatim the same) by a faceless author. Whatever might be the motive behind the case, there is absolutely no way that Moses could possibly receive credit as the doctor (sorry, the author) of such plagiarism from the book of First Chronicles.

It is unmistakably evident that the doctor or author of these verses (Genesis 36:31 to 40 and 1st Chronicles 1:43 to 54) had detailed his record of the Edomites kings after the coronation of the first Jewish king. In any case, the faceless author must have been someone who saw the reign of King Saul. How could this person be Moses? If Moses was not the author of Genesis, who then, was its faceless author? As Thomas Paine had rightly observed in his book, The Age of Reason:

> *Take away from Genesis the belief that Moses was the author, on which only strange belief that it is the Word of God has stood, and there remains nothing of Genesis but an anonymous book of stories… or of downright lies.*

There lies the true depiction of the ageless book of creation, Genesis!

One peculiar and very appalling trait I have noticed amongst Biblical advocates is their inordinate proclivity towards the fanatical defence of scriptural contradictions and discrepancies, which points clearly to the fact that the Bible cannot stand on its own feet. How well might an alleged 'holy book' stand on its own feet when it erratically concocts spurious stories under the cover of divine revelation and faceless authors? Divine truth should not require any mortal defence to survive, because it is an infinite truth which will naturally prevail even when no man has piously defended it.

However, when people with pious reputation have taken it as their stock in trade to substitute the falsehood of mortal men for the wholesome truth of a supernatural god, and fanatically prevaricate by their obsessive enforcement of the falsehood upon humanity as the ultimate truth; in addition to wilfully distorting natural truth through the influence of their religion, something sinister must suspiciously be lying beneath the foundation of such extreme fanaticism.

The manner in which the defenders of Biblical fairy-tales have ubiquitously flooded internet websites with distorted and corrupt information to sustain the falsehood of their religious books, most truly denotes underhand sponsorship of the proponents of religion. It gives a picture of sinister aim to confound the credulous minds of numerous devotees, on account to stay tight in business. These actions are factually consistent with the tricks of businesspersons, as they would stage-manage every ploy and tactic to keep their trade out of the erosion of any threat. These deceptive notions are certainly unedifying and very dishonest to humanity and the very 'God' that these religionists pretend to worship. It is as if the people cannot perceive these numerous contradictions reading between the lines with their naked eyes, or that they cannot discern these inexhaustible discrepancies with their astute minds.

If I have no other evidence to show that the Bible is man's word, fraudulently imposed on divine inspiration, there is the outrageous oddity of the Biblical God, promising the inhabited land of other nations to Abraham, whilst abundant bare lands lay fallow all over the world. There is also the absurdity of Joshua, sharing other peoples' inhabited land to the twelve tribes of Israel, whilst abundant bare lands lay empty all over the wilderness of the Middle East. Therefore, these bizarre absurdities and funny habits have satisfactorily stood as enough evidence for me to conclude that the content of the Bible, in every implication, is man's word fathered on God.

Indeed, the petty story of a God that chose to rain deadly stones to murder the citizens of one nation in bias support of another nation must definitely require the assistance and prolific salesmanship of mortal men to flourish amongst the human ranks. I sincerely cannot make a distinction between the character of the Biblical God and the likes of Augusto

Pinochet of Bosnia, Idi Amin Dada of Uganda, Saddam Hussein of Iraq, etc.

Therefore, the fanatical defence of the Bible by man, and the fervent imposition of its falsehood by pious men who make a livelihood from narrating these words to the dull ears of others, as to appear the wholesome truth, have certainly offered me adequate proof to erect the basis that the Bible is man's word fathered on godly authorship.

Chapter

7

The Tenet of Good and Evil

*"The belief in a supernatural source of evil is not necessary;
men alone are quite capable of every wickedness."*

– Joseph Conrad

The sixteenth chapter of the first book of Samuel verses 14-15 (NIV) states, *"Now the spirit of the Lord had departed from Saul and an evil spirit from the Lord tormented him. Saul attendants said to him, "See, an evil spirit from God is tormenting you."* The book of Judges Chapter nine verses 22-23 (NIV) also states that, *"After Abimelech had governed Israel for three years, God sent an evil spirit between Abimelech and the citizens of Shechem, who acted treacherously against Abimelech."* In addition, the author of first book of Kings wrote in the 22nd chapter verses 21-22 (NIV), *"Finally, a spirit came forward, stood before the Lord and said, 'I will entice him'. 'By what means? The Lord asked. I will go out to be a lying spirit in the mouth of all his prophets, he said. You will succeed in enticing him. Go and do it."* As well, the book of Genesis (3:22 NIV) declared, *"And the Lord God said, "The man has now become like one of us knowing good and evil."* Moreso, the Biblical righteous man, Job, proclaimed in the book named after him, Job Chapter 2 verse 10 (KJV), *"Shall we receive good at the hand of God, and shall we not receive evil?"* Further, the author of the New Testament book of 2Thessalonians (2:11 NIV) also wrote, *"For this reason God sends them a powerful delusion so that they will believe the lie."* Again, the author of the book of Jeremiah 18:8 (KJV) wrote this statement as a direct pronouncement of God, *"If*

that nation, against whom I have pronounced, turn from their evil, I will
repent of the evil that I thought to do unto them." We also read in the
Bible book of Isaiah 45:7 (KJV), *"I form the light, and create darkness: I*
make peace, and create evil: I the LORD do all these things."

From these excerpts of Bible passages, one might truly discern the
primal beliefs of ancient Jews denoting their Jehovah to be the sole
custodian of all powers, both holy and evil. This same belief represents the
exact viewpoint in which the ancient Yoruba spiritual sages had also
discerned the power of Olodumare — the God they believed to be the
supreme creator and ruler of the universe. One of the particular attributes
the ancient Yoruba traditionalists had apportioned their revered deity —
Esu, whom they signified as the General Overseer of the universal justice
system, ably in charge of executing the holy and evil purposes of the grand
ruler of the universe, is that of being the special messenger to the Almighty
God. It is curious to note that modern religionists have basically distorted
this original belief in relations to 'God' being the active custodian of good
and evil, by slyly separating the power of their God into two equal parts.
One half they have kept in the custody of an omnipotent 'holy God;' while
to the contrary, they formulate the other half as residing in the custody of
another omnipotent 'evil God' whom they labelled as Satan the devil.

In every respect, I should for once agree with the thoughts of ancient
Biblical writers alongside the Yoruba ancient beliefs regarding the concept
of holy and evil powers opening from one source, and residing within one
dominion. This perception agrees quite perfectly with all evidence that
nature's laws largely demonstrate to attentive knowledge of humans
through its operations. No power can stand alone on one side without its
opposite side. To keen observation, the whole creation of Mother Nature
has proved in all details to have an equal opposite — the positive and
negative polarity of all matters.

Whenever there is light, there also exists an equal opposite of the light,
darkness. The darkness in that case becomes an essential barometer which
sets in motion, positive reception with which to gauge the real meaning of
the light. If darkness does not exist, how might humans be able to discern
what light truly is? Certainly, we would not be able to determine the true

essence of light, as there would be no means by which humanity can gauge the fundamental nature of the light.

Can anyone imagine a situation where continuous sunshine exists day in, day out, without the coolness of the dark hours to refresh the high temperature the sun had generated during daylight. These two opposing powers—darkness and light—work together as one to create a balanced power base for the universe. Whenever comes the time for the dominance of light, the darkness simply yields to another side. Similarly, when the moment arrives for the dominance of darkness, the light peacefully departs to a different location. This is the simple law of nature that keeps the universe in a stable and unwavering operation from the beginning of existence.

Essentially, death gives the obliged value to life. If death does not exist in our world, humans won't be appreciative of life. If there is no right and wrong, humankind will definitely be oblivious of their sense of lawfulness and lawlessness, as we may perhaps be incapable of making a distinction between righteousness and evil. For, there will be no basis upon which to differentiate morality from wickedness; honesty from deceit; decency from crudity; justice from injustice; reasons from credulity; and so on and so forth.

The intelligence of nature has thoroughly procreated all matters, which exist on planet earth with an equal opposite, for both sides to complement each other for the overall benefits of universal existence. Even as Mother Nature offers existence to all life in the natural world, it equally provides the equilibrium of birth and death to regulate the quality of life on earth. For, if we only have births without deaths in this world, life at a certain point in time will become calamitous and unbearable. Agonizing sufferings and pains would have emerged on earth due to over-population, resulting in excruciating human miseries and intolerable disasters for all life, including animal and vegetation life.

In science, it takes the negative and positive ions to generate electricity, which powers our cooling systems as well as our heating systems. The male folk wouldn't have been able to distinguish their sexual category if the female gender weren't in existence. It is the variety of sufferings in life (these, with the exception of malicious and horrid cruelties that humans have wilfully designed with callous target to afflict fellow humans) that essentially present humans the prospect to appreciate all the pleasures of life.

The faultless order in the midst of mathematical regulation and certainty with which the entire engine room of our awesome universe continually operates most certainly evangelizes the reality to anyone who may find the time to study its operational details that the powers behind these marvellous machineries, indisputably radiate only from one source — Mother Nature.

In my own opinion, religion manufacturers have oddly created two separate power bases for the holy and the evil forces. They have artificially contrived to put the holy powers in the hands of God, and the evil powers in the hands of Satan the devil. Moreover, religion architects have superficially elevated Satan the devil from being an archangel with some degree of authority under their God's command to an omnipotent immortal entity of equal or greater powers to that of their God. I suspect they have done this so that the foundation for setting up myriad of artificial religions might flourish on planet earth.

Empirical revelation of nature's law, which are practically definite to human knowledge, indicates all natural and spiritual powers, whether in the deepest depths or in the highest heights, flows directly from one source — Nature's Law.

Is it the 'Fall' or 'Rise' of Man?

From the Biblical fable of the 'Fall of Man,' which the third chapter of Genesis narrates, it is there written in the first verse (NIV), *"The serpent was more crafty than any of the wild animals the Lord had made."* This is just as the ancient Yoruba in many of their numerous myths and fables would say, *"The tortoise is craftier than any of the wild animals that God had made."* The Bible told us that the serpent had ingeniously deceived Eve into eating from the tree of knowledge of good and evil, which God had placed at the centre of the Garden of Eden and forbade them from eating.

> *You will not surely die, the serpent said to the woman, for God knows that when you eat of it your eyes will be opened and you will be like God, knowing good and evil…*
> *When the woman saw that the fruit of the tree was good for food and pleasing to the eyes, and also desirable for gaining wisdom, she took some and ate it…and they realized that they were naked, so they sowed fig leaves together and made coverings for themselves* – Genesis 3:4-7 (NIV).

An insight into this account would reveal to readers' understanding that the origin of good and evil is entirely of the Genesis God. For, the serpent said, *"you will be like God, knowing good and evil."* The serpent never affirmed that Adam and Eve will be like God, knowing only the good, while they bear resemblance to Satan, knowing its opposing side – evil. The account had simply affirmed Adam and Eve would bear resemblance to God, knowing good and evil. Having thus imbued the knowledge of good and evil into their existence, Adam and Eve therefore became like God, knowing the good and its equal opposite, the evil. Afterwards, the Genesis God upheld the assertion of Satan in the twenty-second verse of the third chapter of Genesis (NIV) *"The man has now become like one of us, knowing good and evil."*

According to this myth of Genesis, God never in the beginning created Adam and Eve as blind people into the Garden of Eden. For, verse six of the third chapter affirmed that, *"the woman **saw** that the fruit of the tree was good for food and pleasing to the **eyes**."* The primordial Bible writers must have referred to Adam and Eve as 'blind' people, because they initially lacked the knowledge of equal opposites — the positive and negative polarity of all matters, which was truly indicative of the fact that they were totally deficient in knowledge. Therefore, their lack of knowledge must have truly made them to be typically unaware of their secular and spiritual condition, which was similar to total blindness. In this myth of Genesis, Adam and Eve were oblivious of their nakedness, because they lacked the exact knowledge of clothing (I wonder how they survived the cold winter of Eden). They were never cognizant of their full existence, because they lacked the conscious awareness of death.

Even, after the Biblical God had blessed Adam and Eve, and commanded them in Genesis 1:28 (KJV) to *"Be fruitful, and multiply, and replenish the earth, and subdue it."* This was a 'blessing' that then stood as divine license for them to commence the business of sexual reproduction; unfortunately for Adam and Eve, they could not practically comply with the order of their God, because they lack the insightful knowledge of doing so. This evidently explained the reason why they had no children prior to their acquisition of the 'knowledge of good and evil' through the aid of the serpent. In short, I observe this as what the manufacturers of the Christian religion and their numerous apologists should have considered as the first disobedience of man to God, while the eating of the forbidden fruit becomes their second sin. It makes one to wonder why the Genesis God had not duly punished Adam and Eve for their defiance to reproduce accordingly; just as he had duly punished them for their defiance for eating the forbidden fruit, when he completely withdrew their license for eternal life. Perhaps the plotters of the Christian religion had suitably considered the personality of the Adam and Eve, portrayed in the book of Genesis, as very comparable to typical robots, who simply roamed about the forest of Eden in their nakedness as morons that did not know their left from right. And, in that case, the pious analysis of priests and Biblical commentators have thus disregarded the first human sin of non-compliant with the order of God to *"multiply and replenish the earth,"* as the product of their naiveté that sprang out of their utter lack knowledge. Then, the claim of many Bible believers, admitting Adam as a perfect being from inception would, on the whole, fall to the ground. Moreover, it would call to question, the rationale behind the 'curse' that religionists had through the Genesis fable made God to place upon the serpent for naturally guiding Adam and Eve from total darkness to self-aware consciousness.

According to the Genesis myth, the serpent had naturally guided the first Biblical human couple from obscurity of insignificance and triviality in the lonesome forest of Eden, into the illumination of wholesome life. And, from the gloom of being naked morons in the forlorn wild, into being an enlightened progenitor of inventors and manufacturers of clothing in all corners of planet earth. From being a dolt and blockhead, who does not even understand the process of making babies, into being a liberated and elucidated progenitor of master scientists that not only reproduced natural babies, but can also re-create or clone humans.

At this point, it is crucial to ascertain the circumstances that suggested the idea of the fabulous 'curse,' which Biblical writers have manufactured by deceit, and put into God's mouth, as an expletive of his vexation for evil to befall the serpent and man, because the serpent had shown Eve and her husband the path to natural truth.

To all accepted indications steered by the veritable wheel of common sense, excepting the absurd doctrines of religion, the serpent had plausibly guided the Biblical Adam and Eve to the path of light and natural liberation. In every logical sense, the serpent had plainly prompted the first Biblical human couples into the reality of what truly laid behind the eating of the forbidden fruit, which the serpent validated did not consist of positive death, but knowledge that was of good and evil.

It is here easy to detect that the circumstance of the painful parturiency that women experienced during childbirth had suggested the idea of the fable in Genesis 3:16. (KJV) *"Unto the woman he said, I will greatly multiply thy sorrow and thy conception; in sorrow thou shalt bring forth children; and thy desire shall be to thy husband and he shall rule over thee."* It is a fact on scientific record that the human females are not the only creatures that suffer the monopoly of painful childbirth. In actuality, most animals that fall into the category of mammals — the class of warm-blooded vertebrate animals — whose females have secret milk glands to feed their babies, also suffer painful labour during childbirth. The giraffes, impala, horses, cattle, including apes, goats, zebra, sheep etc., are all examples of animals that suffer great agony. Their tears, groaning noises, and gesticulations suggest severe pains, like that of female humans, during childbirth.

Only the manufacturers of this 'curse,' which had strangely found its way into the mouth of the Jehovah of the Jews could explain to humankind whether the categories of animal that equally experience child labour pain are also under the curse of Genesis 3:16. If so, which offence had really compelled these animals under the spell of painful labour during childbirth? Perhaps, religionists would say these animals had also eaten of the forbidden fruit. Otherwise, could it be an error or omission on the path of the author of Genesis for failing to untie the fable separately from this category of animals, by not accommodating their own pain in another fabulous Genesis story that has created this loose end?

It is very unfortunate for the generality of the people of this world that even Eve herself, the progenitor of the female folks, never for once experienced any painless childbirth during her tenancy in the Garden of Eden. At least, her testimony should have provided some credible evidence that might afford humanity the yardstick to measure the degree of greatness or severity to which the Christian God had increased her childbearing pains. What a droll fable of the Jewish and Christian religion!

It is also upon the plain fact that the serpent mainly move from place to place by crawling along the ground on its bellies that conjured up the fable of the curse that the Genesis author had equally imposed upon the expletive of God's anger on the serpent for its sin of deceiving humankind into eating of the forbidden fruit. *"And the Lord God said unto the serpent* (as if both God and the serpent are within a speaking distance to each other), *because thou hast done this, thou art cursed above all cattle, and above every beast of the field; upon thy belly shalt thou go, and dust shalt thou eat all the days of thy life"* (Genesis 3:14 KJV).

What a bogus curse from the divine! The fact that its vain potency has not an iota of effect on a very lowly animal for that matter is typically suggestive of the fabrication of the 'curse' into the mouth of the Jewish God. Not even the pretence of divine expletive might well effect the efficacy of the curse upon the serpent to compel it to eat the divinely prescribed food of *"dust shalt thou eat all the days of thy life."* Since the past six thousand years, when Moses allegedly made God to express this bogus curse upon the serpent, never once has the serpent taken to eating dust as its affixed diet. Frankly speaking, has anyone of you ever seen a serpent eating dust? Not at all, I am yet to see one myself! Not in Africa do serpents eat dust; perhaps in the Middle East, from where Moses had written the book of Genesis. It is possible that serpents could be eating dusts as staple food in that region, but the serpents of Africa do not eat dust as food. Serpents are carnivores, and they feed very largely on other animals, including birds and insects, but never on dust.

The author of Genesis cleverly failed to let us out of the mystery of the original form and shape in which his own God had, at first, created the serpent. Maybe his God had originally formed the serpent in the shape of a dragon with multiple legs like that of the centipedes or millipedes, including intelligent ability to reason, speak, and play tricks. Perhaps, the Genesis God had originally created the serpent in the shape of dinosaur walking on multiple feet, we do not know. However, I am not going to involve myself in any speculations regarding another controversy about the serpent; it already has enough controversy over its head. What I am only going to add is that, I have seen numerous publications of artists' impressions in many religious literatures suggesting the serpent originally crawled on its belly. Many of these impressions have depicted the serpent creeping flat on its belly on top of the branches of the "tree of knowledge of good and evil," busy in conversations with Eve during the process of the serpents' presumed instigation of Eve into eating the forbidden fruit. However, this was before the alleged curse that purportedly transformed or downgraded the animal into a crawling reptile. Hmm! Just imagine the kind of dull fable that's a bestseller in the arena where religion and faith is concerned. I sometimes wonder what on earth has gone into the human head; they come to church every Sunday to listen to this kind of stupid story and still donate large sums of money for the spread of such absurd fable!

The circumstance that also determined the curse, which religionists falsely put into the mouth of God and imposed upon Adam's head, as being divine curse to punish Adam because he had listened to his wife, Eve, and ate of the forbidden fruits, was equally put forward by the natural realism of occurrences in humans' everyday life. The normal fact of humans having to work before they could feed is what religion manufacturers have misrepresented to stand for divine curse upon Adam and the generality of humankind.

Essentially, the painful toil that humans pass through before they feed is naturally the stringent principle that applies equally to every other species of animals, including marine lives and flying creatures. If these animals do not practically work by going after their prey, they would likewise not eat. The factors that have made the human toil greater than that of the animals are simply borne out of our choices. Our choice of food, luxuriant shelter, clothing, and other ostentations, which humans essentially desire in life are plainly responsible for the enormity of his toil.

Seasonally, some birds fly for hundreds of kilometres; in some cases, they do fly for thousands of kilometres in search of food to eat and materials to make nests for their shelters. Some herbivorous animals also travel long distances during dry seasons in search of green vegetation and water for their livelihood; this same case is also relevant to marine creatures. Other carnivorous animals like the lion sometimes starve for days without food in the forest, before their pride would finally catch in on one prey. What is the sin that all these other animals have committed to make them equally suffer painful toil like humans before they feed? Perhaps, religionists might also say their ancestors had climbed or perched on the tree of good and evil while in Eden, who knows?

In essence, the reality of the painful toil on human livelihood applies generally to both genders of humankind, the male and the female folks, contrary to the erroneous application of the curse being solely instituted as Adam's cup of tea. An unmarried woman, for example, suffers an equally painful toil to feed and live the decent life she desires in life. Likewise, a single mother would similarly suffer painful toil to give herself and her children a good standard of life. Even married couples could both suffer painful toil together to sustain a good living. Therefore, the reality of the painful toil is not uniquely Adam's cup of tea as Genesis had wrongly portrayed it, but equally that of Eve.

The fable of the 'The Fall of Man' as the author of the third Chapter of Genesis had narrated it, is nothing considerably tangible, but a redundant primordial age deception of the Jewish and Christian religion. It is deceitfully invented out of utter fallacy to bring humanity down to their knees and coerce them into being subjective to artificial doctrines and outdated code of religious beliefs, which the architects of religion have cleverly designed to advance the authority and iniquity of their creeds. The fundamentals of the curse were tailor-made and bespoke to fit and wind itself up in the normal circumstances of every day's natural life; which is that of work to feed; painful labour before childbirth; masculine dominance of the effeminate gender; as well as the crawling of the serpent with its belly on the ground.

At no point in time since the beginning of recorded time did mankind ever fall from his original apex position of favour with his maker, if there exists any. Right from the beginning, evolution of species by means of natural selection had created man as the highest being of all creatures in the known universe, and humans have luminously remained in that zenith position unto this day. With each passing minute, humankind has practically surmounted the insurmountable and, all in all, explored the unimaginable; making premium discoveries of every possibility through science; even beyond the boundaries of our planet earth into the outer world of the heavenly bodies.

Instead of falling, as the Bible had affirmed in its fable of Genesis; humankind has ever since the inception of his life on earth dynamically transcended and progressively soared above the limit of his physical forms into the higher realms of spiritual and mental prowess. Humankind has consistently remained in oneness with Mother Nature. Through the principles of science that Mother Nature had configured into the structure of the universe, humankind has passionately explored the magnificent splendour and wonders that the awesome universe possesses in all its spheres.

In the deep-seated law of nature, it is evident that the overall power that be, which rules all powers, whether righteous or the unrighteous, evil or holy, darkness or light, spiritual or temporal, intrinsically activates and operates from one omnipotent source – Mother Nature – the divine first cause of all matters.

Where is the Lie?

In opposition to all accepted indications steered by the wheel of common sense, the author of the Bible book of Revelation conversely revealed to humankind that Satan the devil was the particular creature and the culprit who invaded the body of the serpent to trick Eve into eating the forbidden fruit in the Garden of Eden. The book of Revelation 12: 9 (NIV) accused Satan as the *"ancient serpent called the devil, or Satan, who leads the whole world astray."* However, the internal evidence of this allegorical drama in the third chapter of Genesis does not suggest that Satan the devil was the actual entity that acted through the serpent to instigate Eve into eating the forbidden fruit of the Tree of Knowledge of Good and Evil.

The Genesis tale asserted that God had specifically positioned the Tree of the Knowledge of Good and Evil and the Tree of Life at the centre of the Garden of Eden. As is usual of the very typical mysteries that wilfully surround religion, the book of Genesis affirmed that God permitted eating from the Tree of Life, so that Adam and Eve might live forever on earth; however, he utterly forbade eating from the Tree of the Knowledge of Good and Evil for reasons very much unknown to any earthlings unto this day. Perhaps, for Adam and Eve to live in perpetual darkness and insignificance, no one could tell.

The third chapter of Genesis narrates the account thus:

> *He* (the serpent) *said to the woman, did God really say, you must not eat from any tree in the garden.* (Verses 2 and 3) *The woman said to the serpent, we may eat fruits from the trees in the garden, but God did say, you must not eat fruit from the tree that is in the middle of the garden, and you must not touch it, or you will die.* (Verse 4) *You will not surely die, the serpent said to the woman. For, God knows*

> *that when you eat of it your eyes will be opened and you will*
> *be like God, knowing good and evil.* Genesis 3:1-4 (NIV)

After Adam and Eve had thus eaten of the forbidden fruits, verses 14-19 of the third chapter of Genesis enumerated a number of punishments that God meted out to the serpent and the Genesis first human couple by placing specific curses on each of them for disobeying his rule. The Bible told us that God had thereafter penalized Adam and his wife, chasing them out of the Garden of Eden that they might, on their own, fend for their livelihood. We equally learn from Genesis that God also rebuked the serpent by placing a curse on his head to become the lowliest of all animals, to crawl on its belly, and to eat dust all the days of its life.

Furthermore, Genesis 3:15 told us, *"I (God) will put enmity between you and the woman, between your offspring and hers; he will crush your head, and you will strike her heel."* However, Christianity has again perverted this plain fact of humans effectively killing the serpent by crushing it on its head; as well as the natural fact that likely compels the serpent to strike the human heel, because that is how high it can go from the ground. The Christian priests have made this plain fact to stand, figuratively, as the hatred between Christ followers and the followers of Satan (whatever that means). Wouldn't the serpent surely strike the heel of the cattle, or any other larger animal that might come unsafely closer to it? I honestly cannot figure out the particular relevance that differentiates this special religious enmity between the serpent and Eve's offspring from the hostility between the humans and the scorpions, or the dragons, as well as between any other reptiles in any positive sense.

If Satan the devil was the one who had slyly acted through the serpent, why then did the Genesis God refuse to punish him by placing a curse equally on his/her/it head? Possibly, to downgrade him/her/it to a crawling reptile just as he did to the serpent that was involved in committing the offence. Why was Satan not hanging forever on the Tree of Knowledge of Good and Evil, and equally eating dust everlastingly in that jungle called Eden, as punishment for his transgressions? Instead, the Christian God had allowed Satan to rove uninhibited between heaven and earth, as the untouchable culprit-at-large. Satan, in this particular circumstance, being the master planner of the transgression, should be culpable, exceedingly above every offender. If truly he was the actual entity that acted through the serpent, he equally ought to have received his own dosage of the divine curse as an accomplice, as moral justice and God's law demanded. Perhaps it would be reasonable to conclude that God did not know that the serpent's deceitful operation was another sneaky act of Satan's ploy to dethrone his government in the Garden of Eden and subsequently the entire world; hence his acquittal from the Garden of Eden's rebellion.

Assuming God did not know of Satan's coup d'état against his government on earth, as to execute his judgment upon Satan's head, how then did John know it in Revelation? I know that Biblical apologists would largely submit that John had received his intelligence report through divine inspiration that revealed the secret to him that Satan was the spirit who cunningly acted through the serpent to deceive Eve. Perhaps, John had also reasoned it out of his head that such insightful information might possibly not be accessible to the knowledge of an ordinary animal as the serpent, unless through the impious influence of Satan. Whether John had received and revealed his intelligence information through divine inspiration, or reasoned them out of his head; one particular piece of information that should be of great interest for the knowledge of man is the actual reason why God had not punished Satan for this offence, as he had accordingly done to Satan's partners in crime.

If Satan was a confirmed accomplice in this case, why then did God allow him to walk away scot-free, and not receive a dosage of his own punishment the same way as his partners in crime? Otherwise, would it not be sufficient to conclude that Satan was above the spiritual law; therefore the Christian God had peacefully allowed the devilish one to go scot-free, because he was weary of another spiritual heavyweight bout. Definitely, not after the fierce fighting, which John, the revelatory author of Revelation 12:7-9 has made the two omnipotent spirits to wage against each other previously in heaven like mortal men or wild beasts; where none of the two omnipotent heavyweights could out-rightly destroy each other in the heavenly insurgence. Only for John to reveal another exclusive scoop indicating the hurling of Satan directly down into our tiny earth, out of all the awesome space in the gigantic universe. If the story of this heavenly expulsion of Satan the devil to the earth were truthful, wouldn't this be another callous and unsympathetic action on the part of the Christian God to the creatures he allegedly made out of love in his own image? Which hoist the question once again, on why God did not hurl this devilish rabble-rouser to the lifeless and gigantic planet Jupiter, or to Pluto to freeze everlastingly in that region, or to roast forever in the scorching temperature of planet Mercury, instead of the very soil of this habitable planet earth that teems with innocent lives?

It may be possible that the Jewish and Christian God had subtly calculated his compassion towards Satan by accommodating him on planet earth, in order to afford him sufficient opportunity to stage a cunning coup d'état through the aid of the serpent, and topple his government here on earth. That the enfant terrible might provide the manufacturers of religion another terrifying means that supported the advancement of their religious trade on earth. However, the author of Revelation who perhaps might have been the promoter or referee of the heavenly bout has terribly failed to provide humanity with the actual reason why his God did not utterly crush Satan the devil in the celestial mutiny, alongside the failure of his God to punish Satan like other culprits in the Garden of Eden defiance.

Fine, I am not a religionist! Perhaps that possibly explains the reason why I still cannot discern to this day, any lie that the serpent had told in this circumstance. The serpent said to the woman, if she ate of the fruits of the 'Tree of Knowledge of Good and Evil,' her eyes would be opened and she would be like God, knowing good and evil, and it exactly turned out to be so. How does anyone call that naked fact a lie? For, the Genesis account truly confirmed this fact in the seventh verse of the third chapter, *"Then the eyes of both of them were opened, and they realized that they were naked; so they sewed fig leaves together and made coverings for themselves."* Then again, we read from the account in the 22nd verse of the third chapter where the Christian God also corroborated the serpent's declaration by saying, *"The man had now become like one of us, knowing good and evil."* Whence, then lays the lie?

The serpent also enlightened the woman that if she ate from the tree of knowledge of good and evil she would not surely die. As a result, the woman heeded the serpent's voice, ate of the forbidden fruit, and positively did not die. How does that constitute a lie? How should anyone consider a person who lived for nine hundred and thirty years, leaving behind numerous sons and daughters who continued to flourish unto this day, as having "positively died?" To the best of my little knowledge, the word 'positively die' in this context means 'absolute and total death.' If the story of their longevity is true, Adam and Eve, having lived for that long period of years on earth, had not positively died, as their genetic traits truly lives on in the life of their progenies that steadily carries the baton of living on their behalf on unto this day.

Very surely, the Holy Bible believers would argue on the premise that the woman and her husband had eventually died. However, I would also posit within that perspective that the eating of the forbidden fruit was not responsible for bringing eventual death upon Adam and Eve. Rather, it was the denial of them by the Genesis God to continue eating from the fruit of the Tree of Life in the Garden of Eden. According to the Genesis fairy tale, what guaranteed Adam and Eve their everlasting life was the periodical eating from the Tree of Life, as this was the only remedy for their eternal life? By implication, even if Adam and Eve had not eaten of the forbidden fruit, they would also have subsequently died, should they not continue to eat from the Tree of Life.

Agreed, if Adam and Eve did not succumb to the serpent's instigation, the Genesis God would not have driven them out of the Garden of Eden, so they would have continued to have access to the Tree of Life. However, the Biblical Adam and Eve, if at all they ever existed in history, would have been eternally useless in that jungle called 'Eden.' For, they would have wandered everlastingly amidst flowering shrubs in the garden all alone in total darkness, as their only way forward was solely dependent on the remedy, which the serpent had naturally prescribed for them, which denoted them to simply acquire knowledge. Because, without knowledge, they would never have understood the significance of the Tree of Life, just as they had never realized the worth of the Tree of knowledge. This possibly was the reason why they never achieved anything tangible during their tenancy in the Garden of Eden.

Therefore, as time goes by, they would have positively died, because they utterly lack the perceptive knowledge to discern good and evil, which also translates into lacking the knowledge to discern life and death. Subsequently, just as their divine licence to *"multiply and become many"* had practically expired and turned out useless in the Garden of Eden, because they lacked the expertise to obey the command of their God as to initiate the business of human reproduction; the purpose of the Tree of Life would most possibly have become useless in that Garden as far as it concerned the Genesis Adam and Eve. Besides, the serpent might turn around in that bush of Eden to deliver a deadly bite on Adam's heel and infect his blood strains with toxins and lethal fluids. In similar vein, a tiny anopheles mosquito could also have infected Eve's blood with the microbes of malaria fever. Alas, with the gullible Adam and Eve knowing not the value of the Tree of Life, because they utterly lacked insightful knowledge, much less knowing the prescription of exact remedy for their ailments as being enclosed in the Tree of Life, they would have positively died.

In fairness to the human race, the author of the absurd story that reported the 'Fall of Man' in Genesis had not told his story the proper way. The story should have been correctly captioned as the 'Rise of Man' instead of the 'Fall of Man.' And instead of depicting the serpent as a deceiver, he should have related his story the other way round; portraying serpent as the protagonist who guided Adam and Eve from gloom to self-aware consciousness; from obscurity into the brilliance of illumination; from the state of undress and nakedness to inventors that could instantly reason and sew fig leaves together to make coverings for their nudity. Instead of calumniating the serpent as being a stooge of Satan the devil who led the world astray, the manufacturer of the myth of Genesis should have told his story in the direction of denigrating and chastising their progenitors (Adam and Eve) for their naiveté and inability to do anything tangible in the Garden of Eden, prior to the serpent coming to their rescue.

How in Eden might Adam and Eve have possibly garnered the knowledge to bear children and become fully conscious of their existence, to be appreciative of their lives and stop living in obscurity as typical robots, if not for the data of knowledge they acquired through the serpent's aid? The natural information from the serpent to Adam through his wife, Eve, had progressively transformed their lives from being unwise morons into becoming vibrant progenitors of great inventors. Even religionists themselves are compulsive beneficiaries of several of these extraordinary proceeds and tremendous rewards that the entire human race has steadily enjoyed through ample inventions and technological progress that sprang from the serpent's emancipation of Adam and Eve. And this is an act they deceitfully castigate from the outset as misleading for the entire world (see Revelation 12:9).

One obvious reason why the Genesis account sounds too odd for belief is that the story is spurious and unreal. Even as a myth, legend, or fairy tale, it is most definite that the narrator of the 'Fall of Man' has not told his story suitably. As a true-life story having the inspiration of the creator of the universe, I am afraid the obvious is a resounding NO.

*****

"Is God willing to prevent evil, but not able? Then he is not omnipotent. Is he able, but not willing? Then he is malevolent. Is he both able and willing? Then whence cometh evil? Is he neither able nor willing? Then why call him God?"

- Epicurus

*****

Chapter

8

The Story of An Evil God

"I form the light, and create darkness: I make peace, and create evil:
I the LORD do all these things."
— God
As Quoted in Isaiah 45:7 (KJV)

People with pious reputations have constantly described the God they claim to serve in a number of ways that is excellent — holy, merciful, tolerant, compassionate, omnipotent, omniscient, omnibenevolent, and perfectly good. However, the opposite of this admirable description of the God of religion is what humans have repeatedly witnessed from true life incidents and familiarities in all ages. Constant evidence of evil on earth has, in effect, denounced the excellent portrayal of God that several attorneys of superstitions have represented to mankind as utter deception and downright fraud. Again, several verses in the 'Holy Bible' that is widely accepted as the *'word of God in print'* amongst people of the Christian faith, constantly relate direct contradiction to the excellent depiction of God that all those who pretend to hear his voice on earth have deceptively shoved down the throats of easy-to-fleece believers.

For example, the Jewish/Christian God reportedly proclaimed thus in the Bible book of Isaiah 45:7 (KJV) *"I form the light, and create darkness: I make peace, and create evil: I the LORD do all these things."* This alleged declaration of God, found in the book of Isaiah, implies the God of religion (if he exists) is solely the source of all evils that often inflict unutterable pain, despair, misery, unhappiness, and sorrow upon the lives of the earthlings.

It is pertinent to note that the prevalence of evil over and over again afflicts those who believe in the benevolence and infinite power of God, the same way it brings tribulations and sufferings upon nonbelievers the world over.

One-time in the past, year 2009 precisely, a South African news publication reported the story of a young woman who was abducted by a bunch of criminals on her way from prayer meeting. This woman was gang raped and tortured to horrid death, and her body was later dumped into a sewage gutter underneath a street corner in Soweto.

Two questions immediately came to mind after reading through the details of this sad story:

- Firstly, where was the *'God'* of this innocent believer at the time this horrific calamity struck?
- Secondly, what was the real meaning of the profound faith that this poor woman had throughout her life devoted to the service of a *'merciful,'* *'all-knowing'* and *'all-powerful'* God in absolute sincerity?

Of course, this young woman had a dream she faithfully believed was to shape her whole life for the better. She had a deep conviction to loyally serve a benevolent and merciful God, and experience the fullness of His divine grace. In order to fulfil her dream, she opted to live a life of a devout Christian, therefore revering God became her number one passion. Of course, her strong affection for God had on this fateful day influenced her resolve to head straight for prayer meeting after the close of the day's work. She could simply have opted to go watch TV in the comfort of her home and engage herself in a couple of domestic works. She could also have opted to go to a pub to have a few drinks as several other youngsters of her age would normally do, or go watch a movie in any of the nearby cinemas. But, as a true believer, the love she had for her *'merciful creator'* and the gospel of Christ was greater than any other thing in her life. She truly had a blazing desire to maintain a steadfast fellowship with her 'Almighty Father' — the 'personal God' with whom she longed for firm companionship and faithful attachment — and with whom she could commune in prayers to seek specially divine favour, care and support as a child of an all-powerful supernatural being she sincerely believed to be present everywhere, watching and guarding over her at all times. Sadly on her return from mid-week prayer service, she met her untimely death in the hands of inhuman tormentors.

Failures and disappointments emanating from tragedies of this nature normally constitute great upsets to the perception of every thoughtful person. Fatal incident of this kind usually opens the floodgate of critical queries concerning the character and true existence of the Christian God. It often fires up outburst of questions after questions: Is this God's plan? Is this the manifestation of one of the pre-ordained days, divinely written in the book of God? Psalm 139:16 (NIV) says, *"Your eyes saw my unformed body; all the days ordained for me were written in your book before one of them came to be."* Is this one of the days the Bible told us in the books of Psalms and Jeremiah that God had pre-planned for believers, even before they were born into this world? And, since 'God' personally declared to be the creator of evil in Isaiah 45:7 *"...I make peace and create evil; I, the LORD do all these things."* Is this tragedy, by the same token, another manifestation of the evils of the Christian God? Again, as Prophet Amos has bluntly affirmed in the third chapter of the book that bears his name, *"Shall a trumpet be blown in the city, and the people not be afraid? Shall there be evil in a city, and the LORD hath not done it?"* (Amos 3:6 KJV). In that case, is this tragedy another evil deed of the Christian God?

Imagine the unpleasant grief that overwhelmed this helpless woman as she suffered unbearable pains in the hands of cruel tormentors who took turns to gang-rape her. Think about all the anguish and sorrow she passed through when her rapists clubbed her to death and dragged her body inside the sewage drain. Where was her God at the time of this unpleasant incident? If this woman truly serve a God who is the Alpha and Omega, having infinite power and knowing everything from the beginning to the end, aren't there so many possibilities opened to God — her *omniscient,*

204 The Crisis of Religion

omnipotent, and *omnibenevolent* deity — in this situation that could have averted this horrific incident from taking place at all? Yet, the 'merciful God' of this faithful believer happily sat on his majestic throne with Jesus flanking him by the right hand side; the Holy Ghost to the left; along with great multitudes of angelic sons of God watching events unfold as criminals took turns to destroy the precious life of a devout worshipper who placed absolute trust in the Christian God as her *all-powerful, all-knowing, all-loving* and *almighty saviour.* Nonetheless, neither God, nor Jesus, nor the Holy Ghost, or any of the great multitude of angelic sons of God could be moved by the motive of sympathy to the grief of this innocent believer, until she gave up the ghost in horrific agony.

If 'God' is Omni everything, why in the first place did he not reveal the impending disaster to the church pastor or any of the prayer warrior in that prayer service, so as to completely overturn the ugly incident before it happened at all? Why did God unkindly ignore the prayers offered to him by the whole assembly of faithful worshippers on that fateful evening? Surely, the entire prayer warriors in that church would have collectively prayed for divine protection against evil for every member attending the prayer meeting. As usual, they would have invoked the blood of Jesus to cover every member of the congregation. Why then didn't God or Jesus heed that prayer? Why did God the Father, God the Son and God the Holy Ghost callously turn deaf ears to the cry of a conscientious and faithful worshipper in her time of distress? Why didn't God create a pillar of thick cloud to protect this young woman from being noticed by the gang of criminals, or send an angel with a sharp sword to scare off her tormentors? How should a 'loving God' allow such an undesirable and brutal suffering when *He* simply had all the spiritual and supernatural powers to prevent this hellish incident from happening at all? What manner of a 'loving God' would design such a hellish plan for his children? As Lin Yutang once wrote, *"All I know is that if God loves me only half as much as my mother does, he will not send me to hell."* Is the God of organized religion, in any sense, a loving God?

The valid rationale in this matter is that, throughout her lifetime, this innocent believer did not have the slightest idea that she had continually been deceived by charlatans of the Christian faith who pretend to be ordained 'oracles of God' on earth. She did not have the least clue that a bogus God who is the symbol of fraud and deceit in the confederation of organized religion had deceptively been imposed upon her consciousness as magnificent icon, worthy of submissive devotion. Little did she know that the all-powerful, all-knowing and merciful God, which the priesthood of her religion had cunningly programmed and embellished in her head is, indeed, a dummy God that *answereth* prayers only on MNET's 'African Magic Movies' channels and on the pages of that big, black book containing outrageous fallacies from cover to cover. But, very regrettably, she trustingly fell for the scam and swindle of self-styled prophets and professional preachers whose stock in trade is to preach outmoded theology of biblical Jews into the dull ears of others. They deceptively kept her mind extra busy by staging useless prayer meetings, now and again, in wasteful supplications to a God who is a full strength fiction — a literature God who is no different from any of African or Oriental idols, or Zeus and Kronos of ancient mythologies. There she innocently placed her entire trust for omnipotent protection that is next to utter illusion — a spiritual defence that never was. Thus, the 'Almighty God' she sincerely trusted as a 'personal saviour' who, by the assertion of her religious faith, is present in all corners of the universe, watching and guarding over her, was totally nowhere to be found when calamity struck. Thus, the merciful hands of her 'all-knowing' and 'all-powerful God' were too short to reach Soweto from his heavenly abode, because this 'saviour' is merely fictitious and unreal; and the stories surrounding his existence were nothing more than sheer imaginary tales by which imperialists of foreign lands had spread abroad to establish and impose their religious hegemony upon the lives of others.

If this God truly exists as the Alpha and Omega who knows all things, how then could he be so indifferent to the agonies of a helpless believer who was on her way home from rendering devoted prayer service to her loving and omnibenevolent creator? Why then was God dormant at a critical time that a faithful child was in desperate need of the saving hands of her supreme protector? Why should God turn blind eyes to the gruesome pain of a helpless child, and deaf ears to agonizing cry of a devoted worshipper? Instead of stretching out his powerful hands, the 'God' of organized religion has once again disappointed a faithful and discreet servant when she mostly needed the fullness of his saving grace at the point of gruesome torture and death. It's like when a vengeful despot revels at the execution of his evil decree: *"Unto the woman...I will greatly multiply thy sorrow... "Thou suffering thing! Knoweth ye not that thine grief and pain maketh my joyfulness and delight?"*

A man who is a loving father will not possess the power and ability to save his helpless child from horrid torture, extreme cruelty and brutal death, and chose instead to allow the child to be callously murdered in cold-blood at the hands of inhuman tormentors. It is very certain that people would banish such a man from the community or avoid him like an infectious disease. He would consequently be labelled as embodiment of evil on planet earth; hated and despised, denounced and condemned as an abomination even amongst his own people. But God, if he exists, has exactly made this cruel choice in the case of uncountable number of his faithful children across the globe. This, in fact, is only one of the overflowing examples of the cruel stories of the 'merciful God,' which humans have fashioned in their own image, and whose worth is the principal object of worship in their respective communities. In the words of Mark Twain, *"Our Bible reveals to us the character of our God with minute and remorseless exactness. It is the most damnatory biography that exists in print anywhere."*

If man is not a credulous animal that must believe something, simply because it seems the most unreasonable, how should any rational human being in his/her rightful senses expect any meaningful help from such a cruel character called 'God' in the Jewish Bible? Why should man persist in wasting his vital hours in fruitless prayer, invoking a phantom that is not only deaf and dumb, but utterly wicked? The key confirmation of what we can deduce from this whole saga is, *"If there are gods they certainly pay no attention to the affairs of man;"* so said Quintus Ennius, the man who is popularly regarded as the father of Roman Poetry.

No matter how unfortunate, anything goes in matters of religion and faith. It merely takes the trick of smart rationalization from theologians and priests to confuse and conciliate the dogmatists. The naive gravity with which dogmatic believers swallow every inconsistent rationalization from theologians is the most outlandish absurdity for any rational mind to ponder.

The most common excuse that theologians always offer to explain away the repeated failures of their God to specially provide believers a safe haven in this kind of tragic situation which they most frequently suffer like anyone else in the world, is the fantasy of eternal life. The sixth verse of the second chapter of the first book of Samuel says, *"The LORD brings death and makes alive"* (1Samuel 2:6 NIV). Dogmatic believers therefore hold the credulous belief in error that, even if their God brings tragic death upon their lives, he also has provided afterlife insurance policy to guarantee their resurrection to eternal life after death.

As Ernest Hemmingway has aptly observed, *"It's an incredible con job when you think about it, to believe something now in exchange for something after death. Even corporation with their reward system don't try to make it posthumous."*

Only the Sceptics truly know the extent to which the poison of insanity and injustice is deeply rooted in dogmatic faith. Otherwise, how else can any sensible person rationalise the notorious verdict that pronounced guilt upon humanity, against every principle of moral justice, for the sin they did not commit? How does any rational person justify the fictitious doctrine of afterlife which perforce eternal cohabitation with an evil God, whom the fifteenth chapter of Exodus proclaims in its third verse as *"a man of war"* (Exodus 15:3 KJV), and *"out of whose mouth proceedeth both evil and good"* (Lamentation 3:38 KJV).

The cruel character of God as portrayed in the Jewish Bible has, for all ages, posed a disturbing source of concern to the perception of several attentive Freethinkers. Helen H. Gardener expressly sounded an added alarm thus in her well-articulated view of the outrageous character of the biblical God:

> *There is no book which tells of a more infamous monster than the Old Testament, with its Jehovah of murder and cruelty and revenge, unless it be the New Testament, which arms its God with hell, and extends his outrages throughout all eternity.*

Normally people help people in times of trouble. Whenever we humans detect that other fellow humans are faced with troubles and tribulations in life, we frequently offer whatever assistance we can, to save the ugly situation. In several instances, I have witnessed other people going out of their ways to provide caring assistance to strangers, and even to animals in distress; especially when the problems are life threatening. In contrary manner, we have also witnessed the peak of man's inhumanity to humanity, where people have felt very much uncaring, like God in this case, to the distress and pain of others. How, then do we exactly make any disparity between the attributes of the God of religion and that of humans? This, of course, reveals the reality of Aristotle's observation that, *"Men create God after their own image, not only with regards to their form but with regards to their mode of life."*

The 121st chapter of Psalms gave false assurance to the believer thus in its 7th and 8th verses: *"The LORD shall preserve thee from all evil... The LORD shall preserve thy going out and thy coming in..."* (Psalms 121:7-8 KJV). The questions thus arise: if an '*omnipotent God*' to whom the deceased woman had just offered faithful worship could not preserve her '*going out*' to prayer meeting and '*coming in*' to her home unharmed, what then is the real meaning of her faith in a 'personal saviour' and 'God' who is utterly dormant? Why, on earth, would anybody want to worship a God who is a complete redundancy in their life and in times of trouble? What specifically is the difference between the idols of African deities — the statue of Isis, the bronze of Orunmila, Ngai, Chiuta, Obatala, Osanyin, etc., and the Jehovah of the Jews/Christians? If this God has neither the power nor the will to specially prevent the prevalence of evil and misery from afflicting the people that long for fellowship with him, why then do they worship him? How is it reasonable that people should continue calling him God? What manner of a 'God' is that? Why should this 'God,' in the first place, deserve our praise and worship?

According to Bertrand Russell, *"The whole conception of an omnipotent God, whom it is impious to criticize, could only have arisen under oriental despotisms where sovereigns, in spite of capricious cruelties, continued to enjoy the adulation of their slaves."* What peak of extreme delusion could be greater than this strange belief in a celestial tyrant who continued to enjoy adulations of his sheep-like flocks, even when it's as clear as the midday sun that he is not worthy of such adoration!

This whole incident presents two definite pictures to the perception of any thoughtful mind. The first picture portrays a bitter and cruel injustice of an evil God who is hell bent on fulfilling his iniquitous decree in Genesis 3:16, *"Unto the woman he said, I will greatly multiply thy sorrow;"* while he enjoys the sight of every wickedness that afflicts humanity as fulfilment of this sadistic decree. What manner of a 'God' is that? The other possible conclusion certainly boils down to the fact that this dormant God is plainly an imaginary, non-existent God. Why would anyone want to worship an imaginary God? How, then, is this God necessary in our life? Again, what is the distinction between the Christian God and all the redundant gods of antiquity? The answer again boils down to the disturbing disorder of living in fools' paradise without realizing it in actual sense.

The valid evidence of what we have always witnessed in the natural world indicates that tragic disasters have, without bias, afflicted both believers and non-believers, plainly on even scale, regardless of what one's theology or religious belief really is. No one will deny the fact that the God of religion does not specially avert natural disaster or tragedies from afflicting devout believers. Despite the fact that the large majority of human population obsessively believe in God, natural disasters still often smash the world with great wreckage, without considering whether its ruinous consequence affects 'God's children' or not.

When the tragedy of Hurricane Katrina struck the residents of New Orleans in America, it indiscriminately murdered several Idolaters,

Catholics, Baptists, Jehovah's Witnesses, Mormons, Pentecostals and Atheists, including Hindu, Buddhists, and Moslems in like manners. Such are examples of life shattering tragedies that recurrently afflict both the godly and ungodly all around the globe. The indiscriminate sufferings of evil by people of faith, despite their religious convictions and enormity of prayers, thus reveal one cogent evidence that the God of organised religion is imaginary and very much unnecessary in human life.

No one has been able to come up with any substantiation that God or any supernatural power beneath the earth or above the heavens has ever had the power to exclude or prohibit non-believers, as a consequence of their non-belief, from enjoying the fullness of nature's life. Whenever there's rainfall in any part of the world, it waters both the farmlands of believers and unbelievers alike. At any time the wind blows, it continually reaches far and wide from Soweto to Honolulu. It is not within the power of the God of organized religion to specially divert nature's wind for the benefit of dogmatic believers alone, leaving out Atheists and non-believers to suffocate and die out of the world. No, we have never heard of any God having such powers! It is therefore evident that every proceeding in this world has naturally happened the same way we would have expected life to come about if God does not exist.

The Fraud of Miracle Healing

My first encounter with failed miracle healers was in 1984. This was in one of Reinhard Bonnke's gospel crusades, held along the Oshodi/Apapa Expressway in the city of Lagos, Nigeria. I was then in my teen-age. At that time, my Mum was a devoted member of the *Deeper Life Bible Church*, a Lagos based evangelical ministry that organized the crusade in affiliation with the Evangelistic Ministry of Reinhard Bonnke. One of my Mum's beloved workers then was a woman we nick-named *'Mama Theresa.'* She too was a rigid *born-again* Christian, whom we cherished very much in our family.

When Mama Theresa got wind of Reinhard Bonnke's crusade, she promptly sent for her younger sister who had a seven or eight years old deaf and dumb daughter. They came all the way from Port Harcourt, a city about 800kms away from Lagos, so that Reinhard Bonnke could heal the little girl of her hearing and talking disability.

As planned, Mama Theresa's younger sister arrived Lagos with her little daughter the night preceding the crusade. When the hour had come, we drove together in my Mum's car to the venue of the crusade. On our way, I noticed great number of people with disability as they moved in droves to the crusade ground. We struggled to secure vantage spot, not very far from the main stage. There, also, I found large number of people with disability. I was very much eager to observe God's miracle — live and direct — for the first time in my life.

The program started with praise and worship songs. Thereafter, prayers commenced, and Reinhard Bonnke mounted the podium to deliver his powerful sermons. The next thing, a number of testimonies of miracle healings began to trickle in from those who claimed that God has touched them. Ushers intermittently interrupted the Evangelist's sermons to announce assortments of miracle healings, but none of the physically disabled people around our section had testified to divine encounter. No lame had jumped out of their wheelchairs or thrown aside their crutches. No blind men around us could still move from one place to another without their guides. Nonetheless, I strongly believed our own turn to witness the power of the Holy Ghost was just by the corner.

The hope was high… Perhaps, lame men and women around our section of the crusade ground would soon begin to stand on their feet. It's just a matter of time, I presumed. Our expectation to witness miracle healings from God was very high. I was particularly eager to see the little girl restored to sound health from her hearing and talking disability.

We fired up relentless rounds of prayers! Hours gone by, and nothing extraordinary had happened. But our trust in God was resolute and constant. Perhaps, the Holy Ghost would touch and transform the life of this little girl the next moment. Perhaps Jesus wanted more prayers from us. We sustained the intensity of our entreaties and intercessions on behalf of our little deaf and dumb baby from Port Harcourt. I eagerly wanted to see the power of the Holy Spirit at work. My Mum and several other prayer warriors around our surroundings were busy invoking the power of the Holy Spirit in the mighty name of Jesus. Kaleidoscope of prayers and supplications were raining cat and dog. Yet, nothing miraculous happened.

Hours later, the crusade ended, and we headed home exceedingly disappointed. I could see that the frustration from this spiritual let down wasn't a monopoly that devastated us alone. Great multitudes of devout participants were also nursing their own portion of disillusionment from Mr Bonnke's miracle shortfall. I expected to see a generous splash of miracle healings on a larger percentage of those with ailments that do not have medical cure, but that wasn't the case. As I looked over the heads of great multitudes of people with disability going back to their respective homes in the same condition they had come to the crusade ground, these questions then flashed across the back of my mind: Why did Reinhard Bonnke call great multitudes to a crusade when a little number of people (having ailments with medical solutions) would be lucky beneficiaries of his supernatural powers. Why should God subject all those with acute physical disability who critically needed miracle healings in their lives to such a big failure of hope? Why did God decide to heal those with ailments that have medical solutions — fibroid, typhoid fever, diabetes, high-blood pressure, cataracts, glaucoma, etc., but has refused to extend miracle healings to those disorders that transcend all medical remedies known to humankind?

I could not understand the logic. I, at once, suspected something wide off the mark was somehow amiss in this whole business of miracle healing. It is either there is a big fraud or deceit involved here or apparently there is no God.

For me, I can only accept any healing as miraculous when I see people with ailments with no medical solutions inexplicably restoring to normal conditions, especially in the case of our little deaf and dumb baby from Port Harcourt. Regrettably, this wasn't the case with the claims of miracle healings on Reinhard Bonnke's revival ground.

About a week after the crusade, I related the little girl's story to one of the district elders in my Mum's church, and enquired from him what could be the problem with her case. I wanted to know what the obstacle truly was that excluded the eight-year-old from receiving her own portion of divine healing — what actually went wrong? The response I got from the district elder was very disturbing. *"Perhaps the mother's faith wasn't strong enough,"* said the church elder. I right away pointed the fact to him that the poor Mum took the trouble to come all the way from Port Harcourt, some 800kms away. Therefore, the trouble of embarking on such a long-distant journey, solely for the purpose of receiving divine healing should stand as a good demonstration of faith. I also referred him to Jesus' promise in Matthew 17:20 (KJV) *"for verily I say unto you, if ye have faith as a grain of mustard seed...nothing shall be impossible unto you."* Then the district elder responded in a clever and more consoling manner: *"Maybe her appointed time has not yet come. It might be her turn next time."* I then had no choice but to agree with the wisdom with which the old man had handled the matter. According to Sir Francis Bacon, *"The general root of superstition is that men observe when things hit, and not when they miss, and commit to memory the one, and pass over the other."*

Similarly, in the first quarter of year 2008, the Christ Embassy Church emblazoned the South African media with intensive publicity blitz from all fronts — Radio jingles, TV promos, Newspaper adverts, Billboards, Posters, Flyers, etc. The paid adverts enjoined South Africans to attend *"A Night of Bliss"* with Pastor Chris. People with disability and other ailments were encouraged to come all out to Johannesburg Stadium to receive their miracle healings through the power of the Holy Ghost. Evangelists of the different chapels of Christ Embassy also embarked on personalized publicity for the crusade.

A day before the event, I drove all the way from Nelspruit in company of my ex-wife (then my wife) to Johannesburg — a distance of about 350kms. My ex-wife loved the 'word of God' so much, but my mission was to verify whether I could find anything different from what I have always observed from miracle workers since 1984.

On our arrival in Johannesburg, we headed straight to the home of our long standing family friends — Lungi and Bongani — the couple with whom we have made pre-arrangements for free accommodation. Our hosts introduced us to two other guests in the house, who also travelled all the way from East London, a city about 1,000kms away, to experience the *'Night of Bliss'* with Pastor Chris.

We exchanged pleasantries, and thereafter discussed general issues and some specific topics relating to faith and religion. It was during our discussions that one of the two ladies from East London shared the testimony of how the power of prayers had miraculously healed her of HIV/AIDS, whilst she was a patient at the Christ Embassy Healing School in Randburg. Lungi and her Hubby also substantiated her testimony and confirmed she, in fact, went to the healing school from their home. *"This woman was terribly sick, but now she's a living witness to God's miracle,"* Lungi joyfully proclaimed. To this testimony of amazing wonderment, we all gave glory to the power of God before retiring to bed.

Lungi gave us breakfast the following morning. It was whilst we were at the dining table that I noticed this woman, in reality, wasn't well. Her hand noticeably shook whenever she put food into her mouth. I found her composure not healthy enough, as I evidently could not observe any convincing indication of someone who is physically sound. She looked visibly frail. I actually wanted to advise her to seek supplementary medical attention, however I kept my suggestion and scepticism to myself. For, I truly know these words of Carl Sagan to be very accurate and truthful, *"You can't convince a believer of anything; for their belief is not based on evidence, it's based on a deep-seated need to believe."* I knew any advice at that moment would fall on deaf ears, especially when she passionately anticipated another round of divine encounter through her spiritual preceptor, currently in town.

Our host reminded us that we needed to get to the venue early enough to secure a seat. So, we hurriedly set out for Johannesburg Stadium at ten o'clock in the morning; although the event was scheduled to commence at 6:00pm. We journeyed to the venue in company of our new friends from East London. Getting inside the venue at 11:00am was a big mission; the queue was exceedingly long. It took another two hours for us to gain entrance into the stadium, as it was fully packed to capacity as early as nine o'clock in the morning.

While on our way to the venue, I rang a bell in my ex-wife's ear. I told her I've been conversant with this kind of event in Nigeria since 1984. I purposely turned her attention to the flood of people with disability who expected miraculous healings at the crusade. Great multitudes were on wheelchairs, others on crutches, while uncountable groups led their blind, deaf and dumb and ailing relatives to the show ground. I then sensitized her to take special note of how these great multitudes of people with disability would, after the crusade, be heading back to their respective homes in the same condition she is seeing them now. My ex-wife instantly became irritated with my comment; she sometimes doesn't like it when I bluntly voice out my atheistic opinions. So I quickly changed the topic to something else.

Eventually, we gained entrance into the venue and had a memorable 'Night of Bliss' with Pastor Chris. We worshipped and praised God in rock concert hymns and melodious songs of praise. He prayed for us and blessed us, but also collected lots and lots of money from us for doing so. We paid him generously through our big-hearted donations when the offering baskets were passed row by row through the great multitudes in attendance.

Well, the blissful crusade was over at the break of dawn. As we struggled to find our ways out of the venue at about 5.00am, I once again noticed the exact situation that had always been the case since 1984. The God of organized religion had done it again! I was afraid to call my ex-wife's attention to it this time around, but I could sense she actually noticed my prediction had, yet again, come to pass. Great multitudes of those who actually needed divine healings had once more been disappointed hopelessly. The disappointed were all trooping out in abject frustrations, going back to their respective homes in the same disabled condition in which they arrived the *Night of Bliss.* Nothing miraculous had happened in their lives. No changes at all could be observed in their physical disorders.

Then and there, the memory of the rationalization I received from the district elder in my Mum's church in 1984 ran across my mind once again. I recounted, perhaps it wasn't their time to receive divine healings this time around; there would always be another *Night of Bliss*. Perhaps, they've also enjoyed the benefit of spiritual transformation from the powerful '*word of God*' which Pastor Chris had ministered to them with great energy and dexterity. Perhaps that was their prime gain from the divine this time around, which actually could be worth the whole trouble. So, I quickly took a moment to ask some worshippers I came across on our way out of the revival venue to remind me what precisely the theme of the pastor's sermon was at the *Night of Bliss*. Alas, several of them did not remember it again! What a big surprise! Nearly all of these believers have forgotten the pastor's sermon the next moment.

The saddest part of this whole story is that about a month later, Lungi called my ex-wife from Johannesburg to relate the heart-breaking news to her that our friend from East London who claimed to have received miracle cure from HIV/AIDS was no more. Her death was particularly painful and devastating to me, especially when I did not have the opportunity again to advise her to seek proper medical attention, rather than persisting in misbelief that God will do it, or God has done it. This case is just one of the numerous examples of how the deceits of bogus miracle healers have brought several premature deaths upon millions of their credulous followers. Several people have died ahead of their time as a result of this false claim to miracle cure by a number of unscrupulous pastors.

Not too long after the *Night of Bliss*, a family friend to my ex-wife lost her life again, after she abandoned her medical treatments for false hope of miraculous restoration to health. She died shortly thereafter in a Bed and Breakfast Lodge near Randburg from where she commuted to this spiritual healing school. Isn't it better if she had died on a hospital bed or in the serenity of her beautiful home?

"Common sense is seeing things as they are, and doing things as they should be done." A pastor is not a doctor; neither is a hired store, converted into a church, a healthcare centre or surgery. Praying and fasting are no remedies to any sort of medical disorder. Depending upon the stage of the tumour or level of the CD4 count, cancer can be treated by chemotherapy, radiation therapy, surgery, etc., and HIV/AIDS can be successfully managed by medical practitioners for as long as possible. Prayers may only be of any kind of help to sick believers who endeavour to seek proper medical remedies in hospitals, not in churches or spiritual homes.

Fortunately for these miracle workers, dogmatic believers indeed do not observe things (when they miss) the way sceptics would critically do; otherwise, none of them would again take whichever advert for miracle healing in the least serious, let alone bothering their lives with the trouble of attending any of such deceitful events. Sadly, no believer ever sees it as fraud for a minister to run extensive advertisement for people to come and receive free miracles in stadiums, and in return ask for generous donations. According to Professor Daniel Dennett, *"Telling pious lies to trusting* (believers) *is a form of abuse, plain and simple. If quacks and Bunco artists can be convicted of fraud for selling worthless cures, why not clergy for making their living off unsupported claims of miracle cures and the efficacy of prayer?"*

Unfortunately, not a single dogmatist will ever ask a pastor what the need is to host a healing crusade in stadiums when only a handful of people among the whole lot of masses will routinely come up with unconfirmed testimonies of divine healing. No dogmatic believer will ever ask why a pastor from West Africa, who claims to have such an enormous healing power, will fly over the nations of Sierra Leone and Liberia where great number of amputees, closer to his home, suffer pains and starvations too awful for words to describe. And, instead of attending to their agonizing sufferings through his acclaimed supernatural power, the pastor will adorn a $5000 dollar suit and head straight to London, New York, Johannesburg, etc., to host healing crusades for people who live in privilege conditions.

No *born again* Christian ever sees it as complete fraud, let alone questioning the character of professional preachers who often sermonize that God wants believers to give 10% (in some cases up to 90%) of their income to the church, and if they don't, they can never prosper in life. Above all, God will haul all those who fail to pay their tithes into everlasting lake of fire. But if they regularly pay their tithes, only then will God answer their prayers and multiply them in millionth folds, and ultimately grant them rewards in heavenly paradise when they die. Hmm! *"Organized religion is like organized crime; it preys on peoples' weaknesses, generates huge profits for its operators, and is almost impossible to eradicate,"* so an anonymous author has aptly observed.

Unfortunately, countless heads today live their lives in false hope and delusion that God will do it for them, because of the helpless situation they find themselves. Several sick people cannot afford paying prohibitive medical bill, habitually charged for treatments by medical practitioners. In most cases, people cannot also afford paying for overpriced costs of pharmaceutical drugs. They, therefore, have no choice than resort to false hope and bogus spiritual healings for succour. Sadly, miracle healers find pleasure in preying on the weaknesses of this group of people instead of setting the record straight that their 'God' cannot do it.

In the last four centuries, the entire continent of Africa has been under the strong-grip of organized religions. From rulers in palaces to peasants in the village huts, nearly everybody from Cape to Cairo is religious. But in my keen study of the African situation, the evidence of a benevolent God is practically not present in any sensible reality from any perspective in the lives of Africans. What we really do have as a substitute for the munificence of God are clear evidence of ever-increasing sufferings, untold poverty, misery, and extreme ignorance. These are the pains that beset Africans through the last four hundred years of our fanatical adherents to the worship of foreign gods.

I really cannot understand why black people are still so exceptionally rapt in religious practices. Any reasonable nation of people would have discerned the nonexistence of a benevolent and all-knowing God from the proof of terrible adversities that, on daily basis, afflict the continent of

Africa, and draw accurate confirmation therein that all proceedings in the lives of their people have naturally happened the way they would have expected life to come about if God does not exist, and if no imaginary sky allies control people's lives from above.

It is extremely puzzling how my people have not exercise the aptness of reason at all with this strange belief system called 'faith.' This is one of the most baffling deficiencies afflicting black people throughout the length and breadth of the continent. Unreason faith conviction is a chronic disease that persistently breeds very awkward delusion for black people, both illiterates and intellectuals, to be contented with not understanding the life they live in. Even if we must engage in religious practices, our delusions do not have to be severely awkward to this extreme folly.

It is true that our former colonial masters who imposed these foreign religions upon us have also in the past undergone their own period of extreme delusion. Instances of religious conflicts and intolerance against thinkers were once rampant in their communities. Time was when they persecuted thinkers and scientists. Men of exceptional scholarly skill have been tied to the stake and burned alive in the Western world. The perfectly accurate scientific finding of Galileo that affirmed the planets revolved around the sun was branded by the Church as *"false and contrary to Scripture."* He was denounced as heretic by the Catholic Church and unfairly placed under house arrest, where this famous inventor of the astronomical telescope later died. But our colonial masters have now acquired new level of reality; and have genuinely modified their life in line with emerging facts from new information that is available to them. A rediscovery of the new world has truly helped their society to evolve out of the dogmas of cruel and oppressive organized religion.

In 1993 the Vatican officially recognized the validity of the work for which they have erroneously jailed Galileo. In so doing, the Catholic Church has thus set a true example of how to do away with static dogmas that lead to ignorance and extreme foolishness. Africans should also emulate this advantageous example, and cast off its obsessive attachment to any form of religious dogma that seeks to lead them into the path of ignorance and inert stupidity. This lovely piece extracted from Tim M. Berra's book, *Evolution and the Myth of Creationism: A Basic Guide to the Facts in the Evolution Debate,* provides us the best clue as to the place of religion in our modern civilization:

> *There is no place in our world for an ideology that seeks to close minds, force obedience, and return the world to a paradise that never was. Students should learn that the universe can be confronted and understood, that ideas and authority should be questioned, that an open mind is a good thing. Education does not exist to confirm people's superstitions, and children do not learn to think when they are fed only dogma.*

When God does not make any sense in our world anymore, we should be courageous enough to cast him off our shoulders, and let the superstitious God of savages rest in perfect peace. It should be morally prohibitive to teach illusions to our children in this modern age. We ought to do our utmost best to give our children up to date knowledge that is profoundly proportionate with intellectual faculty of modernity. Children should be taught the science of going to space and not the fantasy of going to imaginary heaven that does not exist anywhere in the cosmic space.

I strongly hold the conviction that the time has now come for people to wake up from the nightmare of core dogmas and begin to preach observable fact of our natural world, rather than irrational fancies of archaic system of theism. The human intellects have transcended far beyond the limitations of the Dark Age, that it now becomes an appalling sacrilege for us to continue to surrender our brilliant mental powers to the gloom of ignorance, calling it God.

Chapter
9
Alluring Mania

"Religion is probably, after sex, the second oldest resource which human beings have available to them for blowing their minds."

– Susan Sontag

Religion is an alluring mania that commands dominant authority in the society. Its fraternal embrace is so enticing that hardly anyone can resist the potency of the charms that draw great crowds to its rapturous devotions in record numbers. The sermons of divine protection and eternal life, along with the gospel of prosperity and godly bliss, loving mercy, compassion and benevolence are altogether the magnetic allure that make religious practices the most attractive societal obsessions of all times. Allied to this list of attractions is the ecstasy of praise and worship in rock concert hymns, which also constitute a captivating desire that exerts powerful magnetism on a vast number of followers of evangelical denominations of the Christian faith.

In religion resides the passion of admiration in which the fantasies of the collective minds of the mortals ever stimulate in overzealous worship of imaginary supernatural forces. Down the ages, belief in God and religious practices are very prevalent in the human world. The traits of our individual nature excite sentiments to devotional and ritualistic observances, far greater than all other things in the world. To our inherent emotions belongs the vast and impulsive evolution of religious practices in human culture, from which grows sectarian theologies and bigotry.

The question may be asked, if belief in God is so widespread in the tradition of humankind, does it not imply that something sensible and realistic is certainly behind its common affirmation in the society? The answer is a resounding NO...

Our amplified knowledge, through the ages, has evidently helped to expose the false certainty of religion to modern humans; together with how absurd and pointless the beliefs of the ancients really are concerning the vain adoration they obsessively devoted to all the gods of antiquity. We have seen how worthless the intense physical labour and devotion of our ancestors have turned out to become in building magnificent edifices such as the Great Pyramid, the Statue of Zeus in Olympia, as well as bravura Temples and shrines, erected in gold and marbles, in veneration of imaginary and unreal gods. We today know the fact too well that the intense manual labour and efforts invested in these projects are of no spiritual progress to modern day Egyptians, Romans, and Greeks, etc., as they have entirely turned their back on all of these ancient gods. It is therefore evident that widespread beliefs are necessarily not an indication of anything true and sensible or matter-of-fact in the society. As Anatole France has aptly noted, *"If fifty million people say a foolish thing, it is still a foolish thing."*

When God Becomes a Drug

Religion, as appropriately described by Karl Marx, *"...is the sigh of the oppressed creature, the heart of the heartless world, and the soul of the soulless conditions. It is the opium of the people."* The sense of satisfaction that religion brings into play in the mind of its faithful adherents is analogous to the fancied delusion that drug addicts derive in blowing their minds with narcotic substance. They do this in order to be high and happy, while out of touch with the reality of natural life.

Dependency on core dogma is sublime and most vital to every aspect of the believer's life. A new believer finds alluring mania within the fraternity of his religious sect, and succumbs to live angelic model of life according to the dictate and traditions of faith — what is permitted and forbidden in holy books. The artifice of his spiritual preceptors will accordingly program rigid belief systems into his head, and enact pious legislations to control every aspect of his life; much so that he is no longer able to stand on his own feet. There, his mental faculty is touched injuriously. In super-induced obsession, he is a new born bigot of the Holy Ghost — a conformist prisoner of conscience — under the toxin of religious addiction. He is *'born again'* in extreme delusion that places dogmas and creeds far above every other personal responsibility, as his religious sentiments take pre-eminence over all things. Then, the blindness of his intellect surrenders the entire workings of his life to spurious brain rewards, invoking a chant of placebo with no intrinsic remedial values.

The walls of his intellectual refuge are torn to shreds, and he is duty-bound to swallow whatever stupid story, because his faith has subjugated his ability to reason. He must be fearful of the mysteries of God that are beyond the comprehension of normal logic and evidence. The use of fear, guilt, and coercion actively becomes the trick by which his spiritual preceptors lead him by his nose and shove whatever stupid stories down his throat; in that he might be tamed continually in the path of stupidity. He must just believe or face the wraths of God, and be condemned to eternal damnation in hellfire. To the culpability of every transgression against pious legislations enacted in holy books, festered by fear of extreme penalty of everlasting torment in hellfire, belongs the authority and power of religion to rule over the life of every gullible believer.

Addiction can be described as a continued involvement in the use of substance, or taking part in certain activity despite its negative consequence. Spiritual obsession is, therefore, a form of first grade addiction that very much compares with the case of substance abusers and other form of addictive diseases (Arterburn and Felton, 2001). The relationship shows that pious devotees and substance abusers have commonly developed very eccentric and maladaptive behaviours that grow along the ladder of neurotic obsessions, escalating dreadfully into dangerous and extreme fanaticism. As a consequence, believers are mentally rapt, enthralled, and held spellbound to the point of uncontrollable surrender of their life to constant addictive syndrome that's outside the influence of chemicals — cracks, alcohol, cannabis, nicotine, morphine — into an absorbing state of compulsion and preoccupations that enslaves the strength and potency of their minds. Thus, the life of the believer is grossly dependent on intense longing and craving for intermediary agents — the phantom of God, core dogmas, neurotic prayers, miracles, bogus prophecies — in exact manners as substance abusers would compulsively depend on narcotic agents for brain rewards (Arterburn and Felton, 2001).

Emotional high often results in mood alteration that can on its own mutate into becoming severely addictive, even when no addictive substance is consumed. Medical scientists have established the fact that, in most cases, the body internally produces its own addictive chemicals in response to people's addictive behaviours. This explains why a lot of people become addicted to religious practices, sex, gambling, and several other addictive behaviours, even without the use of any narcotic substance.

Some researchers have used the terms spiritual and mental abuse to describe various characteristics of religious addiction. Psychologists believe that psycho-religious problem can be as diverse and complex as mental health problems. Scores of psychologists have offered varieties of definition for the concept of religious addiction.

Arterburn and Felton (2001) state that, *"When a person is excessively devoted to something or surrenders compulsively and habitually to something, that pathological and physiological dependency on a substance, relationship, or behaviour results in addiction."* This explanation clearly points to the fact that extreme and compulsive devotion to religion is certainly another form of addictive activity. Religion, therefore, is like other agents of social dysfunction — gambling, alcohol, narcotics, etc., that breed addictive diseases often injurious to partakers and the general public.

If any rational tourist should visit a country like Nigeria, my motherland; of course, the visitor will not be able to differentiate which one is the greater narcotic between religion and illicit drugs. The evils of religious conflict emanating from devout madness, sectarian intolerance, hates, the acts of killing in the name of God, along with inordinate proclivity for criminality are the realities that confront the so called people of God in a country of countless number of churches and mosques, holy sanctuaries and temples. The present day Nigeria, under the cartel of organized religion, is a nation where anyone cannot differentiate the least disparity between the characters of the godly and the ungodly.

Scholastic research in the area of spiritual abuse and addiction (Ronald Enroth, 1993) indicates that, *"Unlike physical abuse that often results in bruised bodies, spiritual and pastoral abuse leaves scars on the psyche and soul. It is inflicted by persons who are accorded respect and honour in our society by virtue of their role as religious leaders and models of spiritual authority."* Thus, at its extreme end, addictive diseases relating to religious obsessions have led to very dangerous fanaticism where inhuman hatred, murder, and every unspeakable act of cruelty under the guise of sacred articles of faith are altogether gratifying hobbies to fanatical 'men of God.'

Despite our increased level of literacy, what are the factors that compel otherwise intelligent people to succumb the power of their intellect to the belief of ancient narratives that cannot be substantiated by any reliable evidence? What are the aspects of religion that keep people in faith, even when their intellectual capability can discern the truth of the judicious criticisms that expose extraordinary claims of their respective holy books as fantastic exaggerations and downright fraud?

- Emotional highs from praise and worship elicit mood alteration and enslavement of the mind to depend foolishly on implausible influence of imaginary allies. Thus, fixated religiosity and rigid devotion to authorities, which are sacred in the imagination of men, become the nicotine that oddly stimulates a believer's gross addiction into believing incredible things that really do not exist.

- Allied to this notorious factor is early childhood indoctrination. A child is born, and long before he could either examine things or think wisely, his mind is already subjected to believing organized superstitions called the *'word of God in print'* as the ultimate truth. Thereby creating a compelling and dominant institution to propagate and defend bizarre, perverse, and unreasoned beliefs and traditions of their inherited religions. Professor Richard Dawkins scientifically explains the process of conveying customs and traditions from one generation to another through the concept of the "meme" which he introduced in his book (The Selfish Gene, 1976). The concept methodically analyses how memes function in several ways comparable to genes, which are biologically transmitted from the parent to the progeny through the process of natural selection. The concept further examines the commonplace where humans derive the imitative process and transmit ideas, values, beliefs, and practices to each other through repetitive procedures which are transferred to subsequent generations.

- Another of these infamous agents, liable for bonding societal loyalty to religion, is the general assistance of our institutions of learning which specialize from elementary level of education to tertiary education in raising gullible belief engines for different facets of religious sects; as well as training professional preachers in the proficiency of telling lies and preaching fallacious theologies to the dull ears of gullible congregations.

- Apostasy and non-belief in Islam are equal to treason, still to this day, punishable by death in many Islamic countries.

- The Jewish/Christian God is jealous, intolerant, and vengeful. *"Thou shalt have no other gods before me...for I the LORD thy God am a jealous God, visiting the iniquity of the fathers upon the children unto the third and fourth generation of them that hate me."* Exodus 20:1-5 (KJV).

- Our God and Allah will burn you for eternity if you reject the Bible or the Quran. To doubt or question the word of *God,* no matter how ridiculous it may seem, is infidelity. It is a felony to blaspheme the holy name of God. Heretics are legal outcast in the society; they are ostracized and detested. Atheists face social stigma and discrimination; they have been exiled, tortured, maimed, butchered, and burned to death. In this way, the fear petrifies from all fronts; thus, terrified and frightened people are left with no courage to stick to their own convictions, but to accept fictionalized narratives from on high, together with bogus promises of divine redemption and salvation by professing unreasonable faith in manmade gods, willy-nilly.

▪ Furthermore, societal dysfunction is a peculiar case in Africa that fosters extreme belief in god. The precarious level of the human suffering through poverty and diseases is unspeakable in Africa; therefore bogus hopes for heavenly deliverance from the claws of these untold hardships have thus become prevalent in our own part of the world. And, charlatans desiring to feed chunky and chubby on the labour of gullible seekers of falsified divine comfort accordingly took up the trade of preaching false theologies into the dull ears of others, to exploit their credulity.

As Delos B. McKown has accurately observed, *"The invisible and the non-existent look very much alike."* For those of us who hold Atheistic opinions, incredible priest-crafty and pastoral pretension to being oracle of an imaginary God is in grave conflict with our perceptive minds. And, pursuing rewards from imaginary allies in the sky is critically at discord with our considerate thoughts. Much as the big claim to fantastic solutions to people's problems through the efficacy of prayers and miraculous intervention from invisible power of the supernatural is to a large extent spurious to our understanding. Yet, these factors are the notorious agents liable for bonding societal adherence to religion.

The American Society of Addiction Medicine (ASAM, 2011) offers another excellent definition for addiction thus:

> *Addiction is a primary, chronic disease of brain reward, motivation, memory and related circuitry. Dysfunction in these circuits leads to characteristic biological, psychological, social and spiritual manifestations. This is*

reflected in the individual pursuing reward and/or relief by substance use and other behaviours. The addiction is characterized by impairment in behavioural control, craving, inability to consistently abstain, and diminished recognition of significant problems with one's behaviours and interpersonal relationships.

Dale S. Ryan and Jeff VanVonderen (2010) observe that excessive indulgence in religious practices is a symptom of chronic addiction that leads to cyclical exploitation and abuse (Preoccupation > Rituals > Using > Aftermath > Return to Preoccupation). Its characteristics are primarily not different to other addictive diseases such as gambling, smoking, alcohol and drug abuse, etc.

Addictive behaviour, especially in religion, is extremely neurotic, controlling, and regressive. It's a form of life that preponderates the indulger's mind in antiquated dogmas, swinging it out of control. Religious addiction is a life of ritualistic delusion that retards the mentality of the bigots to a cycle of creed outworn, bonded by belief system that is rooted in baseless absurdities. Thus, the believer's mind is always tied to inconsistent and contradictory theologies told from the mindset of primordial mythologists. Tribal version of events that are boorishly untrue and primarily outside the realms of intellectual convictions and value judgments are told and retold in the same cycle of technical theology into the ears of the believer by evangelical priests, propagandists, and professional preachers. Much so, that the story-telling accesses the devotee's mind overpoweringly that he no longer can stop hearing these tales, at least, every Friday or Sunday.

Scholars have established positive links between addictive behaviour and religious backgrounds — belief in God, church attendance, and prayers. The research of Duke (1964) found that church attendance indicated more sensitivity to the effects of a placebo. In a study of 50 alcoholics, it was found that those who were dependent on alcohol were more likely to have had a religious background (Walters, 1957).

True to character, dogmatic believers conduct themselves exactly as the herd of sheep which their 'holy books' precisely categorize them to be—extremely delusional and easily tamed. The personality traits of the religious addicts are remarkably characterized by self-absorbed vanity, deceit, and other traits of psycho-addictive disorder. Their tendency to act and behave in overtly submissive manner to controlled pattern of life best describes how terribly religious dogmas have impaired their willpower and astute self-control. The peculiarity of this excessive compliance, in faith-controlled mode, is strikingly analogous to the kind of impairments and ego depletion that narcotic substance have commonly inflicted upon the mental activities of its users or abusers.

COMPARISON BETWEEN RELIGIOUS AND SUBSTANCE ADDICTION

ALCOHOLIC	RELIGIOUS ADDICT
Mood alters up by drinking; mood alters down by not drinking or simply by thinking about the prospect of not drinking.	Mood alters up by behaving religiously; mood alters down when they don't or can't (attend church, read the Bible daily, pray enough, etc.)
Chooses to be with people who have a relationship with alcohol similar to their own; relationships with others become a casualty.	Chooses to be with people who have a religious belief system similar to their own, withdrawing from friends and even family members who don't.
Gravitates toward places that cater to, are sympathetic to, or even encourage using behaviour (e.g., the local bar).	Attends church and activities with people who believe the same or attends activities that are sponsored by like-minded groups and organizations.

Source: Spiritual Abuse Recovery Resource

It's exceedingly shocking how ignorant most religious people truly are concerning the theology their religion teaches them over and over again from childhood. Most believers have never once read their holy books independently on their own, much less detecting a range of bizarre contradictions contained therein. Multitude of dogmatic believers who call themselves *'born-again'* Christians (whatever that means) actually know a lot less about their Bible than many Atheists do; yet they proclaim themselves to be the most appropriate followers of Christ.

- How then can several hundred millions of poorly informed *born-again* Christians, who are totally oblivious of the spiritual rules and guidelines in their Bible, question church pastors when they abuse their authority?
- How will they know when their priests manipulate biblical injunctions to suit the figment of their ulterior motives and personal intentions?
- How can dogmatic believers, who prefer **not to think for themselves** unless their pastors do the thinking on their behalf, question the absence of financial accountability in the church, while the pastors live in affluence that's visibly beyond their financial means?
- How will any ignorant follower of Christ detect the cunning design that deceitfully equates questioning the wrongdoings of church pastors with questioning God?

In this exact manner too are drug addicts oblivious of the appalling conditions of their addictive life; they, as a result, cannot question drug dealers concerning quality control standards and appropriate pricing. Also in like manner that several gamblers are oblivious of the devious and manipulative programming systems that pre-set the operations of the gaming machines; let alone probing casino operators about hard-hitting and extreme cash-guzzling procedures it takes for pay-outs to be won.

This entire disorder in psycho-religious addiction, lamentably, boils down to the disturbing delusion of living in fools' paradise without realizing it. The terribly submissive manner with which dogmatic believers swallow absurd and silly misconducts of their leaders is a most disgusting reflection for any rational thinker to entertain in his/her sound mind.

Dale S. Ryan and Jeff VanVonderen (2010) emphatically articulate the blight of religious addiction thus in their skilfully written article, entitled, "When Religion Goes Bad," posted on Spiritual Abuse Recovery website:

A wide variety of religious behaviours have the potential for mood alteration and therefore the possibility of becoming addictive. Evangelism, worship, personal spiritual disciplines, church attendance, service, and many other behaviours that are important and praiseworthy in a general sense can be subverted by the addictive process into very harmful and destructive parts of our lives. This is an important point. Just because prayer is good does not mean that addictive prayer is good. Just because worship is good does not mean that addictive worship is good...even getting "addicted to Jesus" is not the solution to our problems with addiction.

Impressions of several dogmatists reportedly imply that their life would become extremely distressing, frustrating, deficient, and very much unbearable without the consolations they derive from religious practices. Much as this is true, the exact sense of consolation that religion brings into play in the mind of its adherents is merely a gratifying comfort in delusion. Only a neurotic addict would consciously choose to live in an imaginary paradise of the deceived and the swindled.

According to Buddha, *"Religion is a cow. It gives milk, but it also kicks."* It is true that different types of addictive activities, ranging from narcotic abuse to alcohol abuse, have provided illusory succour to those who indulge in such addictive conducts; however, the fact we ought to clearly recognize is that these fantasized consolations are borne out of impaired thoughts with which the addict fanatically engross him/herself.

Obsessive thoughts concerning addictive behaviour typically lead to a decreased functionality in rational thoughts, because the focal point is characterized by impairment of behavioural control — mood alteration, craving, dysfunctional brain reward, diminished recognition, and inability to consistently abstain from the cycle of the next '*fix*', irrespective of the grave consequence the present situation brings into bear (Enroth, 1993). The real consolation for the addict in this case is his/her unrivalled imprudence for shutting his/her eyes of reason to undeniable evidence of failures in his/her fanatical activities.

Howbeit, are dogmatists truly happier with compulsive indulgence in religious practices? The answer is no. This quote from George Bernard Shaw captures the state of extreme delusion in psycho-religious addiction very accurately:

> *The fact that a believer is happier than a sceptic is no more to the point than the fact that a drunken man is happier than a sober one.*

In the actual sense of it, dogmatic believers only live their life in fantasy. A great number of factors that educe happiness in human life are certainly not present in religious way of life, but in secular settings. According to the astute viewpoint of the fourth President of the United States of America, James Madison, *"Religious bondage shackles and debilitates the mind and unfits it for every noble enterprise."*

We truly know those things that bring about true happiness in life. We know that *two hands working can do far better than a thousand clasped in prayer.* We also know this practical philosophy from an anonymous author to be very much correct:

> *Give a man a fish and he will eat for a day; teach a man to fish and he will eat for a lifetime; give a man religion and he will die praying for a fish.*

The search for economic paradise in religion is therefore a worthless endeavour. Many of those things that genuinely provide happiness for majority of the people are in fact not available in temples or mosques, neither are they accessible in synagogues, shrines, and spiritual sanctuaries; but these things are practically obtainable only in the secular environment through every noble enterprise. People need good job, physical and mental health, love and affection, as well as enough to eat to be happy in life. Without these things people will certainly remain unhappy no matter their theology and enormity of prayers.

The Perfect Tool for Extortion and Mind Control

The gospel of prosperity and economic paradise are popular hub of sermons, especially in today's Christian church, where priests and professional preachers regularly deceive believers into giving out their hard earned monies to the church.

Indeed, God's ways are enigmatic and sphinx-like; miracles assuredly abound whenever the windows of heavens open its shower of blessings upon faithful sons and daughters of God. These are one of the several ways by which credulous devotees are frequently deceived that they will be rich if they make generous monetary contributions to their church.

It's incredible how the Christian religion has become a perfect tool for fraudulent practices all around the world. Who can imagine how retailing miraculous power of God can so easily turn good people into becoming fraudsters? As the Nobel Laureate in Physics, Steven Weinberg, once observed, *"Religion is an insult to human dignity. With or without it, you'd have good people doing good things and evil people doing bad things, but for good people to do bad things, it takes religion."* Hmm, this is so true!

I have over the years observed with keen interest how the manipulative tendencies of religion have very easily turned good people into doing bad things in the name of God. Years back, I listened on one of the state television channels, to the preaching of a very decent and highly regarded University lecturer turned General-Overseer of a mega Pentecostal church in Nigeria. During the course of the sermon, the preacher related what seemed to me a false testimony, which I considered to be a deceptive ruse to stir Nigerians into bringing generous fractions of their monies to the church where he is *General Overseer.*

The top preacher narrated the story of an unnamed American believer who gave a testimony in one of the crusades he held in United States, of how he (the unnamed business mogul) started doing business with a meagre $100, and five years down the line, became a multi-millionaire in the region of over US$100,000,000 (One hundred million US dollars). The preacher narrated that the American businessman allegedly ascribed his super accomplishments to the "faithful covenant he loyally put into practice with God."

As the story goes, this anonymous business magnet purportedly made a covenant with God to contribute 90% of his income as tithe, in return for divine blessings. The *General Overseer* narrated it on TV to several Nigerians that this anonymous businessperson thought it absurd for his "Heavenly Almighty Daddy" to receive a meagre 10% out of his monthly income, whilst he retains the lion share of 90%. Therefore, he faithfully restructured his monthly tithing contributions, out of his own volition, to a staggering 90%; an amount we were told on television, he religiously contributed to his church on monthly basis. The preacher concluded in his sermon that when the "widows of heaven opened," the unnamed businessman was richly blessed by God in millionth fold, beyond what he could ever imagine in his dreams.

I do not deny the possibility of such exceptional achievement happening in a country like Nigeria where trade manipulations, tax evasions, fraud and corrupt practices are exceedingly widespread; and where believers are so gullible as to bring 90% of their monthly income to the church; but certainly not in the United States where the faculty of reason is predominant. I have sampled opinions of some Americans business consultants about the possibility and truthfulness of this kind of story. Nearly everyone I consulted expressed scepticism as to how a $100 could miraculously multiply to over $100 million within a period of sixty months, especially when 90% of its accrued proceeds were allegedly committed into maintaining church pastors on monthly basis.

Hmm...God's way is indeed unfathomable! Majority of those that I consulted have commonly noted that taxation is compulsory in United States, and that business competitions are very much high throughout American states. They equally put the cost of sundry expenses for running the day to day affairs of this unknown business into critical considerations. Therefore, several of them concluded that the likelihood of this testimony being downright falsehood is exceedingly greater than the probability of its being anywhere close to the truth.

It has really been difficult for me to reconcile the integrity of this respectable General Overseer with what I suspect could possibly be his motive for narrating this incredible testimony to the Nigerian populace on Television, which apparently bears striking resemblance to the kind of deceptive ploy to prop up peoples' faith in baseless miracle stories.

Could it be true that the top preacher is innocent and, in truth, have no idea of the spiritually abusive conduct that consists in the use or misuse of false testimony to deceive people into bringing 90% of their hard earned monies to be redeemed into God's coffer in his church? I honestly find it hard to believe that, after his conversion to a religious professional, such a respectable and innocent looking scholar is not aware that his public conduct constitutes a scam and spiritual crime to the sacredness of humanity. It is thus on the account of this incident that I convincingly arrive at the conclusion that, "for good people to do bad things, it takes religion." This sharp observation of the Nobel Laureate, Steven Weinberg, is undoubtedly a categorical fact.

Observably, as the dubious practices of priests and prophets once existed in the days of old, thus too it fully lingers on, in active force unto this day. *"For from the least of them even unto the greatest of them every one is given to covetousness; and from the prophet even unto the priest every one dealeth falsely,"* Jeremiah 6:13-14 (KJV).

Regrettably, Nigerians have surrendered their capacities and abilities in a frightful way to fear, to such an extent that they have become victims of some confidence tricksters who deceive, disentitle and prey on our fears and frailties in 'gods' name (Fashola, 2016).

Majority of the professional preachers that emerged into the Nigerian religious sector in the last thirty years are undoubtedly gifted scammers who really possessed prolific salesmanship and matchless marketing skills in retailing (dogs as monkeys) to people of faith without much ado. Sadly, the bulk of credulous Africans still hold this invalid belief that the spirituals are actually the controllers of our material world. Therefore, they so gullibly believe the white lies of priests and professional preachers that the mystics and supernatural truly possess the key to miraculous riches on earth. This is the faulty tenet where the whole error of Africans' fanatical adherence to religious practices incredibly lies.

The truth is that, money and material riches are inventions and products of human civilization, not of God or any supernatural forces, as Fashola (2016) has aptly observed:

> *The teaching of science as espoused by Theodoropolous tells me that money is a product of man and not a product of God. It is manufactured in a place called a Mint, by a process of printing, using special paper, ink, engravement and embossment, to make it difficult to fake or counterfeit ... Yes, God is a miracle worker. I believe, but he is not an unjust God who rewards those who make no effort at the expense of those who do... I once listened to a sermon broadcast on television, asking people who are indebted to step forward for prayers that will make their debts disappear. It frightens me. It does not make sense to me... Debts are accounting, matters of credits and deficits. They do not vanish. It is people who live in FEAR who fall prey to such teachings and become victims of misery from poor choices...If we pursue our choices with as much conviction as we pursue our faith, we will certainly be a more prosperous society.*

As a matter of fact, religion represents different things to various categories of people in the world. To the charlatans and the con artists, it is a trap for fools and a perfect tool for feeding chunky and chubby under false pretences. To the common herds, religion is just the right thing that presents illusory succour and false hope for blowing their minds, so as to be able to cope with frequent problems afflicting their everyday lives.

Anything goes in the name of God in today's Christian church, so long as it generates optimal financial returns. Adherent to Christ's spiritual instructions is no longer critical, as avarice of priests and prophets adorns the church with the money of thieves.

The biblical creed of *"seek ye first the kingdom of God, and his righteousness, and all these things shall be added unto you"* (Matthew

6:33 KJV) appeals to no preachers and devotees anymore. *"A wonderful and horrible thing is committed in the land; the prophets prophesy falsely, and the priests bear rule by their means; and my people love to have it so"* Jeremiah 5:30-31 (KJV).

Every profane and worldly attraction has been incorporated into church activities to win as many financial donors as possible. Thomas Paine (1794) in his observation of the Christian church aptly echoed this viewpoint in his book, The Age of Reason:

> *The church has set up a system of religion very contradictory to the character of the person whose name it bears. It has set up a religion of pomp and of revenue, in pretended imitation of a person whose life was humility and poverty.*

Mahatma Ghandi also echoed similar viewpoint to that of Thomas Paine in his observation of the Christian church, *"I like your Christ; I do not like your Christians. Your Christians are so unlike your Christ."*

Through the ages, societal dysfunction has led vast number of people into professing untrue faith in God. The fact shows that uncountable number of dogmatic believers have always resorted to religious practices whenever they are faced with grave adversities — poverty, sickness, misery, destitution, bereavement, lack of money, drug or gambling addiction, job loss, etc. Details of the facts clearly provide undeniable evidence that religion is entirely **incompatible** with the basic aspirations of a refined civil society, as every indication validates the reality that faith is not in any sense objective.

The bully of dreadful conditions in the society recognizably remains the notorious agent that recruits majority of converts into dogmatic faith. How strange indeed that every weak mind must be bullied by appalling conditions for the tyranny of religion to reign supreme over all lands!

The country of Nigeria is world's leading example of how societal dysfunction has led the masses into false belief in God; and how in return, fanatical religious way of life has led to chronic societal dysfunction. Indicators of how societal dysfunction has fostered belief in God could be best seen in the upsurge of daily filings for church registration in Nigeria since the collapse of the country's mainstream economy in the 1980s.

Nigeria is today the most religious country in the world. One report indicates the country has the largest number of Christian churches in the history of human civilization. Today's Nigeria is a country where industries and manufacturing plants are rapidly shutting down, only for those premises and plants to be converted into Christian churches, as if prayer and fasting are of any viable solution to the nation's ailing economy. What a detrimental way for a country to lose headway in the 21st century civilization!

In fact, inclinations of majority of Nigerians now tend towards church operation rather than corporation and business enterprises that can offer professional expertise in transforming their ill nation from a backward country, where all basic amenities have seized to work since the 1980s, into an ideal state where all social facilities and industries efficiently function in perfect state of affairs. Today's Nigeria is a country where presidents and rulers usually prostrate before celebrated '*men of God*' who cannot point to any meaningful development that their unrelenting prayers, revival service, evangelical crusades, and spiritual entreaties have caused into effect in the lives of their people and the progress of the entire nation since the last thirty years of unrivalled boom in their religious trades in the country.

Any tourist who has been to Nigeria in early 1960s up to early 1980s, and again pays another visit to the country in the 2000 millennium cannot help but notice how intolerably the country has idled and decayed into abject poverty in the midst of countless churches and mosques and great multitude of priests and false prophets.

The visitor's candid enquiry will certainly throw him into a state of bafflement as to why these remarkably poor masses of Nigeria are so compulsively devoted to religious practices, even when it's next to impossible to see the proof of God's benevolence in every facet of their daily living. The visitor will definitely be keen to know what exactly is liable for Nigerians obsessive devotion to God, when the vast majority of these devotees who live on less than a dollar a day are not even sure of their next meals. Surely, the tourist will be puzzled, beyond words, amidst visible evidence of collective underdevelopment and poverty as to why Nigerians are building churches rather than factories and industries; as well as why they fanatically adore a God who blatantly has failed to help them out of their extreme poverty and wretched conditions. The visitor's rational reflection will only lead to one valid conclusion: *the more ignorant the believer, the greater his God,* as Charles Bradlaugh has very correctly observed.

This sensible conclusion will further shed light on the piece of evidence that fanatical devotion of Nigerians to the worship of a perverse, blind, and deaf phantom that cannot help them out of their woes, is purely the outcome of incredible con job of their false prophets and priests who regrettably have captured the control of a vast population of ignorant nation of people, whose faculty of reason is appallingly upside down.

This excerpt from *'Bertrand Russell Speaks His Mind,'* very meaningfully captures the subjective nature of faith and the principle of causality in relations to religion and societal dysfunction:

> *I think that if there go on being great wars and great oppressions and many people leading very unhappy lives, probably religion will go on, because I've observed that the belief in the goodness of God is inversely proportional to the evidence. When there's no evidence for it at all, people believe it, and when things are going well and you might believe it, they don't. So I think that if people solve their social problems religion will die out.*

In the immortal words of Charles Bradlaugh, *"The more ignorant the Theist, the greater his God."* Undeniably, belief in God is a neurosis that's very widespread amongst communities of badly informed people. Religion is the most terrible infection ever to infest the rational mentality of humankind. It's a con trade that thrives solely on inherent imbecility of human nature, rather than the hub of mankind's intellectual ability.

*****

"The church hates a thinker
precisely for the same reason a
robber dislikes a sheriff, or a thief
despises the prosecuting witness.
Tyranny likes courtiers, flatterers,
followers, fawners, and
superstition wants believers,
disciples, zealots, hypocrites, and
subscribers."

– Robert G. Ingersoll
*****

Chapter

10

Bogus Doctrines of Afterlife

"I see only with deep regret that God punishes so many of His children for their numerous stupidities, for which only He Himself can be held."

– Albert Einstein

THE DOCTRINE OF AFTERLIFE is a widely accepted dogma in all dominant religions of the world. Reincarnation and resurrection, or as the case may be, the tenet of life after life or life after death is central and deep-rooted in the beliefs of all major religions.

Some religions simply describe reincarnation as a rebirth of the soul in another body. That is, the conviction that after the death of a particular person, the soul departs from the physical body, and is thereafter reborn in another body (in another life) several times without the need to face the final judgment. This is either as a way of reward or punishment for previous life deeds, through the actions of what they refer to as the 'Law of Karma.'

Other religions that profess their beliefs in resurrection plainly define it as the act of rising from the dead. This is the belief that after the death of a particular person, the soul and the physical body of the dead shall rise again at God's appointed time to face final judgment. This is the ultimate sentence whereby the resurrected dead would either suffer eternal pain in hellfire, or reap eternal reward in a paradisiacal heaven, depending on the previous life deeds of the dead person.

From the eye of a sceptic, these two very popular religious doctrines (reincarnation and resurrection) point to one central tenet — man's utmost desire for eternal life. Surely, no man wants to die, but as the mandatory reality dawns on humankind that death is an inevitable adversary to his life — the grim finality that willy-nilly delivers the ultimate end to his earthly existence — it therefore becomes imperative for the human race to design eternal survival for themselves in another world through death. It is upon this desirable inclination to live forever that the architects of religion have erected the very foundation of their implausible doctrine of reincarnation and resurrection. They have subtly employed these doctrines as a means necessary for their evil tendencies to control the destiny of mankind beyond this worldly life unto eternity.

The doctrines of reincarnation and resurrection are two of the world's greatest religious riddles that constantly collide with each other in a state of maximum absurdity. The underlying principles of their respective teachings are extremely repugnant to reason than logic and common sense could ever comprehend in its analytical tangibility.

- What is a soul?
- How does the belief in an immortal 'soul' come into the human way of life?
- Are human and animal souls ever in existence prior to earthly embodiment?

Some schools of thought believe that 'soul' is the central life force of human and animal — the biological mechanism that activates their blood circulatory systems and the mental senses to understand and to engage in various life activities. While, on the other hand, sceptics consider the 'soul' as merely a figment of man's imagination of something spiritual that inhabits the body and acts through it.

Firstly, the various religious scriptures that pioneered the idea of a separate and immortal soul to humans have fallen short in their numerous teachings to elucidate in comprehensible and logical details, how their so-called 'soul' or 'consciousness of existence' deferred from our vital life force. Nowhere within the passages of their sacred books could anyone practically read between the lines, any sensible and realistic difference between this imaginary 'soul' and those biological mechanisms that activate the human nervous systems, thoughts, understandings, consciousness, and liveliness.

The various sacred scriptures (Bhagavad-Gita, Holy Bible, Holy Koran, including the Yoruba Odu Ifa and Opele, etc.,) that told us of the concept of afterlife, did not describe in clear terms, how exactly the 'soul' interacts with the physical body, and its influence on man's everyday life. The only clever thing these sacred books and their various apostles have done was to mystify the description of soul as an *"immortal spirit or the conscious aware self that survives the death of the material body."* Of course, their various illustrations have totally failed to explain anything cogent to the human understanding.

If an institution claims to be an electric bulb producer, but on the contrary cannot prove its ability to produce any electric bulb on the realistic field of performance; by implication, what else is left of that institution, except to list that institution in the category of charlatans and deceivers?

Secondly, many religions that informed us of the doctrine of afterlife, under the pretence of divine revelation, also have informed humans of several other misleading doctrines under the same pretence of holy inspiration, revelation, and prophecies. A lot of these, I have exposed in earlier chapters as utter suppositions, outright fallacies, and deceptive notions. How then should we again trust these religions when they brandish their sacred books, and preach from therein, such doctrines as life after death? This is a notion that no one can experimentally confirm simply by taking a trip to the great beyond to conduct realistic research into its truth, and returning to earth with reports of empirical findings. Religion manufacturers are cognizant of the fact that going to 'heaven' is not like taking a holiday or business trip to Tokyo, London, or New York. No one ever comes back to the earth from any 'heavenly' trip with report that exposes the falsehood of these bogus religious doctrines. In our lifelong experience and knowledge of the ever-consistent law of nature, has anyone ever seen any dead person coming to life again? Of course, the dead are never known to live again! As a result of this plain fact, humankind has no cogent means under the umbrella of empiricism to verify the truthfulness of life after death (the tenets of reincarnation and resurrection) as taught by all religions of our world to their followers.

Many of the world's popular religions have chiefly defined 'soul' as the self-awareness or the self-consciousness, distinctive to every individual. Their various teachings relate that the soul is peculiarly separate from the body, and transcends the death of the physical body (Swami Prabhupāda, 1982). However, these religions have never told us, in clear terms, how our soul differs distinctively from our active life force, and how it interrelates with our physical body, detached away from the biological life-spark that animates the body and differentiates animal life from stones and other non-living things.

The American Heritage dictionary of the English Language, fourth edition, defines 'soul' as:

> *The animating and vital principle in humans, credited with the faculties of thoughts, actions, and emotions and often conceived as an immortal entity.*

From spiritual indicate, the same dictionary also defined soul as:

> *The spiritual nature of humans, regarded as immortality, separate from the body at death.*

Comparing these two definitions of 'soul' that the American Heritage dictionary had given, one would find logical and coherent meaning, synonymous with the principle of vitality – that biological mechanism that activates the human nervous system – in the secular definition. On the other hand, the spiritual definition remains hollow, pointless, and fraught with imprecise meaning that does not practically explain the principles of active vitality, which is a typical portrayal of the absurdity of religion that customarily veils the reality of life in spoof and parody.

Many religions are of the belief that their God accordingly formed each individual soul directly at conception. While some religions, on the other hand, believed that the soul pre-existed prior to the moment of conception. A religion such as Traducianism holds the belief that the soul comes from the parents through the process they usually refer to as

Natural Generation. Admittedly, the doctrine of afterlife and immortality of the soul are very widespread and deep-rooted in all known religions of the world, including paganism and idolatry.

For Dust Thou Art

Turning the focus of analysis to the Biblical account of creation that the Jewish and Christian scriptures offered to us (that is if we can believe the story). The book of Genesis reported that God created the first man, Adam, out of the dust of the earth, and respired the *"breathe of life"* into his nostrils, and Adam became a *"living soul"* (Genesis 2:7). Before the creation of Adam from the dust of the earth, there existed no Adam anyplace, in any form; be it in spirit soul above the heavens or beneath the seas, or in any pre-human existence whatsoever. Likewise, Eve had no existence in any pre-human being.

The book of Genesis says, *"Adam became a living soul,"* that is, Adam came into living existence after God had formed him and respired the "breathe of life" into his nostrils, meaning that the physical formation of Adam from the dust, and God's breathe of life into his nostrils made him a living soul. Besides, Eve also came into existence after the God of Genesis formed her from the ribs of Adam. Furthermore, all of Adam and Eve's offspring came into way of life as 'living souls' through the divine reproductive design and capability that the creator had endowed upon the first human couple, which might possibly be what Traducianism always referred to as the process of Natural Generation.

Admittedly, Cain and Abel and all of Adam's offspring were all in a state of non-existence prior to Adam 'knowing' of his wife. *"And, Adam knows Eve, his wife, and she conceived, and bare Cain"* (Genesis 4:1 KJV). Therefore, the product of Adam 'knowing' his wife was Cain, thereafter, Abel, Seth, and so on. On the contrary, if Adam had not 'known' his wife, Cain and Abel, including all humans that have reportedly descended from their lineage would definitely not have whichever existence on earth; is that not so? What chance would be in there for this so-called 'soul' if successive human and animal generations have not derived their existence through the process of Natural Generation? It consequently means the presumed soul would also have no existence. Is this fact, therefore, not an indication that this religious imaginary soul is actually our active life force?

The Bible did not indicate in any of its numerous passages that Adam and Eve and all of their offspring formerly had pre-human existence as 'souls' or 'spirits' in heaven or anywhere in the extra-terrestrials, which the supposed creator had commandeered into existence through their bodies on earth. Nowhere in the entire passages of the Bible was it written that God created the first human couple, purely by transferring pre-existing souls from heaven into their bodies. Even nature's law and science did not support the notion of pre-human existence, as all succeeding human and animal life have indeed derived their existence through the result of sexual intercourse – the natural reproductive device.

According to biblical account, Adam and Eve were created out of dust, while the breath of God reportedly made them a living soul or a living being. Therefore, all of Eve's offspring have truly come into existence as a result of the fixed (Natural Generation) that comes about through the reproductive system of cohabitation between a man and a woman. This is the wonderful design that Mother Nature had provided in support of steady reproduction, so that humankind may multiply and replenish the earth ad infinitum.

The questions that here arise for the attention of those apologists of reincarnation is this:

- Before the first human death on earth, whose souls had then reincarnated in Cain and Abel, and other children of Adam and Eve? Since the Bible affirmed that Adam and Eve gave birth to other sons and daughters (Genesis 5:4).

- Assuming that after the death of Abel, his soul had reincarnated in the body of Seth or one of his siblings, where then did the other sons and daughters of Adam acquire the souls that inhabited their own bodies and acted through them? Except that we might possibly fancy consigning this case to utter assumption, and surmise that God had specially created souls for the bodies of the first sets of human generation before the advent of death into their lives. How then would the ground of assumption be a reliable precept for a true religious belief? Moreover, this assumption would then call to question, the inherent life force that Mother Nature had fixed into the biological mechanisms of the human body, which distinctively separates the living from non-living.

Nonetheless, the ground on which the religion of Christianity had erected their belief in pre-human existence is the expression found in the book of Jeremiah 1:4-5. The New International Version reads,

The word of the Lord came to me, saying, before I formed you in the womb I knew you, before you were born I set you apart; I appointed you as a prophet to the nation.

By now, readers should have known a little bit of the character of Jeremiah, the purported author of these biblical verses; that he actually was not a genuine prophet of God, but a questionable schemer and double agent, who took the trade of prophesying as a lucrative business for amassing wealth and royal favours that go well with his personal interest. One or two of his false prophecies I have earlier exposed in previous chapter under the subheading, *Biblical Fraud Prophecies*. Furthermore, I will like to recommend that readers learn more about the double-faced character of this lying prophet in chapters 18:5-10; 37:11-15; 38:14-28; 39:11-12 of the book that bears his name. If possible, read the entire book of Jeremiah.

At death, the Bible affirmed Adam had simply returned to his former state of non-existence before his creation from the dust of the earth. *"For dust thou art, and unto dust shalt thou return"* (Genesis 3:19 KJV). At the time the Genesis God pronounced the death decree upon Adam, he never promulgated, 'for soul thou art, and unto soul shalt thou return' for a reborn of another parent, in another body of thy offspring, either in Japan as Yokohama Suzuki, or in Scotland as Donald Brown. Neither did God decree the soul of Eve for numerous rebirths in another body in Soweto as Zibuyile Komape, nor in Las Vegas as Hillary Rice; either to suffer for the

248 The Crisis of Religion

sins of their disobedience to God in the Garden of Eden, or to reap the reward of their past life deeds in the bodies of their progeny.

When the first human couple disobeyed God's order, the Bible clearly detailed the punishments that God delivered upon them as retribution for their sin in the third chapter of Genesis 3:16-19. However, the penalties did not include any such thing as reincarnation in the physical bodies of others, or resurrection to final judgment in eternal paradise or eternal hellfire. Therefore, the foundation upon which all the dominant religions of this world had deviously developed and erected their bogus doctrines of life after death clearly remained the tyrannical tenacity of religion rulers to punish man beyond this world, as a means of enslaving his sense of right and wrong into eternity. The judgment of the Biblical God upon Adam and Eve did not include such pugnacity of vindictive cruelty to punish man unto eternity; however, the verdict was quite clear and definite in its ruling, *"For dust thou art, and unto dust shalt thou return."* This simply meant that Adam and Eve were nothing but the dust of the earth before their existence, and unto nothing but the dust of the earth they should return at death.

Furthermore, the Genesis creation account told the story (if the account is also true) that in the beginning, God's original purpose for man was to live eternally on earth without dying, hence the divine provision for the 'Tree of Life' in the Garden of Eden. This purpose had allegedly derailed, because the serpent purportedly deceived Adam and Eve into disobeying God by eating from the forbidden fruit of the Tree of Knowledge of Good and Evil, thus the advent of death into the human world.

From the details of this account in Genesis, it would be right to conclude that reincarnation and resurrection were never part of the Biblical God's original purpose for humankind. Of what use would they stand for, if the human destiny is everlasting life on earth? None, my readers would agree.

Now that there is death in man's life, does it therefore mean that the soul or vital life force of the dead are then reborn in other peoples' physical bodies—born of other parents in some strange lands—according to the teachings of reincarnation? Alternately, has the soul or active life force of the dead practically expired, and therefore at rest in their various graves? Otherwise, are these souls hovering around somewhere unknown to the knowledge of man in the extra-terrestrials, while waiting the *"final sound of the trumpet"* to re-unite with their former physical skeletons in the graves for revitalization into eternal life or eternal damnation, according to the doctrine of resurrection? At death, do we simply return to our former state of non-existence just like Adam, according to Genesis 3:19?

Before giving any answer to these questions, it is reasonable that we consider some illustrations that relate to the doctrines of reincarnation and resurrection as propounded by the apostles of both canons.

The Judas Iscariot's Reincarnate

Several years ago, a very close friend of mine, who is an ardent believer in the doctrine of reincarnation narrated an illustration in the direction to establish and clarify the morality that associates with the imperative of reincarnation, under the actions of the Law of Karma — what you sow is what you reap.

My friend bluntly affirmed in his illustration that Adolf Hitler was, as a matter of fact, Judas Iscariot's reincarnate. He offered some explanations from the 27th chapter of the Bible book of Matthew in support of his illustration. The summary of his story goes thus:

After Judas had betrayed Jesus, and the Jewish order of priesthood arraigned the Christian Messiah before Pontius Pilate for trial. Following the trial session in which Pilate was unable to find Jesus guilty of the flimsy accusation preferred against him:

> He (Pilate) took water and washed his hands before the multitude, saying; I am innocent of the blood of this just person, see ye to it. Then all the people answered and said His blood is on us, and on our children (Matthew 27:24-25 KJV). Then Judas, which had betrayed him, when he saw that he was condemned, repented himself, and

> *brought back again the thirty pieces of silver to the chief priests and elders; saying, I have sinned in that I have betrayed the innocent blood. And they said what is that to us? See thou to that. And he cast down the pieces of silver in the temple, and departed, and went and hanged himself Matthew 27:3-5 (KJV).*

In rendering his illustration, my friend declared that the irrevocable justice of the Law of Karma is inescapable, unavoidable, and very certainly to happen. He affirmed that it is only when a person's soul had attained liberation through the process of reincarnation in several circles of life, and the soul had fully paid all karmic debts that stemmed from previous life deeds; just then could such a soul attain freedom from the grim inevitability of the law of karma.

Furthermore, he strongly established in his explanation that Judas had certainly reincarnated in another life as Adolf Hitler, to ask for vengeance from the Jews with the same anger and fury with which he had committed suicide after he realised that the Jewish religious leaders had tricked him into betraying his master for crucifixion.

My friend provided further illustration that the curse, which the Jewish people had spiritually invoked upon themselves when they proclaimed, *"His blood be on us, and on our children,"* was another overhanging action of retribution that the inexorable Law of Karma would certainly execute in its appointed time. Finally, he recounted that the several millions of innocent lives that the Jews had unjustly slaughtered in scores of their unrelenting Old Testament wars were also another impending actions of retribution that the Law of Karma would unavoidably recompense.

This ardent advocate of reincarnation asserted that at God's appointed time and hour, the 20th day of April 1889; about one thousand, eight hundred and fifty six years later at the little town of Braunau Ann Inn, Austria, the soul of Judas Iscariot reincarnated with the anger and fury of 33CE. Fuming profusely in great wrath and vehemence, the spirit of Judas Iscariot, the fallen Apostle of Christ, rematerialized again in another body of baby Adolf to ask for the innocent blood of his unjustly crucified master, Jesus Christ, from the heads of the Jews and their children. The results, he said, were the torturous executions of about six million Jews within a period of six years in the hands of Adolf Hitler and his soldiers.

When I expressed my fervent disagreement with the logic of his illustration and theory, this question then arose from him: "What else could have been the acceptable logic or motive behind the torturous executions of six million lives?" He continued, "Mind you, this figure was not a mere six hundred lives or six thousand lives. Neither was it sixty thousand nor six hundred thousand, but a staggering six million precious lives, in the hand of the leader of a civilized country like Germany, and as recently as the 1940s. If not for the factor of retributive fate, what else could have been the logical judgment behind the historic holocaust?" My good friend resolutely affirmed the notion that, "Adolf Hitler's actions would have been a little excusable, if it were in the Dark Ages. The mystery surrounding the ways and manners in which Adolf Hitler had executed his mission and mysteriously departed this world, most evidently signified some esoteric acuity to several population of insightful spiritualists that Adolf had purposely come into this world to fulfil some divine tasks," the zealot reincarnation apostle insistently concluded.

After I have carefully considered the above illustration according to how this fanatic campaigner of reincarnation had presented it; admittedly his illustration sounded very logical, but not quite convincing for my belief. This is not because of the atheistic opinion that I appreciably held, but because the illustration lacked tangible evidence to prove that Adolf Hitler was truly Judas Iscariot's reincarnate. Despite the fact that it might be true that the motives behind the cruel execution of a staggering six million Jews in the hand of Adolf Hitler and his soldiers have to this day remained mysterious and irresolvable. And, despite the fact that Adolf Hitler once asserted thus in his famous speech of 1936: *"I believe today that I am acting in the sense of the Almighty Creator. By warding off the Jews I am fighting for the Lord's work;"* however, the gloomy nature of the doctrine of reincarnation still stood very repugnant to my sense of reasoning.

Moreover, I have earlier read other Gnostic Gospels concerning the account of Jesus; conversely their reports of Jesus' crucifixion deferred miles apart from what the Christian Bible narrated. Although, no one reliably knows where the truth of the entire contradiction accurately lays, as religionists enjoy painting their stories all over the place in disjointed and incoherent fallacies. With my background knowledge of the discrepant stories that wilfully surround the historical Jesus, I have no doubt in my mind that my friend's illustration was just another typical coat of illusory paint on the fictionalized wall of religion fantasy tales.

I just could not take it for my rule of faith to admit the unjust rationalism that would put the creator of the universe under such an extreme necessity of vengeance. In that, a compassionate God would compel the soul of a sinful dead person, about 1,856 years after his death, to inhabit the body of an innocent infant. Thereafter, this ancient soul would channel the course of this baby's destiny towards tyranny and despotism in committing more dreadful and shocking sins, while living a presidential life of affluence at the costliest expense of millions of German taxpayers. Such act, simply to me, does not portray any reasonable justice that is consistent with the fine character of a merciful God.

If this is what the apostles of reincarnation had spiritually christened, as being the concept of retribution under the Law of Karma for the despicable or holy deeds of past lives, then the decency of moral justice is bankrupt in religion. I solemnly believe that the rationale of reincarnation is primly in conflict with the virtuous quality of natural justice. Of what purpose would it serve moral justice, if the Law of Karma should piously punish the innocent and the just in the place of the offenders?

Let us consider together, the logic or the absurdity that holds fundamental connections to this illustration offered under the actions of the Law of Karma.

Firstly, the Jewish generation of sinners in Judas day, who crucified Jesus and accursed the Christ's innocent blood upon their heads, including their children's head have all passed away several centuries ago. In addition, the Old Testament generations of Jewish warmongers, who during their lifetime slaughtered many innocent persons in numerous wars have all died some millennia in the past. Why then would a god be under the inevitability to take revenge for the sins that these two separate generations had committed several centuries apart, in Adolf Hitler's day?

Let's assume the soul of all the sinful generations of the Old Testament warmongers and the generation of Judas day had all reincarnated in the bodies of their descendants that suffered the brutality of the 1940s holocaust in the hands of Adolf Hitler. The question, therefore, is how exactly would the souls of those ancient generations of Jewish sinners have suffered the pain that Judas Iscariot's reincarnate had inflicted on the bodies they inhabited; insomuch, that the soul is regarded as *'immaterial,'* and therefore suffers neither pain nor death?

More to the point, when Adolf Hitler inflicted systematic agony and pain on those six million Jews and eventually tortured them to death, very surely he did not kill their souls. If their soul had thus survived the retribution and death inflicted upon their bodies by the purported Judas Iscariot's reincarnate, for the reason that the soul is supposedly immaterial and thus encompassed immunity against material or corporal destruction, what then is the merit or meaning of the karmic punishment upon the culpable souls? Moreover, where is the justification for the operation of the Law of Karma in this case? Honestly, this cruel vengeance of the Law of Karma comprises nothing tangible that supplies any rationalism to my discernment.

Furthermore, how in this case had the soul of Judas Iscariot paid for his own appalling sin of betrayal and suicide during past life? Surely, the soul of Judas, which purportedly reincarnated in the body of Adolf Hitler was also highly culpable, and ought to have received his own punishment as the law of karma has prescribed. Perhaps, the advocates of reincarnation would corroborate the premise that the soul of Judas Iscariot had actually paid for those sins he committed in his previous life by reincarnating to life again as Adolf Hitler; who became the President of the Republic of Germany, and lived a flamboyant and grandiose lifestyle befitting the status of a National President. Perhaps, they might say Judas' soul had duly paid for his past sins by issuing flagrant orders as Commander-in-

Chief of the German Armed Forces; liable for the loss of over six million lives in a regime that saw several trillion dollars' worth of properties and equipment perishing worldwide. Maybe, the soul of the reincarnate Judas had paid for his previous sins by committing suicide again the second time; with every possibility of this notorious soul escaping unscathed to reincarnate several times in the distant future to terrorize humanity again, asking for more blood. Remember also, there is still the personal soul of Adolf Hitler himself looming in reserve, and waiting for God's appointed time to reincarnate and inflict another terror on humanity. Ah! Humankind is helplessly doomed with this reincarnation terror, if truly the tenet is real.

How I wish these apostles who truly know the profound science of reincarnation could sincerely decode the past owner of the souls that are presently acting through their own personal bodies. Apparently, it would be interesting for everyone to know whose soul is it that presently acts through their individual selves.

Where exactly lies the probity of justice in this case, if the Law of Karma should punish a physical body merely because a sinful soul had superciliously inhabited that body uninvited and unsolicited? If the soul that inhabits a particular body should receive divine punishment or divine reward, prompted under the requisite of the Law of Karma, why then, must it be a material or physical punishment and reward; which, of course, is inconsequential relative to soul that is allegedly spiritual and immaterial, and as a result, cannot enjoy or suffer ephemeral things?

Just as the soul is spiritual, why then are spiritual arrangements not obligatory to solving spiritual matters? In other words, why must it take the punishment of the physical body to castigate a spiritual soul? What meaningful sense is there for the Law of Karma to deliver punishment or reward on a soul that cannot feel the pain of corporal or mortal punishment, or enjoy the bliss of worldly reward? Why must the physical body of another person receive retribution or reward for the evil or the good that emanated from past deeds of another unknown and unrelated person; especially when the recipient cannot even realize or keep in mind those actions for which the Law of Karma recompenses him from past life deeds. Why, for heaven's sake, must it take the physical body to trap or cage a spiritual soul? These loads of unending questions surely require coherent answers from the advocates of reincarnation towards clarifying their inexplicable doctrines.

I honestly decline to accept or subscribe to any doctrine that is too gloomy for my acuity, and too repugnant for my comprehension. What benefit is therein for moral justice, if the rule of karma is under the inevitability of castigating the soul of a doomed sinner for transgressions in past life, and for that reason, would punish the innocent physical body that the sinful soul had tyrannically invaded and occupied without the knowledge and consent of the owner of the body?

I can only liken this doctrine of reincarnation to the scenario of a criminal who unfairly invades the residence of an innocent person and resorts to using the residence as shield to evade justice. It will therefore be rational upon ethical justice to design a suitable way to safeguard the innocent person, while it works out appropriate means to search out the criminal from his illegally acquired haven, in order for the offender to face proper justice. Definitely, moral justice would become ruinous and damaging if the law does not respect the feeling and life of the innocent in authorizing the bombardment of this temporary hideout with missiles and artillery fire, because there is a criminal element shielding in there.

How rational would be this abstract illustration, say for example, divine fiat, under the inescapability of the Law of Karma, compels the soul of the late Pablo Escobar, the notorious drug lord of the infamous Medellin Cartel in Colombia into our world once again. This time around, Pablo's soul had tyrannically invaded the womb of a pregnant Zulu woman uninvited; took an earthly embodiment through a rebirth in another mother to reincarnate again as Toks Dube in a remote street of Soweto, South Africa. As a result, this reincarnated soul of Pablo channels the course of Toks destiny towards becoming a chronic drug addict on the notorious street of Hilbrow, Johannesburg. In reality, would this karmic act of comeback be an efficient retributive justice that constructively or destructively recompenses the soul of the late Pablo Escobar for his atrocities, on account of past life, for being an unrepentant drug lord? Alternatively, would it be an unfair punishment for Toks, the direct recipient of the penalty with his own physical body? Without any controversy, the direct answer in this case is that, it would surely be an unfair retribution to Toks, and equally an injustice for the emotions of his parents, relatives, and wife (if he has one). Because, Toks would steal from everyone, lie to everyone, and commit all sorts of atrocities to sustain his drug addiction, which would in return tarnish the image of all relatives around him (who has no relationship or connection whatsoever to Pablo Escobar). Each and everyone around Toks in Soweto and Hilbrow would swallow a dose of the bitter pills from his appalling drug addiction. In this case, only the invincible and immaterial soul of the late Pablo, which the karmic retribution had actually set out in pretence to cage and punish in Toks body, would surely escape the punishment safe and sound, because the soul possessed the power of immunity that transcends above destruction.

What rationale is readily available for me to believe such fallacy that the soul of my late father, who died some 38 years ago, could have somehow by divine stroke of the law of karma, reincarnated in the body of another strange person in some far away land, say for an example, Haiti or Uzbekistan. Where, presently, the soul is busy moulding the destiny of the person whose body it has inhabited, to reap the consequences of his karmic compensation according to past life deeds in Nigeria. After the soul has finished with recompensing its newly inhabited body, either with rewards or with punishments, it then survives the body safe and sound at death, and is again ready for another adventure in another body. Where then is the actual punishment or reward for the soul in this case?

If a strange soul tyrannically invades the body of another person, and unjustly superimposes its spirit on the body, as to act through it, where now is the personal self-aware consciousness of that person, which the apostles of reincarnation affirm in their doctrine as distinctive to a particular individual? In other words, where is the person's own distinct self – the self-realization? Where truly is his/her own personalized soul?

The soul that could rightly be called his/her own, which s/he is truly accountable for in his/her present life.

Let us assume Adolf Hitler's body had become the remote controlled robot for the strange soul of Judas Iscariot, which had invaded the direct control of his mind from infant without his being conscious of the strange soul that acted arbitrarily through him for the purpose of paying karmic debts. At what stage in life would Adolf possess his own personal soul distinctive to his individual self that might reincarnate in future to suffer punishments, or reap fruitful rewards for his personal past life deeds that were free from the influence of Judas soul, or any other strange soul? If the soul of Judas Iscariot had acted through Adolf, and the soul of Pablo had acted through Toks, where is the person of Adolf and Toks? Which life would these two people personally be accountable for, in their individual way of life? Furthermore, at which circle of life should Adolf and Toks take possession of their own personal souls that could reincarnate to reap rewards or suffer punishments on the merit of their own personal life deeds? I mean the deeds that are truly free from the controlling influence of foreign souls, but wholly distinct to their individual selves.

If Elijah's soul had become the controlling compass that navigated the body of John the Baptist, as to channel his destiny to the palace of Herod Antipas for beheading; on the Christian resurrection day, how would John the Baptist account for a life on earth that was based on his personal life deeds, which were out of the influence of Elijah's soul, but wholly distinct to John the Baptist's own personal life deeds?

As I have already asked, who amongst these apostles of reincarnation can truly tell whose soul it is that acts through their own body? How exactly do they determine whether a person is in his first circle of life or the second? In other words, how do they determine how many circles of life a soul has gone through in earthly embodiment?

Many other teachings of reincarnation are also bewitched with faltered convictions. One of these bizarre beliefs is the factor responsible for why one child is born to a rich family, and another born to a very poor family. Under the retributive actions of the law of karma—what you sow is what you reap—the concept of reincarnation has wrongly accepted it as truth that a child born into a wealthy family has reincarnated into the world to reap the rewards of past life deeds. On the other hand, they also accepted it as the truth that a child born into a poor family has reincarnated as well to suffer the retributive punishment of past life deeds.

What a gross misconception of religious belief this precept is! The foundation of its incoherent and conflicting realism, in any ramification, does not come into any sensible agreement with the actual course of life. It is very unfortunate that this inconsistent belief system has ardently enraptured the minds of many credulous believers.

Let me quickly narrate this true-life story to buttress my point of disbelief for this particular principle of reincarnation regarding people born into either wealthy or poor family, as a retributive reward or punishment for previous life deeds.

In the mid-1940s, a baby boy was born to very poor parents in my home village. His father worked as a labourer in a sawmill factory in another village some eight kilometres away from home. The sawmill proprietor was indeed a rich and affluent man in the society. He owned several properties that included vast acres of rubber tree plantations, which supplied raw materials to tyre and plastic manufacturing companies. The rich sawmill boss also had sons and daughters born to him.

As the little poor boy grew in age, his life also developed amidst blatant fraught and complexity; as if he had truly come into this world to reap karmic retribution of past life sins. To make matters worse for him, I do not know which one of these two terrible disasters first happened to him. Whilst still a young man, he lost his mother; also, his father lost his right arm in an accident while working as a sawmill factory labourer. These terrible disasters, undoubtedly, had spelt more poverty and hardship for the little poor boy as he was left without a mother, and a father with partial ability.

All the same, the father of this little boy firmly committed himself to a vision of living a good life, and of bequeathing fine legacy to his children. As a result, the old man did not allow his disability to obstruct his vision and progress in life. Of course, many other people with similar disability would lazily rescind to fate, begging for alms to feed themselves and their family. Instead of yielding to the dictate of fate and earn a peasant living at the mercy of others; this old man had skilfully undertook tailoring apprenticeship to learn dressmaking with his remaining left hand. With the aid of the little income from his new vocation, he was able to hire labourers to work in his farmland. Gradually, he commenced trading in cassava flakes between surrounding villages and the city of Lagos to source extra funds for his children's education.

The winning conclusion of this story is that the unassuming poor boy, who happened to be the first son of the family, recently retired as the Group Managing Director of the largest petroleum corporation in Africa. This was after holding various senior executive positions in the petroleum corporation since the 1970s, including being a special adviser on petroleum affairs to a number of Nigerian presidents.

Here lies the big irony of life. Where today are those children born into the wealthy and comfortable family of the sawmill proprietor from where the old man had lost his right arm while working as a factory labourer? The sawmill shut down operations shortly after the proprietor's death, and up unto this day, no one has heard of any tangible achievement from any of his children. In this case, who has truly come into this world to reap karmic compensations? Is it the little boy who was born into abject poverty, but transcends above the wretchedness that fraught his early days to accomplish monumental successes in life; or the children of the sawmill proprietor, born into affluent riches that did not last the test of time?

The American legendary politician, Abraham Lincoln, was a child born into an underprivileged family; even so, he rose above the poverty of his early life to become the president the United States of America. So too was Barack Obama, the first black president of the United States of America. Likewise, Nigeria's greatest philanthropist of all time, the Late Chief M.K.O. Abiola, was also a child born into a very wretched family. He too transcended beyond the curb of abject penury to become a multi-billionaire. During his lifetime, he was undeniably the richest man in

Nigeria with investment interests that spanned across extensive business spectrums. So, how then does the doctrine of reincarnation credibly relates to the factor of having a child born into either a wealthy or underprivileged home?

In good conscience, the gloomy principles of this popular doctrine of reincarnation illustrates nothing cogent and logical to my understanding, but an overcast misconception that is bedevilled with extreme absurdity. It's exceedingly cruel for belief, and too demoniac for credence as the moral justice of any compassionate god. It's simply the worst of vindictive vengeance.

As for the doctrine of resurrection taught by the religions of Islam, Christianity, Jewish, Zoroastrian eschatology, etc., its belief is intrinsically founded upon the same tenet as that of reincarnation. This, I have earlier mentioned in the opening part of this chapter, as man's inordinate desire to live forever. Therefore, its faith equally follows that of her twin sister, reincarnation. As accurately observed by Shaun, *"The finality of death is the coldest truth one must face. Religion makes the perfect distraction."*

The Doctrine of Resurrection

In the eleventh chapter of the Bible book of John, Jesus said in verse 25, *"I am the resurrection and the life. He who believes in me will live, even though he dies, and whoever lives and believes in me will never die."* Furthermore, the Christian Bible narrated the story of Jesus crucifixion, and his resurrection on the third day.

We also read the story of Lazarus; a man the gospel of John claimed had died and been buried four days. When Jesus received the news of Lazarus' death, he journeyed from Jerusalem to Bethany on a condolatory visit to the bereaved family. Verses 21-24 (NIV) recounted,

> *Lord, Martha said to Jesus, if you had been here, my brother would not have died..., and Jesus replied your brother will rise again. Martha answered; I know he will rise again in the resurrection at the last day.*

The story told us that Jesus followed the deceased family to the tomb where Lazarus' body had been buried four days, verses 43-44 narrated,

Jesus called in a loud voice, 'Lazarus, come out!' The dead man came out, his hands and feet wrapped with strips of linen, and a cloth around his face. Jesus said to them, take off the grave clothes, and let him go.

The story of Lazarus' resurrection from the dead had there ended abruptly without the gospel writers giving Lazarus any further slot in their book to narrate the account of his four-day sojourning to the great beyond. As plentiful and as detailing as those words the gospel writers had put into the mouth of Jesus in the New Testament, not once did they allocate the Messiah a slot to narrate a slight description of what the 'great beyond' truly looks like after his purported resurrection from the dead. Up until this day, no one is sure whether the Christian paradise is located eastwards of the moon, and their hellfire situated northeast of the sun. In any event, the Biblical biographers have totally failed to allow their Messiah a slot to narrate a bit of these details to humankind; however, they take pleasure in bothering our heads with petty narratives of every Martha and Magdalene and that of a fish that swallowed a coin inside of its belly.

As I have earlier noted, when the reality dawned on man that death is the inevitable end to his life, whether he likes it or not, it therefore becomes necessary for him to design the idea of eternal existence in another world, in pretentious denial of the reality of death being the grim finality to human life. The conversations that verses 21-24 of the 11th chapter of the book of John, recorded to have taken place between Martha and Jesus, are further revelations that correlated man's eternal wish for everlasting life. Without doubt, no man truly wishes for death. Through the fantasy of reincarnation and resurrection, depending on one's religious faith, humankind has falsely hoped for everlasting life that is beyond the mortal world.

The concept of the Christian resurrection teaches that when a person of faith dies, there is hope for him to continue eternal life from the point where death has stopped him in earthly life, whether in infancy, youth, or adulthood. Depending on his previous life deeds, he would however resurrect on the last day to final judgment, either to reap his rewards with compensation in eternal paradise, or suffer damnation in everlasting fiery furnace.

Some Christian sects are of the conviction that their God would host the resurrection drama into paradise and hellfire in the amphitheatres of heavenly territory, while other sects affirmed the showground would be here on earth. Wherever the venues of the religious hellfire and paradise might be situated, whether the theatres of planet Jupiter, Uranus, or the Andromeda Nebula or the blue planet; one could certainly perceive a glaring case of man not wanting to die, from the resurrection idea. As a result, humankind has designed a hopeful wish to continue with life eternally after death.

From the reality of what the wonderful laws of nature, which is the natural medium of expression to all humans, have consistently conveyed to our knowledge; we know for sure that it is appointed unto man to live his life only once; thereafter, the finality of death would come. The entire world of nature — the vegetation, animal, marine and human life — evangelizes universally to us in this evident order that denotes death as the ultimate end of all consciousness of existence.

Contrary to nature's law, did Lazarus and Jesus actually rise from the dead? In certain terms, no details of empirical record existed anywhere in the Bible, or anywhere in history that wholly signified Lazarus and Jesus truly rose from the dead. Except for the discrepant testimonies of four faceless authors, who impersonated the personality of Jesus' apostles, and covertly gave illusory fabrications to render assistance to the cause of their establishing another false religion on earth, there's no empirical record anywhere in history to validate that Lazarus and Jesus actually rose from the dead.

In actual sense, the discrepant testimonies that these gospel writers narrated in their account regarding Lazarus and Jesus' resurrection would merely be admissible as neurotic evidence, directly in point to the doctrine and cause of another neurotic religion, in the court of yet another neurotic jury. As for the lawful court of certainty and firmness—where reality and truth rule over spurious claims, and where juries demand evidential facts to verify bogus claims—those testimonies would at once fall to the ground, and be thrown out of the court of law with immediate alacrity.

As I have always suspected, it would be an unmistakable fact to conclude that the architects of religion have self-interestedly incorporated the spurious canon of the *'last day resurrection to final judgment'* into man's natural lifetime; wittingly to serve as a means required for their authoritarian propensity to control the destiny of man into eternity.

From the outset, the intelligence of nature knows that it would not be too long before the earth becomes excessively over-populated, later becoming too deplorable and unhealthy for pleasurable habitation if the human race should continue to reproduce and live forever on earth without dying. Therefore, the process of natural creation has effectively designed adequate provisions for wear and tear, which makes human and animal grow old and age to the point where they can no longer reproduce and continue with life, but must surrender to the inevitable end that nature has divinely provided through death.

Let us take a brief moment off, and digress a little to reflect on one fundamental teaching of religion that fervidly contradicts the fact of life. The Bible told us in the book of Genesis that the original purpose of the creator-God for humankind is to live forever on earth without dying; hence, the planting of the Tree of Life in the Garden of Eden. According to the account in Genesis, the serpent had subsequently overturned God's original plan when he deceived the first human couple into disobeying God's order in the Garden of Eden; thus death came into man's life.

If the original purpose of God was for every man to live forever in this world, and it therefore happened that all humans from the first generation to the present have remained on earth, hale and hearty and reproducing accordingly without any death; could anyone imagine how many trillions or Zillions of people would be populating the entire globe at the present? If our world is devoid of any death like those that emanated from the global deluge of Noah, the destruction of Sodom and Gomorrah, the annihilation of several Egyptians in the Red Sea, counting all the deaths from the first and second world wars, and natural causes, etc.; at what figure would the world's population possibly be standing by now? If every single person from creation to date has remained on earth, and have all consistently reproduced from Adam to now, with no deaths ensuing from natural disasters such as tsunamis, hurricanes, floods, earthquakes, including the numerous deaths from plane crashes, terrorist attacks, and so on; imagine the attendant human miseries that would prevail on earth due to over-population. It would undeniably be catastrophic; anyone would agree! Man, at his own volition, would have long devoured the entire *Tree of the Knowledge of Good and Evil* without the aid of the serpent, but essentially out of starvation.

Where on earth, would man have found enough land to cultivate as farmlands, and rare cattle and livestock that would adequately feed the whole lot? Let alone building magnificent golf courses for pleasure, including such spectacular nature's reserve park as the South Africa's Kruger National Park. Where in this world would the various races of humans have found sufficient land to build all the necessary industries, roads, airports, oil refineries, motor parks, power stations, recreation centres, including schools, hospitals, shopping malls, train stations, and many other facilities that would be most required to service the need of such an astronomical population? How would humans have survived the problems of industrial pollution, as there would be colossal production of everything, ranging from various utensils to clothing; varieties of food items, toiletries, motorcars, trucks, home appliances, and many other apparatus, as well as heavy duty equipment. How might humanity endure the problem of waste disposals, water and electricity supplies, oil and gas supplies, the dilemma of mass transit, environmental degradation, financial problems, and the problems of health care delivery to mention but a few. Imagine the limitless number of thieves that would be populating the earth, and the vast number of law enforcement officers that would be required to combat crime and police the entire world. The general population of humankind would have repeatedly wreaked havoc upon themselves where they jostle for food and allotment of any small piece of land to either farm for food or erect shelters. That is if there is any available piece of land left anywhere again, as excessive population of humankind would have spread across every available piece of land. These problems would have been so calamitous, such that man on his own volition would employ the service of death contractors into his own world, and make huge budgetary allocation for such service as effective remedy to ease the monstrous problems of over-population and shortage of everything.

In the face of this illustration, which of these two points of view is more reasonable to believe as the truthfulness of the creator of the universe, if there exists any:

a) Should we continue believing Biblical fallacies that the original purpose for which the creator-God (if there exists any) had designed life was simply to, *multiply and become many, subdue the earth, and reside in it forever without dying;* only for this grandiose plan to be derailed by the bare trick of a serpent, thereby suggesting the creator-God as a dim-witted divine being who could not see beyond his/her/its nose, let alone foreseeing the horrible end result that would befall the existence of life, should our planet earth become over-populated because of the faulty *eternal life* plan?

b) Alternatively, should we believe that the process of natural creation is vastly intelligent and had essentially foreseen these calamitous consequences should natural laws have decreed *eternal life* on earth; therefore, the intelligence of nature had, for that reason, made natural provisions for reproduction, ageing and death, to allow for limitless circles of life to progress in organized sequence through the genetic traits from generation through generation, as we witness it today?

I also wish to leave the right conclusion on this matter at the discretion of the reader as it is here easy to detect that the proponents of religion have contrived the *doctrine of afterlife*, in fervent denial of the finality of death being the real end to all consciousness of existence.

The ability of man to reproduce and become many, replenish the earth with offspring or successors, as it naturally prevails in our world, is the genuine reincarnation and resurrection of life. It is the only reasonable idea we can have of living another life in our children and descendant who are carriers of our genes and DNA traits from one generation to another, to time eternal. The reality of human reincarnation and resurrection does not consist in bogus fantasies and gullible beliefs of many religious dogmatists that represent ridiculous and false hopes to humanity, which artificially imply that their earthly life shall continue beyond this world after the death of the physical body. Since the beginning of this world unto this day, never has the living identified any dead man ever to live again. The author of Ecclesiastes 9:5-6 (NIV) wrote in the Bible:

> *For the living know that they will die, but the dead know nothing; they have no further reward, and even the memory of them is forgotten. Their love, their hate, and their jealousy have long since vanished; never again will they have a part in anything that happens under the sun.*

The life that we live now is the life that nature has appointed for us to live once only. Thereafter, the inevitable end of humankind – death – would demand the baton of life from us and pass it over to our successors, who at their own appointed time would likewise hand over the baton of life to their individual successors and so on, for life eternal.

Whoever the anthropological Adam and Eve might be, they are still very much in existence on earth today because their offspring have continually flourished from generation through generation, carrying their genetic data with dignity. As always, the posterity of human civilization shall forever refer to them as the progenitor of the human race. So also are the souls and spirits of my primal ancestors alive today, as several of their offspring are alive with their genetic traits. The greater fractions of the human folk undeniably bear striking resemblance to their ancestors, because of the genetic materials (DNA and RNA) that directly live in them. Therefore, the actual resurrection or reincarnation of humankind does not consist in those misconceptions and lies that all the religions promote. As we bear children and our children continue to bear their own children, thus the genes of our ancestral lineage endure forever.

If we make the best out of our earthly life, where we only have a singular option of residence, posterity will judge us and record our good deeds eternally in the annals of world history. If otherwise, the same posterity will discredit our vile deeds in those same annals of history.

If reincarnation and resurrection is what gives life to human again; then, the real reincarnation or resurrection of man's existence is that life and that gene, which has truly reincarnated or resurrected in his offspring to add continuity to his lineal descent from generation through generation forever and ever.

In the words of Allah Verpint, *"The idiots killing people in Mumbai honestly think they're going to heaven for it... while the relatives of the victims console themselves their loved ones are going to heaven... and the truth is they're all just dead."*

Here is a word of wisdom suitable for the conclusion of this chapter, an excerpt from a factual devout leader who is free from the claws of theological programming and the fraud of religion, Stephen Grellet (1773-1855):

> *I expect to pass through this world but once. Any good, therefore, that I can do or any kindness I can show to any fellow creature let me do it now. Let me not defer or neglect it. For, I shall not pass this way again.*

*****

*"Wandering in a vast forest at night,
I have only a faint light to guide me.
A stranger appears and says to me: 'my
friend, you should blow out your candle
in order to find your way more clearly.'
This stranger is a theologian."*

– Denis Diderot

*****

Chapter

11

The Blind Guide

"Theology is an attempt to explain a subject by men who do not understand it. The intent is not to tell the truth but to satisfy the questioner."

– Albert Hubbard

Organized religions contrive to make the continent of Africa a blind alley of the world. Over our continent, complacent imbecility reigns supreme, as ethical science and wisdom that stand for irrefragable logic suffocate under the folly of religion. The dogmas of popular superstitions blossom in every part of our communal society beyond what my words can describe. Those in whom the faculty of reason is vital solution and means to the advancement of African civilization struggle for recognition amid the dominant influence of preachers who propagate nothing but outmoded customs and traditional beliefs of uneducated worshippers.

Today, the entire world yearns for more light, but the faith mentality unreasonably suppresses the rewards that nature and common sense firmly place on reality and ethical truth. That, which we consider universal enlightenment and call reason, the despotism of faith unfairly subjugates for the hag of superstitious belief and ancient system of theism. The big claim by ignorant men who pretend to be oracle of God on earth excites the reverence and cheerful gratification of my people in Africa, far greater than the deeper fact that pragmatism best indicates in the philosophy of insight and scientific knowledge.

In religion resides the Dark Age with humankind. The iron grip of organized religion forbids that old things should pass away — it is thus written. Ancient theologies and worship of the old still lamentably dominate the control of human lives and rule their world in the 21st century civilization. Under the subterfuge of spiritual illumination and wisdom from the divine, the superiority of religion gives victory to the reign of stupidity over our land in a modern world. Unto this day, spurious claim to sacred authority by artificial priests and self-styled prophets absurdly rule our new age through the practice of outdated belief systems.

As far as we can trace the natural history of theology, the Bhagavad-Gita, the Sanskrit, the Torah, the Quran, and the Bible, *etc.,* are not by any means Holy Scriptures. They are altogether a bunch of historical records, written by primitive men — savages who told tribal versions of events that entrench bigotry and intolerance, unruly deeds and violence, including hatred, brutality, and slavery into the culture of humankind, at the fabricated commands of imaginary gods of antiquity.

It's out of the ordinary to imagine how unrestrained fallacies of pious men, in their despicable con job of heralding spurious 'word of God' to others, have made persistent mockery of the human race through all ages. Imagine how thinkers and men of astute nobility can no longer find a new emphasis of their own amid repressive rule of faith that saddles their critical faculties with the domination of absurd and contradictory theologies; which of course can be so easily proven false by any adolescent schoolboy. It's much baffling to imagine how humans can no longer think for themselves in their own world. Just imagine how the despotism of faith has built extensive territories of gullible bigots across the length and breadth of Africa!

If we should ask ourselves, what precisely are the benefits of the mental cruelties that program countless heads all over the globe into believing embroidered myths that are totally untrue? Of what gain does it profit humanity when organized religions compel the worship of fictionalized gods upon the general populace? As far as the generally accepted history of religion is concerned, where exactly has the journey of dogmatic belief systems led humanity, except for the business of *'propheteering'* and fattening the wallets of preachers and proponents of religious trade?

The enduring mental manipulations that fill the heads of little kids with the dogmas of the greatest lies of all times, and pre-set infants long before they could either reflect or think wisely into subjective believers of popular superstition called the *'word of God in print,'* clearly depict the suppressive nature of faith. The very essence of this despotic propensity goes all out to show how organized religions commonly covet for no autonomous logical thoughts, born out of one's own reflective views and convictions, to ever exist in this world; and for every sound mind in whom the rational mentality is truly alive to perish with the logic of his/her personal intellect. In fact, I am sincerely at a loss as to how the commission of this infamous system of suppression has been of any significant benefit to the progress of human civilization.

My early childhood indoctrination into the Christian religion culminates into the study of nothing but a confused fable, featuring the character of a mythical, three-headed 'supernatural God' who is a lead actor and commander-in-chief of brutal wars amongst earthling creatures; together with gullible obedience that is inconsistent with freethought. Who can imagine what the world has lost by the evil execution of this notorious plot of dominating the minds of the world's most valuable future resources with mountains of theological gibberish!

The looming danger that today poses grave menace to the progress of Africa's civilization and the survival of its people exists not in the plague of incurable diseases such as HIV/AIDS or cancer, but the faith mentality that greatly deludes the entire population of the Dark Continent. Yet again, a new Dark Age in the history of human civilization is more than ever before endemic in the continent of Africa, as booming pious trade that deeply engulfs the totality of African society since the 1980s, dangerously advances to a new level of discomfort. The artifice of trading in the name of God terribly gears to bind the dark species of humankind eternally to the gloom of ignorance and the pillage of pious extortion.

Sinister misapplication of faith that now rules the entire nations of Africa has inherently become the real threat to the progress and survival of its civilization. Regrettably, the faith mentality that organized religion has bred into the entire continent remains the evil virus that absurdly deludes Africans into becoming perplexed servants to the service of foreign gods without them realizing the grave implications of losing one's own cultural heritage and traditional identity in tangible logic. Very appallingly, our moral outlook and eyes of reason are tightly closed to this perilous mentality that terribly infests the critical faculties of our entire people and imposes malignant retardation upon the progress of our land. In order to see through irrational bearings of faith, we gullibly embrace repugnant absurdities, mislay our connections with reality, and plague our lives with strange superstitious beliefs that foster acute societal dysfunction across the length and breadth of our fatherland.

Beyond words is the outrageous manner in which otherwise intelligent people in our society have taken up the business of religion as a full-scale trade. The most disturbing of it all is how credulously majority of African intellectuals in various areas of discipline have subverted the cool validation of science and common sense in ludicrous obedience to the rule of faith. In spite of all compelling evidence against the absurdity of faith, several African intellectuals have gladly thrown rationalism to the winds for preposterous belief of fairy-tales that are very much untrue.

It is increasingly becoming impossible to come across any intelligent person on the continent of Africa whose rational views have not been somewhat distorted or twisted out of order by religion. Even worst is the vast total of intellectuals who have so much lost their footings on rational thoughts that they accept the slavery imposed upon their minds by priests and con preachers who know far little than they do. The awful condition into which the faith mentality has badly altered the astute minds of so many intelligent people in Africa is surprisingly beyond what the language of my words can find satisfactory expression to convey to readers of this book. It's incredible how huge number of African scholars have been programmed to reason wrongly by charlatans whose stock in trade is to preach the dogmas of mythical gods into the dull ears of gullible congregants. Uncountable academics who as one would expect to be rational thinkers in our modern age have credulously donned the fanciful garb of mental illusion, because religion and faith are here concerned.

To wilfully sacrifice the application of common sense on the altar of unfounded faith convictions is a terrible transgression against humanity. And, to toss away scientific findings in firm devotion to ancient works of religious fiction is indeed moral blindness, especially after one has empirically recognized such valid results as reliable verifications that are overtly devoid of underhand falsity. The commission of such wrongdoing is a gross misconduct against the ethics of moral knowledge. There is no other way to describe the folly of such errant misdeed, in the spirit of intellectual honesty, than to condemn it in strong terms as objectionable crime of academics that is extremely detrimental to human civilization. Of course, it's the height of abhorrent inconsistency and disloyalty to coherent and valid knowledge, which the conduct of intellect must at all times preserve and respect. But, to the contrary, majority of the human race have all in the name of religion naively shut down the appliance of their vital faculties in order to live by faith and continue believing illogical things which are, by all inferences, foreign to reality; and as such can never be justified by any atom of reasoned facts. The famous mathematician, William Clifford, very sternly denounced the folly of such errant misdeed in expressive clarity in his book, *The Ethics of Belief:*

> *If a man, holding a belief which he was taught from childhood or persuaded of afterwards, keeps down and pushes away any doubts which arise about in his mind, purposely avoids the reading of books and the company of men that call in question or discuss it, and regard as impious those questions which cannot easily be asked without disturbing it—the life of that man is a long sin against mankind.*

It's exceedingly baffling how intellectuals on African soil have basically thrown logic into the winds, especially in the midst of overwhelming evidence that are day to day accessible to them. The credulity of shutting one's mind to the truth is by every implication a noxious sacrilege to humanity. It's without doubt, "*a long sin against mankind,*" as William Clifford has aptly condemned it.

Just as the dogma of pious stupidity hath practically surmounted all societal functionalities in the name of God, so, in every manner, hath despotism of faith subverted the natural impulse of human reasoning. Humanistic values and our entire sense of being, along with every trait of our critical judgments have clearly been blotted out of the horizon of rational stance by absurd and contradictory theologies cunningly imposed upon the human conscience as the word of the creator of the universe.

At the present, the only reasonable way for the bulk of Africans to celebrate their outrageous backwardness and revel in the stupidity of their poor industrial, technological and scientific progress is nonsensically through retailing the name of the Nazarene in every corner of their towns and cities. Incredible priest-crafty and confidence trick of professional bigots now contemptibly represent general idiotic guides as to how Africans should live their life under the pretence of divine command. This shameful error that plagues our culture is especially prohibitive for comfort — objectionably baseless and disgusting — beyond what is fair and acceptable in any civilized society.

If our boundless hypocrisy and obstinate self-deceits permit our minds to affix the right facts to things we evidently observe in our natural world, we must inevitably come to the realization that if any **God** positively exists, scientists would have come across compelling evidence to believe the existence of this **God** more than theologians or people with pious reputations do on planet earth. But the 1998 survey conducted by Edward J. Larson and Larry Witham clearly revealed the level of Scepticism amongst world's leading scientists. Details from the research disclosed that 93% of the associates of American National Academy of Science out-rightly reject God; while the total number of non-believers in the British Royal Society climbed the chart table to a very high record of 97%. The study shows vast total of these topflight scientists – physicists, biologists, mathematicians, astronomers, geologists, etc., doubted the story of God, because there is no scientific evidence to prove that neither the Jehovah of the Jews nor Allah of the Turks or Vishnu of Hindus truly exist. Result of the research is detailed on the next page:

Figures in %

BELIEF IN PERSONAL GOD	1914	1933	1998
Personal Belief	27.7	15	7.0
Personal Disbelief	52.7	68	72.2
Doubt or agnosticism	20.9	17	20.8

BELIEF IN HUMAN IMMORTALITY	1914	1933	1998
Personal belief	35.2	18	7.9
Personal disbelief	25.4	53	76.7
Doubt or agnosticism	43.7	29	23.3

Source: 23 July 1998 issue of Nature by Edward J. Larson and Larry Witham.

This group of people have meticulously carried out in-depth studies far above our galaxies and solar system into extensive depth of the earth beneath. Different branches of Organic Chemistry have conducted thorough research and experiments on every part of atoms and molecules, the same way as Quantum Physicists have methodically provided mathematical insights into the discrete, indivisible units of energy in the universe.

Thomas Edison, the prominent scientist and inventor of the electric light bulb, motion picture camera, the phonograph, etc., insightfully observed that, *"I have never seen the slightest scientific proof of the religious ideas of heaven and hell, of future life for individuals, or of a personal God. So far as religion of the day is concerned, it is a damned fake... Religion is all bunk."*

If the biblical account of creation as recorded in the book of Genesis is correct, scientists who have dedicated the larger part of their lives into exploring and discovering nature's life through all possible experiments would have come across convincing evidence to admit such account as infallible; but the case isn't so. Instead, several meticulous observations and experiments that these scientists have carried out entirely provide irrefutable facts that expose the scriptural account of creation as patent fallacy.

For example, the creation story in the book of Genesis asserts that God created the sun, moon, and stars on the fourth day, barely 72 hours after he created the earth, water, and vegetation life. Yet scientific observations evidently reveal the contrary to our understanding that the sun came first, and then the planet and its rotation around the sun, which causes day and night (light and darkness) to occur on a daily basis on our planet; then came the earth's water and all life in it. Experimentally provable information goes to show us that all these did not happen in just six days or 144 hours as biblical account has asserted, but over the course of several millions of years.

Years back, some religions used to believe in errors that the earth is flat, with four giant elephants holding it at each corner. These giant elephants are believed to be standing on the backs of sixteen giant turtles, one turtle carrying each of the elephants' leg. Perhaps the turtles are, in turn, held up by other set of turtles or they magically float in space, the inventor of this mythology did not give further details. But as the age of scientific illumination progressed in human civilization, geographical facts clearly detected the tenet of this religious belief to have been founded upon downright fallacy. The truth became very clear to mankind that the Earth is not flat, but has a shape that is very close to that of an oblate spheroid, revolving in an elliptical path around the sun at a very high speed of approximately 29kms per second. There are no supporting elephants, and no turtles. It is, therefore, evident from all fronts that ignorance of nature has, in effect, given birth to this fallible account, as they merely represent the works of primitive mythologists who blindly attempt to explain a subject for which they totally have no iota of fact.

Despite increased literacy and the realistic light that modern science has shed on the tenet of these religious beliefs as provably incorrect, billions of faithful followers still fanatically profess faith in the theologies of these religions as divinely inspired word of the creator of the universe. It's incredible how people subordinate their astute minds to the belief of errors, propagated by blind guides popularly known as theologians, clerics, rabbi, prophets, and priests, imams, etc.

According to Bertrand Russell, *"Man is a credulous animal, and must believe something; in the absent of good grounds for belief, he will be satisfied with bad ones."* If man isn't a credulous animal that must believe something even in the absence of good grounds for belief, our increased knowledge of nature and cosmology ought to have prompted us to relegate religion to the back seat a long time ago. As Heinrich Heine has very aptly observed, religion only serves as *"best guides in dark ages,"* but *"when daylight comes, however, it is foolish to use blind, old men as guides."*

The tragedy of great disasters like the Asian Tsunami and Hurricane Katrina further ascertain the scale of pointlessness and redundancy that religion and God have turned out to be in our modern society. When Hurricane Katrina destroyed the city of New Orleans in 2005, not a single one of the so-called prophets of God, who kept preaching bunkum to Americans, could come up with any revelation to indicate to American populace that a killer disaster was in the offing; much less proffering safety measures that would secure peoples' lives from Katrina's deadly path.

Where was God when more than a thousand people of faith lost their life and earthly possessions to Hurricane Katrina? Why did God not avert the disaster by revealing it to any of the numerous prophets and priests in America? If, truly, God had averted impending disaster for the inhabitants of biblical Nineveh through Prophet Jonah, why did he not do it again in our present-day for the very religious people of America through Pastor Kerry Jackson or Evangelist Bryan Bush? Why didn't the word of the Lord come to Prophet Ronald Kennedy, saying, "Arise, go unto the city of New Orleans, that great city, and preach thou unto the people the prophecy that I bid thee... "Behold a great hurricane cometh their way; beseech thou my anointing to flee the city that they shall not perish alongside idolaters and sinners."

Howbeit, only through satellite imagery and meteorological calculations provided by the means of science were residents of New

Orleans able to receive advance warnings of Katrina's path. Had the inhabitants of New Orleans, by the motive of faith, been so thoughtlessly insistent to rely on the benevolence of God or Jesus as their mighty saviour, or had they anticipated prophetic word of God through any of the so-called *'prophets of God'* in America, they wouldn't have known that a catastrophic hurricane was fast approaching their city until all their bodies have laid entirely wasted on the streets and drain channels of the city.

As I have earlier mentioned, if our reckless hypocrisy and adamant self-deceit permit our minds to affix the right facts to things we evidently observe in nature's world, we must undeniably come to the realization that the God of organized religion is an unnecessary postulate in human life. The fact is undeniable today that the death of Ogun — the Yoruba god of iron — has not in any way prevented the people from mining and producing abundant iron ore for prosperity in their lands. Also, the death of Inca and Ra could not stop the sun and the moon from shinning their lights unto every part of the world. In the same way, the death of all ancient gods has not affected natural phenomena from taking place in the universe.

It is evident therefore that if the human reasoning faculty permits the monotheistic God of organized religion to die out of our modern world, the outer-space, our earthly home, and everything in the universe will be unaffected by his demise.

Chapter

12

Lamentation for Africa

"I freed a thousand slaves; I could have freed a thousand more if only they knew they were slaves."

– Harriet Tubman

Here is one chapter I truly wish I could write in my mother tongue, supposing established status permits me doing so. This is plainly because of the constraints of expression in English language, which compels certain limitations on those of us who use the language as our second verbal communication. Oftentimes, it becomes very impossible for us to render cogent explanations in English language without losing a quantity of measures in the meaning of what we actually intend putting across to our readers.

Ever since my childhood days, I have always wondered why it happened that the black race — a race of people that I humbly belong to — have been so backward in all areas of endeavours, excepting the art of music and churching; this in comparison with the outstanding successes of the white race, and recently the Asians. Whenever I read or hear about the backwardness in the life of the entire black race, whether in America, Brazil, Jamaica, Haiti, or Africa, worst in fact in Australia, my heart resentfully laments for the emblematic deficiencies of the totality of the black people in whichever continent we find ourselves all over the world.

At any rate, I think I have been privy into a pinch of the evidence of what is responsible for our backwardness as the black race during the period that I commenced the writing of *The Crisis of Religion.* It is through the course of my research into this book that I accurately come to discover some endemic factors that have significantly devastated the black African societies, which no longer have any religious and cultural identity they could call their own.

The huge disparities that continue to exist, miles apart, between the black race and other races of the world have evidently transpired out of one singular factor, which is discipline. By implication, the black race is exceedingly deficient in this foremost factor of nation building — discipline. It takes a nation of disciplined people to embrace and uphold their native culture and religious identity in the uppermost esteem. A nation of people with astute discipline will always cultivate a dignified respect for state laws, doing all things the proper way, and to the best of their abilities. In whatever tempo of change that life may bring at any given time, a nation of disciplined populace will always strive, with grand dynamism, in keeping a steady pace with the reality of life. A nation of people with insightful discipline will not just credulously adopt every strange system of things in an exceedingly baffling manner.

The tragedy of this case is that, the black race has not a dot of the strikes that meet up with any of these very few attributes of a disciplined nation of people. To the contrary, black Africans have totally allowed organized religion to strip their nations stark naked of its native religion and cultural identities. What is now left of us is the bare carcass of our stack dependency and complacency on the stereotypical doctrines of foreign religions that several of these business missionaries have subjugated our native culture in its place. As things now stand, the two dominant faiths on the continent of Africa today (Christianity and Islam) are not original to us; they are introduced. Therefore, our survival for livelihood, our cultures, our indigenous religions, and languages as Africans are altogether dependent on foreigners and their imported religions.

Extreme delusion in the dogma of foreign religion has become the fanciful way of life for millions of credulous Africans. It is by this means that business missionaries from foreign lands have lamentably suppressed and laid to rest, the relics of our ancestral heritage and edifying identity as a distinctive nation of people, at the subterranean vault of our own land. Wherever they go, we gullibly follow like the zombies; and whatever they do, we trustingly imitate and turn upside down, like morons.

Today, all African countries are free from the command of colonial rule, as the entire continent is now self-governed by its native owners. However, if an alien visitor should undertake an assessment trip from space around the continent of Africa, the opposite of its independence from colonial rule would at once become the obvious and the observable fact for such a visitor.

The evidence of Africa's gross dependency on the Europeans, Americans, and Asians for their livelihood would unmistakably become open to the alien visitor within the range of the first few kilometres of the tour. The African culture, education, and government, as well as her economy and trade are all directly dependent on foreigners. Even the way to God for Africans is entirely dependent on foreigners, and under effective control of foreigners.

If anyone should show genuine interest in conducting a study into the pragmatic application of the numerous crises that foreign religions have brought upon Africans, I would honestly advise such a person to commence his or her case study from Africa's most populous nation – Nigeria. Nigeria has now become a country where all the industrial units, warehouses, and factories, which I grew up to know as a child, have in reality been shut down and bought over by churches that converted these industrial premises into redundant properties. Very regrettably, these former industrial buildings now provide my fellow compatriots with ample sanctuaries for the inglorious adoration of paltry and extraneous narratives of the defunct Biblical Israelites. Such trifling tales in the vein of that of Ruth—the Moabite widow of either Mahlon or Kilion—for the Bible did not clearly state who amongst the two sons of Elimelech Ruth's husband was. What is more, my fellow countrymen would ecstatically revel, as if God directly leads their church service, at the narration of such flippant tales that glorify Ruth, who under the trickery supervision of her bereaved mother-in-law tiptoed cunningly to bed with her father-in-law's cousin, whose name is Boaz. In the midst of this unholy affair, Ruth became grandmother to Jesse, father to the juvenile David who slaughtered Goliath, and later became the famous king that once upon a time climbed unto his palatial rooftop to peep at the nakedness of Bathsheba, the wife of Uriah. Through the profane trick of assassinating Uriah in the warfront, King David afterwards became husband to Bathsheba, who begat to him, another adolescent Israelite King named Solomon blah... blah... blah... As a child born out of the grossest scam of infidelity and adultery, King Solomon consequently became the wisest and weirdo king of all times, including being the world's most terrific polygamous husband to three hundred wives, alongside seven hundred concubines. And since the past three and a half millennia, King Solomon has continuously held this matchless record unbroken blah... blah... blah... blah...

In any case, through this adulterous lineal descent, came the promised Christian Messiah to save the world. And, this is an act which by implication stood in direct contravention of the decree of the Jewish God. Prophet Moses expressly decreed through divine inspiration in the book of Deuteronomy 23:2-3. The New International Version reads, *"No one born of a forbidden marriage or any of his descendants may enter the assembly of the Lord, even down to the tenth generation. Verse 3, "No Ammonite or Moabite or any of his descendants may enter the assembly of the Lord, even down to the tenth generation,"* blah... blah... blah...

Instead of Nigerians to thread the path of industrial capability for their nation in providing for stronger economic resources that gainfully offer employment to millions of their jobless youths, just as the Chinese and many other Asian countries have done in the past three decades, they alternatively preferred the failure of their industries for these sorts of worthless tales from ancient Jews.

How irrational and silly for a nation that teems with immense human and natural resources to unreasonably opt to trail the gloomy path of devout madness by encouraging the establishment of churches in the place of factories that provide for gainful employments to her citizens, and pay Company Taxes to her government! This disgusting, absurd, and shameful preference of my people for the inglorious exaltation of strange religious tales over industrial, scientific, and technological advancements, has regrettably subverted our country's potentials for becoming a great nation like Japan, China, Singapore, Taiwan, Malaysia, South Korea, etc., to an insignificant shadow of herself. Sadly, this is an appalling religious activism that modern day Israelis do not in any way perpetrate!

If petty narratives have become the desired objects of our happiness in Africa, do such paltry narratives not greatly abound in the ancient Zulu Kingdom, the ancient Karnem-Borno Empire, the Yoruba and Edo Kingdoms, the primordial Kikuyu and Ashanti Kingdoms, and so on?

We have never known the church paying Income Taxes to the state, neither do they provide gainful employment to the masses as the industries and companies do. Rather, churches are notorious for fleecing their devotees through the imposition of tithes, levies, and offerings. In majority of the cases, only the crumbs of the enormous amounts the church generates week after week are ever passed down into charitable courses, while the larger portions go into providing ostentatious living for the priestly class.

Now that the Nigerian fraud industry is fast dwindling due to intensive prosecutorial campaigns that successive governments have mounted against it, many of those professional scammers in Nigeria have switched their get-rich-quick businesses into floating of churches. Instead of financing viable projects that would renew their nation's ailing economy, they chose the option of floating churches all over the streets of Nigeria, South Africa, Britain, and a number of English-speaking cities around the world. This disturbing trend has now become the latest snare for fleecing the people another time around, on an unholy third missionary journey.

There is hardly any street or any nook and corner in all the cities, towns and villages of Nigeria where one will not find astonishing number of churches of different denominational faiths. The same trend is gradually building up in South African cities, where record numbers of West African church operators are profoundly investing in commercial evangelism. In Lagos, mushroom churches have displaced several shop owners out of their stores, making them take to street vending to accommodate the countless number of churches that have sprung up overnight in that country.

The Nigerian Corporate Affairs Commission could bear out a clear data of evidence to the explosive rate at which most Nigerian youths have filed for registration of new churches from their agency in recent years. The number of daily filings for church registration in Nigeria in the last ten years far surpassed the number of filings for company and enterprise. Since the Nigerian local law required that public notices containing the name of a new church and their trustees be duly published in at least two national newspapers before registration approvals, the Nigerian print media could as well attest to this disturbing development, as paid advertisements for registration of new churches have continually over-flooded their newspapers on daily basis.

To make matter worse, Nigerian youths are happy and simply proud of it that God has taken over their country. While their foremost pastors and preachers joyfully revel in the obsession and frenzy that Nigerians are now the biggest operators of Christian churches all over the world. However, their industries and manufacturing plants, as well as their social infrastructures have collapsed, and many offices of company Directors have given ways to becoming church premises and Pastors' offices, thereby festering a very prohibitive level of unemployment rate in that country.

As things stand now, if the number of churches in Nigeria were to be converted into industries, unemployment would instantly disappear. Good heavens, what a shocking act of spiritual recklessness hast my people adopted in espousing their inordinate ambition to making hasty bucks in the name of God! Instead of developing the Nigerian ailing economy and opt for technological capability like the Taiwanese, the Chinese, the Malaysians, etc., and begin to export their products to other parts of the world, my people are happy and arrogantly boastful that God has made them the biggest and the best of all species of humankind in the art of churching.

There's not a single dilapidated church in Nigeria, but thousands of dilapidated schools are all over the places. All public schools and libraries in Nigeria are neglected to rot away while my people are busy erecting magnificent church buildings all over the nation. How can any nation make considerable progress in the face of crumbled educational system?

The Holy Bible oddly declared in the first verse of the fourteenth chapter of Psalms, *"The fool hath said in his heart there is no God."* My insistence to the contrary is: *the fool hath said in his heart there is a god.* Of course, it is only the fool who will gullibly admit of the evidence of a benevolent god in a land where majority of the people are jobless and poverty stricken, because the bulk of their industries have collapsed and converted into churches that glorify prehistoric trivial tales. As Charles Bradlaugh has aptly observed, *"The more ignorant the theist, the greater his god."*

Religion is undeniably the most terrible infection ever to infest the rational mentality of humankind. It's a con trade that thrives solely on inherent imbecility of human nature, rather than the hub of mankind's rational faculty. Only the fools would devote early mornings at work to prayers with their staff, while productive hours tick away as is commonly the practice all over Nigeria. Nowhere in the civilised world would anyone find such appalling practice.

Where precisely is the evidence of a benevolent of God in a country where majority of her citizens presently suffer the most intense hardships compared to any other nationalities in the whole world? A country that ranks the sixth largest exporter of crude oil in the world, but unto this day cannot provide any functional basic amenities that a civilized and godly country requires to make her citizens enjoy the good things of life. In fact, Nigerian citizens do not at all enjoy any good life in their home country.

It's mind-boggling to imagine how life has become exceedingly hard for Nigerian masses in their home country in the 21st century civilization, especially amidst countless churches and mosques. Many would not readily believe the bitter truth that a country like Nigeria has not had steady electricity supply and running tap water for over thirty years on the trot. As Fashola (2016) has aptly observed, *Sango is the god of lightning and thunder, but all the sacrifices made to Sango (in Yorubaland) has not generated 1 (ONE) kilowatt of electric power.*

It is such a shameful thing that the world's sixth largest exporter of crude oil and several other petroleum by-products cannot provide for good roads and automated traffic lights all around its major cities and towns, instead they allot staggering amount of their resources into building magnificent places of worship.

Since the 1980s, Nigeria has had dilapidated public schools from primary education up to tertiary level, the same as healthcare facilities, but their communities are busy erecting wonderful churches and mosques. Likewise, the country has no efficient public transport system, but mega churches and mosques flourish everywhere.

The World Bank and other global financial credit providers have, since the 1980s, continuously assisted the Nigerian government through loans and aids, sinking billions of American dollars into the Nigerian water projects. While, the water project in the tiny country of Lesotho perfectly runs, the tap water pipes into all Nigerian homes are practically dry unto this day. Even the United Nations' Special Programme that targeted to provide portable water for the Third World countries has hopelessly failed in Nigeria.

To the best of my knowledge, the Nigerian nation started to witness epileptic power supply since 1982; thirty-six years later, the entire country now suffers the startling confines of absolute darkness. This, also, after the World Bank, the International Monetary Fund, including several other international donors have equally assisted the Nigerian government in pumping billions of American dollars in loans and aids to revive the Nigerian white elephant electric power supply project.

Where then is the presence of God in a country that's in total gloom and darkness? Where truly is the manifestation of God's kindness in a country that has never once experienced any atom of good governance since more than half-a-century of its independence from colonial rule?

Where unerringly is the true reward for Nigerians and their neurotic fanaticism towards religious worship? This, especially when the Nigerian ethical and astute values have become so ruinous to an appalling level that corruption has completely enveloped the country, compelling millions of its citizens on self-exile that's attributable to shattered dreams of not being able to live the basic life of normal human beings in a country they called their home. This is a miserable and wretched condition of national shame!

It is only in the country of Nigeria — the make belief 'Head Office of God's Kingdom on Earth' — that one would not find any bit of disparity between the churched and the unchurched. A country that lays the claim to being God's own country, but cannot provide for decent healthcare delivery services, advanced shopping malls, decent abattoirs and butcheries, including world-class entertainment facilities and excellent recreational parks all around the country, except for building mega churches and mosques.

Fifty-eight years into self-rule, the alleged 'Head Office of God's Kingdom on Earth' cannot boast of any world-class infrastructure for its citizens to enjoy good life. On the contrary, my country can only boast of dilapidated facilities on remarkably filthy streets where its citizens derive pleasures from indulging in neurotic religious practices. Such manners of irrational religious practices do not in any way exist in Israel, Rome, and Saudi Arabia from where the Christian and Islamic faiths had originated. No one would find degrading living conditions in the British homelands where inventors and exporters of Anglican Christianity live in privileged conditions. Not in America, the founding community of the Methodist church and the different colours of Episcopalian and Pentecostal churches that now decorate the entire nooks and crannies of Nigerian villages, towns and cities, would one find shameful living conditions as in Nigeria.

A people that resorts to culturing neurotic and gullible religious habits, which in effect do not translate into astute and civilly virtues vis-à-vis their respect for state laws, save for exposing their appalling tradition for stealing public funds, and their extreme proclivity for criminality, has artificially attracted deceptive swindle and representational blight upon its existence as a nation. Rather than nurturing the path of rectitude in judicious service and faithful worship of God, it has artificially cultured the murky path of spiritual fraud and scornful hypocrisy. The practical revelation of these unspeakable afflictions upon a country of countless number of churches and mosques is a direct exposure of her walking in total obscurity under the guide of false religions. These terrible acts of spiritual fraud and deceitfulness have practically relegated the Nigerian national status in the new world order, merely to an insignificant nation that is deficient in every facet of social cohesion.

Of all the continents of the world, Africa is the only one that does not make any money through the business of 'Religion Export.' Right from the time when the Europeans have practically usurped the religion of Christianity from the Jews and repackaged it for export into all parts of the world, they have consistently made remarkable amount of money through the religion, the same way as the Islamic religion is generating enormous foreign exchange earnings for the Middle East (please confirm this fact from Rome, London, Germany, Poland, and Saudi Arabia, etc). Similarly, Hinduism and Buddhism are both making a great deal of money for the Orientals. The Americans too are quietly making billions of dollars through the export of their Adventist, Methodist, Witnessing and Moronic Christianity to all corners of the world. Regrettably, Africa does not feature anywhere, at all, as a player in the exploit of this incredible money spinning *Religion Export Processing Sector.*

During the course of my research for this book, I stumbled upon an overwhelming fact that has shocked me into total disbelief. It is hard to believe, even though it's true, that in the 21st century civilization, foreign historians are still largely the authors of over eighty-percent of all the histories of ancient Africa in print, including the history of our religions and cultures. Foreigners still virtually write Africans stories for Africans in the presence of their numerous scholars. My further investigation into this matter revealed some very unconvincing excuses that blamed our inability to publish our own stories in prints on racism.

Consequently, I have interviewed many African writers on this matter. As usual, everyone has pointed accusing fingers to the dominance of the white race in the publishing industry. They ineffectively blame white publishers for rejecting the greater percentage of the manuscripts coming from black authors. It is as if over fifty years of Africa's self-rule is not enough for many African entrepreneurs to invest substantially in the publishing industry like the whites.

In brief, my simple rejoinder to our flimsy excuses for failing to bring our history into print boils down to two major factors. Firstly, majority of black Africans lack foresight, as we tend to invest the larger percentage of our money on things of insignificant values. How possibly might an African invest in the publishing industry when he/she does not even appreciate the deeper essence of documenting the history of his tradition in print; or when he/she has not driven those luxurious cars to his villages and towns that have no tarred roads, tap water, and electricity? As long as abundant ready-made products saturate our lands from overseas, then we are fine. In short, the bane of our backwardness as Africans still boils down to our complacency on other people doing things for us. It is very annoying to discover the stretch of extreme irresponsibility that our over-dependency on others doing everything for us could draw out. We are absolutely dim-witted and lazy to a fault. Our inferiority complex and lack of confidence have relegated our race into an insignificant shadow of itself. The Europeans have sailed all the way from their shores into Africa to conquer us, build our cities, open our eyes, and give us the civilization that we enjoy today. However, we have absolutely refused to take responsibility for ourselves, but have decided unto this day to leave the key to our powerhouse in the possession of foreigners.

When a nation of people has deemed it fit to surrender the entrance key of their traditional powerhouse to the control of an interloper, then there remains no inherited powerbase for such a nation of people, but a wretched and imaginary powerbase. The very moment this interloper locks up the access to the powerhouse, and beat a swift run-away with the key, ruinous consequences would accordingly befall the indigenous occupants and submit their entire life to effective retribution and reckoning because they do not in reality possess the key to take valuable control of their lives.

Long after our colonial masters have left us alone to fend for ourselves, the entire continent of Africa has practically refused to adopt their own system of making a life for themselves and effectively possess the key to their own powerhouse. Very unfortunately, Africans still grope and fumble about under the regulation of their colonial masters' dictum for everything they do.

For an African man to name his child, he must have to firstly conduct a research into the reservoir of foreign names. If he professed faith in the Christian mythology, he would opt for Biblical or European names. If he happened to be an Islamic believer, he would accordingly consult the Koran for Islamic or Arabian names. Africans do not look inwardly into their native history any longer before they name their child. It is prominent for Africans to address their children as Daniel or Ahmed, instead of Ikechukwu or Bulelani; as Aminat or Maureen, instead of Nkosazana or Adesuwa; or as Zainab and Jackson in the place of indigenous Nomthandazo and Ayodele.

To the contrary, it would be an absolute sacrilege for an Arabian man to name his child Ikechukwu, or for a European to name her daughter Khanyisile. Whence in Europe, America, Asia, or the Middle East has anyone heard of such? Not even the Afrikaner whites in Southern Africa give African names to their children. Of course, it is very illogical to go with a name that one does not even know its meaning. What sense is there for a European man to name his daughter Matshidiso when he does not even know the actual meaning of the name? In the same vein that I could not comprehend any sense in an African man going by the name Haastrup, Willoughby, Francis, Oscar; or an African woman going by the name Jacqueline, Valerie, Cynthia, and so on.

The words of Onyeani (2000), taken from his book, Capitalist Nigger, are truthfully of black Africans, *"We (Africans) have transgressed against the Black race beyond what our creator had in store for us. We will have to atone for our transgression; because what we are facing is purgatory."*

The continent of Africa is the only one that does not make any money from the religions they engaged themselves in its practice more than any other race; even more than the inventors of those religions do. However, our crude obsession is to erect proliferate churches and mosques to fleece our own people. How else can a people of artificial identity make any reasonable progress in life?

The Chinese, Japanese, Koreans and other Asian nationalities have basically resisted all attempts of western imperialists to re-colonize their people culturally and religious wise, but strongly held on to their own culture, language, and religion. At present, the result of their unique identity is clearly demonstrated in the natural understanding that's predominant amongst their people, which has driven the rapid level of civilization and industrial advancement they have progressively attained in recent years. These groups of people are now at par – head to head – with their former colonial masters. They have been able to accelerate their advancement to the very top through the steadfast and patriotic commitment they obliged their native culture, language, and religious identity.

Just like the Caucasians, the Asians too have delivered every form of education, including the teaching of mathematics and other varieties of science to their people in their own indigenous language and culture. In fact, the Chinese have, at some point, closed their nation away from the tricky economic and religious invasion of the Western world, engaging in every aspect of their national development and civilization, strictly their own way, as against the credulous follow-follow attitude that Africans have gullibly adopted.

Unfortunately, Africans still remain perplexed servants to foreign gods, as the fictionalized gods of ancient theism still enchant and fascinate the entire black nations, even when the popularity of these ancient gods have continually dwindled in Europe, the Americas, Asia, and several civilized parts of the world. The Jews themselves have never believed the stories of Jesus as the Bible narrates it, which the Romans, English, Dutch, and American people have embellished, repackaged, and exported to us via

Catholicism, Anglican, Methodist, and Baptist, including Pentecostal, Adventist, and the Dutch Reformed Churches; as another means of wealth and power for their nations. To the contrary, many Africans have credulously adopted these foreign religions as their own ancestral faiths and traditions. As a result, they could commit irrational act of bloodsheds, should anyone venture to say it to their face that those spurious stories concocted in the so-called sacred books, with which the Europeans, Arabians, and the Orientals have subjugated their ancestral faith, are highly suspect materials and sheer fabrications of ancient con artists, because of reason a-b-c and d.

Africa's Native Culture Eroded

In the ancient Yorubaland of my birth, distinct religious devotions developed in our various communities out of the uniqueness of the people's occupation and trade, which then became sacred observances for our ancestors to accomplish thriving harvests and divine fortifications for their diverse occupational endeavours. The different communities and clans that engaged in specific form of occupation would normally worship those particular gods they so deemed suitable for their work-related purposes.

The farmers of ancient Yorubaland would idolize Orisa-Oko—the land fertility god, and serve their god at peace without any fear of losing sleep. Those who were hunters and blacksmiths would naturally worship Ogun—the god of Iron. The communities that engaged in fishing would venerate Olokun and Yemoja—the river god and goddess. Others that were oracle priests and herbalists worshiped Ifa, Orunmila, or Obatala— the gods of wisdom, divinity, and knowledge. Those who engaged in traditional nursing and midwifery were natural worshippers of Osun—the goddess of childbearing, and so on and so forth.

Furthermore, by the side of all these gods, the ancient Yoruba people would deify Esu—special messenger to Olodumare and custodian of the universal judicial power—who takes their prayers and sacrificial offerings directly to Olodumare—the supreme God. It is very painful to see the precious beauty of our unique unity in religious diversity totally worn down and out by the imposition of foreign religions on our land.

The fraternities of the different religious sects, for the observance of seasonal festivals and religious rituals, in appreciations of the munificence of their respective gods, especially during seasonal harvests, have totally washed away with the advent of foreign religions that handed us a bequest of religious fanatics who derive pleasure in killing each other (over as trivial as differing interpretations of religious dogmas). Through intense misinformation and the peddling of half-truth, many of the virtues that abound inside of Africa's native culture have simply eroded and washed away.

When I was growing up, nearly every home in my village had Esu (God's special messenger) deified either at its frontage or at the backyard; as my people duly recognized Esu as the special messenger of the supreme God, who takes their supplications directly to the throne of the creator of the universe. Sequel to this belief, the Yoruba people would customarily venerate this special messenger of the supreme God (Esu) in high esteem, and would deify his statue in their homes, next to the statues of their various gods.

As soon as the missionaries of the Christian religion had duly infiltrated our land and imposed their strange religion upon the Yorubas, the first task these missionaries had then accomplished was to blacken the religious quality of Esu, while they deviously imposed a caveat on the deification of our revered deity as a devilish idol. At the time the late Bishop Ajayi Crowther translated the King James Version of the Holy Bible from English into Yoruba, he out-and-out misrepresented Esu, and deceitfully substituted the Yoruba sacred deity for the equivalent of the Biblical Satan the devil. As a result, my people began to despise and abhor their traditionally known messenger of the supreme God. Their consecrated deity, who had customarily taken their supplications to the Almighty God for ages, had thereafter become their number one enemy. The deified god that duly rewarded their deeds and accordingly punished their offenders had, at the double, become Satan the devil that nobody wanted to associate with anymore, let alone offer sacrifices in his worship. I wonder what in this world has become of the one deified in my paternal grandfather's front yard after he became the chairperson of the Anglican Church in my village.

I strongly harbour the suspicion that the Yoruba story would most likely be the same in scores of other African nations, where operators of foreign religions would, by design, calumniate the peoples' most traditionally revered gods, in order to suppress their aboriginal religion for the credulous worship and adoration of strange son and prophet of God, imported from ancient Israel and Turk, via Rome and Mecca into their homeland.

It is so sad that after fifty years of the Nigerian so-called independence, the misinformation of the Yoruba people deeply endures in the presence of their numerous great scholars, out of which come a respectable Nobel Laureate and a Pulitzer Prize winner for Journalism. Nevertheless, our great scholars have not deemed it suitable to correct the errantly perverted history of the Yoruba traditional beliefs, along with wilful suppressions that foreign religions have meted out mainly on the Yoruba indigenous culture, to give room for exclusive operations of their con religions.

One of the quotes of Les Brown affirmed, *"If you take responsibility for yourself you will develop a hunger to accomplish your dreams."* Every culture had at some points in history of its civilization attained a turning point, where the old and unworkable techniques of the past become very much absurd, useless, and are therefore discarded for a fresh and unsullied feasible solution.

According to the history of Africa, our continent once ranked among the first to attain early civilization in the world, but at the present, ours now sluggishly trails behind at the bottom last. The Asians have achieved monumental successes believing strongly in their very own. All the same, they have smartly fixed an eye on their colonial masters' resourceful, scientific and secular ideals, instead of allowing some strange and spurious religious dogmas to retard their progress. Now is the turning point for the entire continent of Africa, when we ought to ingeniously begin to look inwardly to our native potentials, and from within, take responsibility for ourselves in determining the next step forward. It is now essentially important for Africans to develop the proverbial hunger to accomplish their dreams.

There is no time too late to make a good life. More than ever before, Africans should now uphold every scientific initiative of their former masters, because the scientific path is the only logical path that has truly proven to be very dependable, instead of allowing the folly of religion, conceived in baseless esoteric mysteries to enclose and restrict our scientific and technological potentials. It is of utmost necessity that the people of the black continent should rather uphold the astute path of science, in order to experience authentic results.

It should now become imperative for Africans to design a workable approach under which they could break free from the stronghold of organized religions. If at all Africans must engage in religious practices, we should endeavour to uphold, reform, and propagate our very own, just as the Caucasians, Jews, Arabs, and the Orientals had done. It is an incontrovertible fact that several of the foreign religions with which we have gullibly suppressed our own inherited religions are simply on the same level as ours—they are all works of fiction—as Thomas Jefferson has irrefutably observed in the past: *"I have examined all the known superstitions of the world, and I do not find in our particular superstition of Christianity one redeeming feature. They are all alike founded on fables and mythology."*

The only difference between our ancestral faith and those being propagated on our land by organized religions (Islam, Christianity, etc.) is that they have undergone several stages of reformation to keep abreast with the progress of modern civilization. We also can reform our cultural inheritance to meet with the requirements of modern civilization, in order to create global acceptability that will also put the black African religion on universal trade chart. This will enable us generate substantial foreign exchange earnings for our continent.

Those fetish and absurd sacrifices of ancient Jewish religion, which the Bible specified as divine verdicts of God, and expressly code-named the

Law of Moses, have all been cleverly expunged out of Christianity to give way to a very new system of devotion that is conformable with modern civilization. Praise and worship in rock concert hymns, tithing and generous offerings in US$, GB£, ZAR, €uros, etc., which are much more convenient and less burdensome to modern day disciples of the Christian religion, are now the valid sacrifices acceptable to the Christian God in Christendom nations. This reformed system of the Christian faith has thus become effective substitute for antiquated burnt offerings of cock and bull, ram and duckling, male goat and she goat, blood and incense that the Jehovah of ancient times originally approved of in his purportedly *"inspired Holy Scriptures."*

The adulterated subsidiary of Judaism, which has been reformed and repackaged under the management of European pious men and finely tuned as Christianity is what majority of the masses have easily accepted today in every corner of the world, only because it is without burdensome sacrifices, whilst Judaism—the Jewish aboriginal religion—interlarded with antiquated sacrifices and arduous spiritual observances could not go beyond the shore of its native land.

Of paramount obligations, Africans should learn to believe in their own cultural identity. The turning point for Africans to begin to adjust their over-dependency on foreign religions and cultures is now. It is without doubt that Africa's dependency on these foreign religions and cultures, to every perceptive observation, has never taken us to any progressive height, and Africa will never advance progressively while riding on the back of these foreign religions, because they are intrinsically founded on utter fallacies.

In the 1980s, the campaign for reparation to Africa for the atrocities of slave era effectively kicked off in Nigeria. I remember quite well that as soon as the reparation campaign had flagged off, the white race had equally launched their own counter propaganda, contesting the legality of the reparation claim as invalid and dishonest of Africans, because the black race had actually sold their own people into slavery. This singular piece of misinformation and deceit had on the whole delivered a deadly blow to the reparation crusade. As a result, no African leader could again summon enough courage to demand satisfactory explanations from the white authorities, how exactly the black Africans had in effect sold themselves into slavery. Even to make further enquiries into how all our captured ancestors had chained themselves, neck, wrist, and leg; and how they by themselves pierced holes into their own lips with hot iron rods and padlocked their own mouths to prevent themselves from eating and talking at will, have become extremely difficult for all African leaders.

Never again could any African leader demand justified reparation for the bodies of countless millions of their ancestors, which the slave traders had dumped into the sea to feed marine creatures during the Trans-Atlantic crossings to Europe and America. Our former colonial masters have cleverly suppressed the campaign for any reparation to Africa, and cunningly vindicated themselves of any evil doing, as if the brutal atrocities the slave traders had inflicted upon African ancestors were not substantial enough for any compensation.

What is bothersome about this matter is truly this: ultimately when we Africans at last realize the truth that the proponents of foreign religions have totally misled us into casting off our own ancestral traditions and cultures; and we try to seek cheap reparation for indefensible extirpation of our inherited traditions and religions; knowing how clever the white race is, it is very definite that they will, once again, point the same accusing fingers at us that we are certainly the idiots who's guilty of gullible follower-ship towards other peoples' strange religious affairs. Undeniably, the Europeans, Americans, including Asians and Arabs would, by implication, turn the heat back at us the second time. And this time around, they would be damned too right to label the entire black race as 'Gullible Zombies' in the complicity of other peoples' religious competitions. Certainly, all of us Africans, including our universities and scholars, owe it a dear duty to restore our inherited traditions and cultures to ourselves.

The question may therefore arise: is there possibly no alternative to religion?

The fact of the matter is that, *"Nobody can deny but religion is a comfort to the distressed, a cordial to the sick, and sometimes a restraint on the wicked...,"* as Mary Wortley Montagu has aptly observed. Religion is undeniably a delightful, magical device for invoking the phantom of God to explain mystery, while we happily throw out logic and common sense. For this reason, religion will continue to thrive in the African continent.

However, it is my resounding opinion that belief should have some ethics, as Hypatia of Alexandria (c.350 – 415 AD) has very accurately observed:

> *Fables should be taught as fables, myths as myths, and miracles as poetic fancies. To teach superstitions as truths is a most terrible thing. The child mind accepts and believes them, and only through great pain and perhaps tragedy can he be in after years relieved of them. In fact men will fight for a superstition quite as quickly as for a living truth – often more so, since a superstition is so intangible you cannot get at it as to refute it.*

It is undoubtedly true that religion provides comfort to the distressed, and sometimes a restraint on the wicked. However, it has also been the root cause of more crises in the history of human civilization than anything else. As Blaise Pascal had more suitably phrased it, *"Men never commit evil so fully and joyfully as when they do it for religious convictions."* Buddha also express a similar opinion, *"Religion is a cow. It gives milk, but it also kicks."*

The fact cannot be denied that religion had through the ages attained a disturbing trend in the human society, which makes its practice lethally dangerous in our modern world. Religious practices indisputably become mischievous and lethally dangerous to any refined society once it adorns that deceptive mask for twisting the cock-and-bull tales of humans into godly commands, for the purpose of extortion, power, and mind control.

As Richard Dawkins has very correctly observed:

> *Revealed faith is not harmless nonsense, it can be lethally dangerous nonsense. Dangerous because it gives people unshakable confidence in their own righteousness. Dangerous because it gives them false courage to kill themselves, which automatically removes normal barriers to killing others. Dangerous because it teaches enmity to others labelled only by a difference of inherited tradition. And dangerous because we have all bought into a weird respect, which uniquely protects religion from normal criticism.*

At the present, I very much doubt whether any computer memory can keep track of the countless numbers of abominable iniquities and horrendous cruelties that religious conflicts and intolerance amongst sectarian extremists have brought upon the continent of Africa and the entire world. The effect of the cunning imposition of this so-called 'word of God' upon several other societies has brought unbearable miseries, horrid cruelty and bloodshed upon humanity, as opposed to their false claim of peace and joyfulness to the world in the name of their Lord.

The evils of revealed faith still largely reside in Africa, the Arab world, and Asia. Several of the First World countries have outgrown the troubles of revealed faith. It is therefore imperative for Islamic clerics and Christian priests to change the ways in which religion is being delivered to new generations of Arabs, Asians and Africans. Fortunately, the United Arab Emirate is opening a new, commendable frontier in this regard in the Arab World, Asia and Africa also need to follow suit.

13

The Rational Choice

"My only wish is to transform friends of God into friends of man, believers into thinkers, devotees of prayer into devotees of work, candidates for the hereafter into students of the world."

– Ludwig Feuerbach

He who hath ears to hear, let him hear. In spite of all threats, the rational property of truth can never be shattered or suppressed. Instead, its realistic vanguard will continue to advance in progressive dynamism to help heal the delusion of the world. Amid the hound of hypocritical prating, oppression and tyranny of organized religion, the revolutionary infinitude of moral truth is steadily motivating the forward movement of secularism in Africa, to sustain the constancy of legitimate truth and reality, over the propagation of the greatest lies of all times by different sects of organized religion. At the frontline of a new worldview radiates the luminous hope of rationality to free souls held in bondage by imprudence of faith-based unreason, in order to lay the foundation for a new and more excellent society that upholds the purity of human ethics and most satisfactory virtues of reason and common sense without the dictate of absurd religious dogmas.

As the stand for humanistic liberty gathers universal momentum along the sullied tracks of oppression and universal deceit where the tyranny of organized religion has for millennia reigned with repressive control, the eternal fidelity of rationality intrepidly rewrites the sacred cause. In spite of all brutalities, sinister bigotry, mind control and shackles of suppression designed against the spread of atheistic opinions and secularism in Africa, it has not in any way been possible to smother the rights of conscience. In fact, no cage has been strong enough to imprison the liberty of rational thoughts, as the hammer of the God of religion has dismally failed in crushing the quest for freedom from the yoke of theological programming.

How dear, how soothing for rational minds to see logic and reason streamlining the mentality of several people of the world into becoming more rational than being religious. In defiance of brutal suppression and restraints, the alliance of Freethinkers, Secular Humanists, Agnostics, Atheists, and Sceptics of organized religion has advanced the gradual revolution that is now reshaping religious thinking of the populace in all corners of the world. It has been unattainable to subvert the bravery of the Freethinker, as the very act of devotion to principles constantly fortifies his intellectual freedom.

The velocity of change in faith, in a world that's been under the stronghold of organized religion for millennia of years, can be best seen in the upsurge of interest in secularism in over 85% of the First World countries. This progressive interest in rationalism very clearly indicates the desire of the informed and well-meaning people for a healthier world that is free from the nightmare of theological gibberish and babbles, oddly rooted in organized superstitions of religion proponents. Several people from different walks of life are now coming to terms with the truth that taking a stand for rational and well-substantiated reasoning is much more comforting than revelling in the dreamy realms of fantasy and illusion.

Owing to the inroads that have been made possible by the alliance of Secularists, Humanists, Atheists, and Freethinkers, the liberty of rational thought is increasingly weighing down the sustained spread of absurd and dogmatic evangelism. From every indication, people are rapidly straying away from the misfortunes of fixated belief and now coming into the path of reality based on reason. The unrelenting spread of the age-old theology of fallacies and of strange superstitions is, for the first time in the history of human civilization, facing considerable resistance all around the globe. More than ever before, the touchstone of reality and logical insight into absurdities of ancient system of faith is fast signalling the inevitable end of dogmatic belief system.

The facts indicate that the dominant authority of religion is as never before in danger of losing significant patronage in its con trades, even within the enclave of its greenest zones in Africa. To a greater extent, the resolute stance of the alliance of Freethinkers, Secular Humanists, and Atheists to defend the truth in eras of universal deceits, along with their unswerving courage to deny illogical gods fashioned by men, for the purpose of power and lucrative profits, is now reshaping a new world attitude against the absurdities of core dogma, which religion has bred into the culture of humankind. Today, more and more people are progressively becoming rational than being religious; which, of course, is a better alternative to living a life of estrangement, delusion, and false hope of salvation.

Religion is indeed the most horrible infection ever to infest the rational mentality of humankind. The grave error in the course of human civilization is undoubtedly the defective judgment that allowed religious authorities usurp the foundation of societal morality, in which all collective ethics of humankind must take a cause. This appalling blunder is comparable only to assigning the leper exclusive franchise to run beauty clinics in the society; this can only lead to cycles upon cycles of common infection syndrome.

No one can deny the fact that discordant religious doctrines have prevented the priceless values of common humanism from blooming forth amongst the entire human race. The evidence of how religious practices have terribly Balkanized our world into troubled and conflict-ridden communities today disturbs and irritates our personal knowledge. We are all baffled observers to outrageous bigotry in the name of God. Each and every one of us is a dazed eyewitness to unthinkable, disgusting intolerant conditions where diverse religious sects cannot live at peace with one another. Unto this day, religion still remains a potent force for enmity, violent behaviour, hostility, and hate in all human communities as it was, indeed, from the beginning of recorded time.

It is common knowledge that dogmatic believers do not only despise the infidels, they by the same token, extend extreme hatreds to each other. Pentecostals have refused to worship in the temples of Catholics; and the Sunni Muslims abhor the worship of Allah in the mosques erected with the monies of Shiite Muslims. Devotees of these religious sects forbid one another with passion, and horribly despise each other's faith with abysmal fervour. Between Muslims and Christians, the terrible history has been that of unrelenting conflicts. It has been brutal war amongst Islamist Arabs and the Jews. Recurrent clashes and bigotry endure between Orthodox Christians and Protestants, Muslims and Hindus, Buddhists and Hindus, etc. Many indications clearly show that extremists of these religious sects are becoming more and more dangerous in the society. Ugly memories of the 9/11 terror attacks still worry Americans to this present day. More recently, Nigerians can no longer sleep with their two eyes closed, because jihadist suicide bombs are increasingly being detonated in their country by Islamist terrorists group known as *'Boko Haram.'*

For humanity to uphold its own inviolability, we indeed must expose the false certainty of religion and remove the spirit of worship from our communities. Religion demands worship — the very thing that man should give to no being, human or divine. Robert G. Ingersoll gave humanity this argument in his work, titled, *The Enemy of Individuality:*

> *To worship another is to degrade yourself... It is the spirit of worship that elevates the one and degrades the many; that builds palaces for (liars), erects monuments to crime, and forges manacles even for its own hands. The spirit of worship is the spirit of tyranny. The worshiper always regrets that he is not the worshiped. We should all remember that the intellect has no knees, and that whatever the attitude of the body may be, the brave soul is always found erect. Whoever worships, abdicates. Whoever believes at the command of power, tramples his own individuality beneath his feet, and voluntarily robs himself of all that renders man superior to the brute.*

Rationality, certainly, is a better choice to religiosity. The resonant chord with uttermost echoes of commonsensical validity in any admirable society is the stern ethics that upholds the sacredness of humanity in taking a stand on reason. In this way we make every effort to build a rational alternative to faith-based unreason by erecting our ethics and moral outlook on humanity rather than imaginary gods of religion that do not exist. The entire human race owes it a dear duty in our modern civilization to consign the terrible history of religion into infinite abyss of memory gone astray. Our most obligatory sense of duty in this contemporary age of reason is to decisively relegate all forms of religious practices into a fringe activity in our various societies. This, exactly, is the level that the Europeans have effectively attained with religious practices.

The big questions are:

- ✓ How best can Africans begin the journey of building a secular society that is free of religious domination and control; free of its conflicts, bigotry, hates, and the acts of killing in the name of God?

- ✓ How effectively can we kick-start the transition of relegating all forms of religious practices into an insignificant activity in the various societies of African countries, in such a way that the fraternity of humanity to humanity will reign supreme without domination and control of organized religion?

- ✓ How do we engage this colossal course of action in a way that is constructive rather than destructive?

Of course, with great determination, we can truly effect this significant change; all it takes is our sincerity of purpose. According to Sam Harris, *"Only a fundamental willingness to be reasonable — to have our beliefs about the world revised by new evidence and new arguments — can guarantee that we will keep talking to one another."*

For humanity to do this resourcefully, we need to build and uphold an effective system of thought in the society. We need to encourage each and every individual heart and mind to engage in critical thinking and sceptical enquiries into religious myths. We also need to undertake personal and scientific investigations into the origin of all religious *holy books*, and compile a critical assessment of the great harm the highly questionable claims in these 'holy books' have brought upon the human civilization down the ages.

Professor Daniel Dennett advocates for this in his book (Breaking the Spell, 2006) that humanity needs to institute scientific investigations into the causes of religious beliefs in order to abate the immense influence it commands in human culture. Scientific scepticism is definitely a reliable method of probing into the truth of religious claims lacking empirical evidence, reproducible research, and direct observation. Once the larger percentage of humans better recognize and become aware of the mythical origins of religious fairy-tale through extension of certified and tested scientific enquiries, conceivably they could be free from the spell of its addictive influence. Once we scientifically get to the root of our belief systems, perhaps, we would not have any need for faith.

If our astute minds genuinely permit us to affix the right ruling to the outcome of our in-depth investigation and review of religion history, we should clearly discern as Anne Nicol Gaylor has long before now observed that:

> *There are no gods, no devils, no angels, no heaven or hell.*
> *There is only our natural world. Religion is but myth and*
> *superstition that hardens hearts and enslaves minds.*

Once we recognize and comprehend this plain fact, the first leg of the problem is solved. At this stage we will be very convinced within our personal minds that our indulgence in illusory activity such as religion is plainly a waste of precious time.

The second step is to share the news with others. We should always endeavour to spread freethought books and philosophies amongst like minds. This can be done through sharing of links on Social Media (Twitter, Facebook, WhatsApp, etc.), including personal or community websites, blog posts, as well as by words of mouth. One will be amazed at how far and wide the news has spread; and the remarkable inspiration it has produced in stimulating people into becoming more rational than being religious. Before we know it, religion and its practices would gradually become a trivial and negligible activity in our various communities as it has gradually turned out to be in highly civilized countries like Sweden, Norway, Canada, Iceland, Australia, Switzerland, Belgium, Japan, the Netherlands, Denmark and the United Kingdom, etc.

It is imperative for Secularists, Freethinkers, Sceptics, Humanists, Agnostics, and Atheists to use each and every opportunity at their disposals to share the 'rational gospel' with others; and let as many people as possible become acquainted with the false certainties of religious beliefs, its deceptive notions and fallacies. When we, over and over again, persist in relating the rational message to the entire world, perhaps its moral truth will sink into peoples' ears and begin to transform *"friends of God into friends of man, believers into thinkers, devotees of prayer into devotees of work, candidates for the hereafter into students of the world,"* as Ludwig Feuerbach has wholeheartedly desired during his lifetime.

As Isaac Asimov once wrote, *"Properly read, the Bible is the most potent force for Atheism ever conceived."* Again, one of the most effective ways in which we can easily relegate religion into an unimportant activity in the society is for rational believers to properly delve into the study of their respective religious books, and not gullibly rely on bigoted deceits of professional preachers and evangelical propagandists. Once a rational believer starts reading his/her religious books with critical minds, surely the false certainties of religion will totally become exposed to his/her judicious mind. The fact will open to everyone like the midday sun that, *religion is but myth and superstition that enslaves minds.*

I highly recommend it to all those who seek the path of natural truth to read a number of the freethought related books available in print and share these books with friends and family members. This is a sure catalyst that could easily stimulate one's attentive thoughts to opt for the rational choice.

The truth remains that, at some points in time, every aspect of the human culture must reach a turning point where the old and redundant system of the past becomes very much absurd, worthless, ineffective, and are therefore discarded for a fresh and unsullied feasible solution. The time has now come for us to wake up from the nightmare of unreason delusion in outrageous superstitions, and uphold that which is legitimate and valid in our natural world.

In a nutshell, my opinion agrees with the very incisive advice of Francisco Ferrer Guardia, *"Let no more gods or exploiters be served. Let us learn rather to love each other."* In a world without gods, the fraternity of humanity to humanity will positively thrive at a better rate of knots amongst the human race. Only when a secular and humanistic alternative to religion — the association of ethical people who live in peace and harmony, loving mercy, cheerfulness, and compassion outside the influence of dogmatic belief — is firmly established across the length and breadth of our modern world that the entire human race will have a lasting peace. Only then would we all be convinced that man had never from the beginning of existence worshipped anything but himself — the gods are all in our heads.

Conclusion

In my usual tradition, I made it crystal clear in the preface of the first edition if this book — *The Crisis of Religion* — that I have not written the book to compel Atheism or non-belief upon the mind of anyone, because the freedom of every world citizen to religious or irreligious practices is constitutionally protected within the full ambit of the law. It is imperative for religious fundamentalists in every neighbourhood to clearly recognize this legally endorsed universal right of every citizen of the world.

Let me clearly restate it again that my intention for writing *The Crisis of Religion* is not to turn the Irish into Spanish; neither is it to turn the Catholic into Muslim nor to make any religious person become a nonbeliever against their wish. I very sincerely recognize the fact that the preference to become religious or irreligious is a free choice that every world citizen is at liberty to hold. However, it would be most delightful for me to see some valid information and arguments in this book converting great multitudes of fanatics and credulous believers, out of their own volition, into the ranks of rational believers and thinkers.

Comprehensive usage is the only condition attached to nature's gift of reason. The use of reason and sceptical enquiry appends no senseless creed and unreasoning obedience to its ethical values; rather it bequeaths upright consistency to those who genuinely search for natural truth. Therefore, people should not hesitate to resourcefully make use of this free gift of nature at all times, so as **not** to become complacently contented with several apparent errors that religion continues to engender in our society. As Baron d'Holbach has rightly held, *"The Atheist is a man who destroys the chimeras that afflict the human race, and so leads men back to nature, to experience and to reason."* This is purely the fundamental essence of the freethought philosophies I have espoused in this book.

Ever since dogmatic preachers have cunningly resumed their pretence to speak and act for the creator of the universe (if there exists any), and under the shadows of fabricated revelation began to burden humanity with these outrageous things called revealed religion, the entire world of humanity has known no peace. In several parts of the world, people can no longer sleep with their two eyes closed, because of the erratic outbreak of religious conflicts that might trigger at anytime, anywhere in the world.

Earlier in previous chapters, I did mention that the gullibility of man has been the chief medium that has aggravated the advancement of false religions on earth. People are too credulous to believe any fairy tale without enforcing the traditional requirement of logic and scepticism to verify the claims of such narratives put forward to them; as a result, they most ill-fatedly become prey to charlatans who have ensnared every corner of our world in search of gullible victims to consume. I'm strongly of the opinion that the numerous problems that religious fanaticism have brought upon humankind could have been averted, if only the people had applied the gift of reason to subject their actions to sceptical evaluation.

The disastrous penalties that befell the Millerites and the Xhosas, in addition to the detestable executions of fellow humans (an appalling blot on moral landscape that we have repeatedly witnessed during the numerous uprisings of religious conflicts), including the massive fleecing of the credulous 419 victims, are all observable tragedies that humankind should have possibly averted if the people had resorted to astute path of common sense, instead of taking the reckless path of blind faith which their respective religions recklessly promote.

I have also re-examined some prophecies of the Bible to expose the utter supposition and fallacies of the Christian scriptures, which the church incredibly fathered upon the command of the creator of the universe and christened as divine inspiration or revelation. Meanwhile, the belief of this word of man smugly turned inside out as the 'word of God' is what the dominant religions of the world have enforced upon the psyche of man as religious dogmas that are obligatory to gaining everlasting life in unknown heavenly kingdom.

As I have previously mentioned in the introductory part of this book, it is not my intention to condemn religious practices where it upholds ethical and natural truth. It is encouraging for me to put on record, the reality that religion has helped put together many social assemblies for several nations all around the world, most especially in Africa, where people of the same faith embrace each other in trust, and share their common views together in happiness, praise and worship, and loving mercy. I most sincerely adore some intrinsic virtues that religion has encouraged in the human societies all around the globe. However, religious practices in this modern age must surpass the boundary of sectarian faith to embrace all and sundry. For the modern religion of today to attain the credibility that would appeal to all, the fallacy of religious revelations and prophecies, miracles and ritualistic observances must be thoroughly wiped out of its practice.

Of necessity, we should stamp out the false promise of eternal life in heaven or eternal torment in hellfire. The bogus dogmas of reincarnation and resurrection, and the falsehood of religious tithing, and all other deceits that grossly abound in religious practices must totally give way to the decency of moral truth. Afterwards, religious conviction would naturally transform itself into communal and secular organization that simply appreciates the decorum and affability of ethical truth, loving mercy, and the benignity of humanity-to-humanity by reflection into the goodness that consists in the natural world, which the entire human race universally beholds within every passing minutes of their daily living.

One of the basic intentions of my writing this book is to defuse, from an ex-Theist's eye, that there is not a slight of any credible indication that the god of religion truly exists. This is very evident from the numerous discrepancies and contradictions I have exposed to the discernment of the reader in previous chapters, which makes it undeniable that not a single word of the bible had truly come from the so-called creator of the universe. In short, the Bible is a lie for a line, a line for a lie, as almost all the claims of bible authors have been proven downright fabrication by scholars and modern science.

The propagation of several of these religious fallacies has been responsible for breeding bitter seeds of discord and horrid brutality into the human culture. I therefore find it very obligatory to add my voice to intensifying stance of several sceptics and critics in exposing the fraud of religion, lest humanity lose sight of the loyal and dutiful fraternity that is unadulterated and pure, all embracing, and free from the manipulations of theological doctrines of false priests and clerics – this is Secular Humanism.

At this age, humanity should recognize the wholesome truth that Mother Nature had in the beginning of existence spoken directly to everyone through the divine works of natural evolution. Throughout the ages, nature's word and its revelation changes not; and this we clearly observe in the natural world. Mother Nature has NOT spoken (specially) to any nation through any particular prophet; but nature has spoken collectively to all, through life and matter in the universe.

The true revelations of the creator of the universe (if there exists any) are in nature's laws. Evidence of nature's laws does not support such spurious things as divine promise of eternal bliss in a heavenly paradise and godly wrath of eternal torment of the human souls in fiery furnace. Assuming the spiritual soul does truly exist, the burning fire is in fact a physical element that cannot destroy any spiritual soul; therefore, it is downright gullibility for anyone to continue believing this impractical and ridiculous religious doctrine.

Many religious dogmatists have recurrently given myriad of false testimonies through numerous religious literatures in support of this bogus religious doctrine of hellfire and paradise, which are all in all fallacies to terrify humanity into submitting to the dominance of religion in their lives.

With the Christian religion, we do not know what and who to believe anymore, be it the scriptures or the priest, or the false testimonies of gullible devotees. Whenever their Holy Bible emphatically affirmed a thing in its passage, the priests would deceptively twist it around to imply something else. For instance, the author of the book of Jeremiah 7:31 (NIV) clearly inscribed this statement in the Bible as the true declaration of God, *"They have built the high places of Topheth in the Valley of Ben Hinnom to burn their sons and daughters in the fire – something I did not command, nor did it enter my mind,"* however, the Christian priests dearly loved preaching the word of their own God to the contrary. If something sinister and devilish is not sitting inside of the bellies of those priests, why should they over and over again continue to terrorize their gullible followers with contradictory sermons of everlasting hellfire? Similarly, if something sinister and devilish is not sitting inside of the bellies of those gullible devotees, why should they continue to believe and promote false testimonies in support of a cruel act that their 'God' had plainly condemned as, *"Something I did not command, nor did it enter my mind?"*

It is my hope that some revelations in this book will give those who stagger under the confusion of what to believe or disbelieve, the informed position to make their loyal choice. This (dear choice) was what our ancestors did not have in Africa when foreign imperialists then imposed the cartload of imported religious doctrines upon their minds. Therefore, if your head aches with the fallacies of religious programming, simply say no to religion. If, on the other hand, your head tickles with the propagation of these absurd dogmas, simply engage in your religious practice as you so desire. For I have always known this quote of Albert Einstein to the true:

"There are two ways to live your life. One is as though nothing is a miracle. The other is as though everything is a miracle." The precious choice to religious and irreligious practices is constitutionally protected and guaranteed within the basic human rights of every individual. The United Nations' charter for fundamental human rights duly guarantees the freedom of everyone to religious or irreligious practices.

Some factors I have earlier identified as the notorious culprits that constantly glued the human conscience to religious practices include man's uncontrolled fanaticism for storytelling, alongside his emblematic lack of caution for irrational beliefs, and his extravagant search for security and tainted spiritual enlightenments. The common tendency of humans to socialize and interact with people in their community also constitutes another major factor that closely attached the human conscience to religious practices.

Furthermore, societal dysfunction is a peculiar case in Africa that fosters extreme belief in god. The precarious level of the human suffering through poverty and diseases is unspeakable in Africa; therefore false hopes for heavenly deliverance from the claws of these untold hardships have thus become prevalent in our own part of the world. And, charlatans desiring to feed chunky and chubby on the labour of gullible seekers of bogus divine comfort accordingly took up the trade of preaching deceitful theologies into the dull ears of others, to exploit the extremism of black Africans' reliance on those superstitions.

Although it remains without a doubt that the human sense of reasoning is wholly responsible for the formation of several religions that today rule their world. As every rational mind examines his own sense of existence, he consequently marvels at the invisible power behind the sustenance of his life, and accordingly gives praiseworthy glory to his imaginary creator through the means of his inherited tradition. Also, as our universal home abundantly declares its wonderful splendour, thus too, the human comprehension of the inconceivable whole becomes astounding; thereby submitting to compelling motivation as to why he should appreciate the supreme powers that caused these amazing things into existence. I personally find no fault in the choice of adoration that humankind gives to Mother Nature, or God, or any name that the human civilisation might give to the cosmic intelligence that is behind the formation of the inconceivable whole in the universe.

Anyone who has read this book up to this point would probably wonder what exactly my bona-fide conviction about religion truly is. My direct answer is that I am a Secularist, a Freethinker — truth-seeker as defined by rational enquiry — who refuses to profess any credulous belief in a god whose status is truly not clear to me. I guess the basis of my atheistic stance is critically influenced by the severely contaminated and false religious teachings I've passed through in my early years in the Christian faith.

As I've earlier mentioned in the opening part of this book, my purpose for writing *The Crisis of Religion* is mainly to promote the awareness of secular values in Africa, seeing how strongly the iron-grip of organized religion has retarded our continent into extreme dormant position since the 16th century, and how obsessive religious practices have attained very, very disturbing trend in our modern society.

I have been very conversant with how majority of the people in the First World have lived a very excellent, high-quality life without religion. It is therefore my opinion that our attention as Africans should be rightly focused into making our society a tolerant and liberal society where religion is relegated to the back seat.

I positively do not know if there exists any supernatural creator of the universe, but what I do know with absolute degree of certainty is that, if there exists any creator-God, he/she/it is certainly not the Jehovah of the Jews, neither is he/she/it the Allah of Arabians, the Vishnu of Hindu, nor any of the gods alleged to have spoken to humankind in all of the numerous *'Holy Scriptures'* of organized religions.

Nature has indeed spoken without mincing any words, and I have positively come to the ultimate realization that the sermon of nature evangelizes better theologies than the fabricated word of man, cunningly turned inside out as the word of the creator of the universe, which all the dominant religions of our world incessantly flaunt as Holy Scriptures.

As I examine the awesome wonders of nature, I clearly see the hands of intelligent creator(s) in the perfect finesse of the natural world, pointing clearly to the reality that these creations have not merely evolved haphazardly at random. For this reason, I have always referred to the supreme power(s) that fashioned these things into existence as Mother Nature. Charles Darwin scientifically discerned this *'creator-God'* as *'Evolution of species by the means of natural selection.'*

Throughout the ages, it is evident that no man had been able to give a clear-cut answer to the puzzling question of how the universe truly came into existence; the same way as all the pages of the sacred books that claim to contain the revelation of the creator-God in print could practically not offer any clue. From Judaism through Christianity to Islam, including Hinduism, Shintoism, Idolatry, through Rocicrucianism to Confucianism and every other religious confusion; all these manmade religions have disconnectedly painted the description of the universe and their creator-god in total obscurity. From this plain reason, it is absolutely clear that the creator of the awesome universe, if there exists any, is indeed not the personal God that several sects of organized religion have fabricated for their respective trade. In every respect, I am wholly convinced that the invented words of the sacred books are definitely not the word of the creator of the universe, but that of human inventions and fantasies concerning a fictionalized creator-God.

As I have earlier concluded in the preface of this work, the bane of religious extremism has eaten too deeply into our society, turning vast number of people into dogmatic extremists who live under pretentious fanaticism of abiding by the word of God. For that reason, the scourge of religious resentments must be wiped out of our modern way of life. The act of killing in the name of God must now give way for the fraternity of humanity to humanity to thrive beyond the dictate of bogus religious doctrines, but simply by reflections into the goodness of our natural world. The priceless virtues of cordiality, ethical uprightness, loving mercy, and the benignity of wholesome dispositions towards one another should definitely be beyond the dictates of bogus religious doctrines. Sacred devotion to imaginary gods should henceforth cease to cause any act of pious brutality, hate, and violent conflict amongst humankind, for they are plainly not worth the while.

In all, it is my resounding opinion that belief should have some ethics, devoid of believing every fairy tale in an extremely baffling manner. As Bishop John Shelby Spong has rightly put it, *"People need to understand that questioning and doubting are healthy, human activities to be encouraged not feared."*

As a matter of utmost necessity, the perspicacity of checks and balances must reign supreme in every civilized society. The candour of Scepticism and Freethought must fully be accepted in our modern society as the necessary checks and balances against evil authoritarianism of organized religion, as well as the feral excesses of the gullibility of man. To this end, those who took outrageous delight in credulously accepting every fragment of religious fantasy tale should cautiously cultivate the fine habit of questioning. For, it is always better to figure out things than make them up in clusters of organized superstitions. In the same vein, those who took contentment imposing their beliefs upon the innocent mind of others should totally refrain from perpetrating such extreme nonsense.

According to the German Poet and Freethinker, Heinrich Heine, *"In dark ages people are best guided by religion, as in a pitch-black night a blind man is the best guide...When daylight comes, however, it is foolish to use blind, old men as guides."*

I leave the variety of opinions and propositions articulated in this book, which are genuinely conceived in liberty of rational thoughts, to rest in the mind of the reader. Undeniably, as Gloria Steinem has very truthfully asserted, *"The truth will set you free, but first it will piss you off."*

I here close this work in the immortal words of Thomas Paine, *"When opinions are free, either in matters of government or religion, truth will finally and powerfully prevail."*

Your friend in reason,
Adebowale Ojowuro
January, 2019

BIBLIOGRAPHY:

A. C. Bhaktivedanta Swami Prabhupada (1982)
Coming Back: The Science of Reincarnation
Based on the Teachings of His Divine Grace, A.C. Bhaktivedanta Swami Prabhupāda
Founder, International Society of Krishna Consciousness.
The Bhaktivedanta Book Trust

Adebowale Ojowuro (2011)
Echoes of Common Sense
Verity Publishers

Alexander Heidel (1963)
The Gilgamesh Epic and Old Testament Parallels
University of Chicago Press

American Heritage Dictionary (4th edition)
Published by Houghton Mifflin Company

American Society of Addiction Medicine (2012)
https://www.asam.org/resources/definition-of-addiction

Anthony Campbell (ND)
Online Essay on the Origin of Religion
www.acampbell.ukfsn.org/essays/skep...

Aterburn & Felton (2001)
Toxic Faith
Shaw Books

Babatunde Raji Fashola (2016)
Freedom from fear, choices before the new generation
Published in 01 December 2016 issue of The Guardian Newspapers,
https://guardian.ng/opinion/freedom-from-fear-choices-before-the-new-generation/
The Guardian Press, Lagos, Nigeria, Accessed, 03 March, 2018

Bertrand Russell (1952)
Is There A God?
The Collected Papers of Bertrand Russell, Volume 11: Last Philosophical Testament, 1943-68, ed. John G. Slater and Peter Köllner (London: Routledge, 1997)

Bertrand Russell (1974)
Bertrand Russell Speaks His Mind
Praeger Press

Charles Bradlaugh (1895)
A Plea for Atheism
America Atheists website: http://www.atheists.org

Chika Onyeani (2000)
Capitalist Nigger
Timbuktu Publishers

David Barrett, *et al* (2001)
World Christian Encyclopaedia: A Comparative Survey of Churches and Religions in the Modern World vol. 2
Oxford University Press

Dale S. Ryan and Jeff VanVonderen (2010)
When Religion Goes Bad
http://www.spiritualabuse.com

David Hume (1748)
Enquiry Concerning Human Understanding
Oxford University Press (rpt. 1999)

Dale S. Ryan and Jeff VanVonderen (2010)
Soul Repair: Rebuilding Your Spiritual Life
INTERVARSITY Press

Daniel C. Dennett (2006)
Breaking the Spell: Religion as a Natural Phenomenon
Penguin

Donald E. Johnson (2010)
The Programming of Life
Big Mac Publishers

Douglas Adams (1998)
Is There An Artificial God?
Biota.org

Douglas J. Futuyma (2009)
Evolution (2nd Edition)
Sinauer Associates, Inc.

Dylan Evans & Howard Selina (2005)
Introducing Evolution
Totem Books

Emanuel Haldeman-Julius (1996)
The Meaning of Atheism
http://www.positiveatheism.org

Encyclopaedia Britannica Online
www.britannica.com

God Is Imaginary Website
http://www.godisimaginary.com

Frank Lorey (1997)
The Flood of Noah and the Flood of Gilgamesh
Institute for Creation Research
https://www.icr.org/article/noah-flood-gilgamesh/

Grant Edwards (1996)
Planets, stars, and orbs: the medieval cosmos, 1200-1687
Cambridge University Press

Guy P. Harrison (2008)
50 Reasons People Give for Believing in a God
Prometheus Books

John Locke (1905)
Essay Concerning Human Understanding Books II & IV
(with omissions) selected by Mary Whiton Calkins
University of Michigan Library

L. Piccardi and W. B. Masse (2007)
Myth and Geology - Special Publication no 273
(Geological Society Special Publication)

Life–How did it get here? By evolution or by creation (1985)
Watchtower Bible and Tract Society of New York

Moshe Averick (2010)
Nonsense of the High Order: *The Confused and Illusory World of the Atheist*
Tradition and Reason Press Inc.

Robert G. Ingersoll (ND)
The Enemy of Individuality and Mental Freedom:
A Lecture on Why the Church Hates a Thinker
https://ebooks.adelaide.edu.au/i/ingersoll/robert_green/lectures/chapter4.html

Richard Dawkins (1976)
The Selfish Gene
Oxford University Press (rpt. 2006)

Richard Dawkins (1996)
The Blind Watchmaker: Why the Evidence of Evolution Reveals a Universe without Design
W.W. Norton & Company Ltd

Richard Dawkins (2006)
The God Delusion
Bantam Press

Ronald M. Enroth (1993)
Churches That Abuse
Vondervan

Sam Harris (2006)
An Atheist Manifesto
Truthdig.com
https://www.truthdig.com/dig/an-atheist-manifesto/

Tim M. Berra (1990)
Evolution and the Myth of Creationism: *A Basic Guide to the Facts in the Evolution Debate*
Stanford University Press

Thomas Paine (1794)
The Age of Reason
Citadel Press (rpt. 1988)

William Clifford (1877)
The Ethics of Belief
Prometheus Books (rpt. 1999)

Wikipedia
The Free Online Encyclopaedia
https://en.wikipedia.org/wiki/Evolutionary_origin_of_religions

Contents by Chapter

Brother Pluto Sister Eris

**Aspects Between the Dwarf Planets
Through 800 Years of History**

Thomas Canfield

www.ingramcontent.com/pod-product-compliance
Lightning Source LLC
Chambersburg PA
CBHW060040100426
42742CB00014B/2649